Extremist Propaganda in Social Media

Extremist Propaganda in Social Media

A Threat to Homeland Security

Michael Erbschloe

CRC Press
Taylor & Francis Group
Boca Raton London New York

CRC Press is an imprint of the
Taylor & Francis Group, an **informa** business

CRC Press
Taylor & Francis Group
6000 Broken Sound Parkway NW, Suite 300
Boca Raton, FL 33487-2742

First issued in paperback 2021

© 2019 by Taylor & Francis Group, LLC
CRC Press is an imprint of Taylor & Francis Group, an Informa business

No claim to original U.S. Government works

ISBN-13: 978-0-367-77907-8 (pbk)
ISBN-13: 978-1-138-49367-4 (hbk)

Library of Congress Cataloging-in-Publication Data

Names: Erbschloe, Michael, 1951- author.
Title: Extremist propaganda in social media : a threat to homeland security / Michael Erbschloe.
Description: Boca Raton, FL : CRC Press, 2018. | Includes bibliographical references and index.
Identifiers: LCCN 2018005234 | ISBN 9781138493674 (hardback : alk. paper) | ISBN 9781351027380 (ebook)
Subjects: LCSH: Social media--Political aspects--United States. | Polarization (Social sciences)--United States. | Internet and terrorism--United States. | Radicalism--United States. | Extremist Web sites.
Classification: LCC HM742 .E73 2018 | DDC 302.23/1--dc23
LC record available at https://lccn.loc.gov/2018005234

**Visit the Taylor & Francis Web site at
http://www.taylorandfrancis.com**

**and the CRC Press Web site at
http://www.crcpress.com**

Contents

List of Tables

Preface

There has been a great deal of attention focused on the impact of extremist propaganda and how it can radicalize individuals or groups into antisocial or even violent behavior. That has all been in the name of anti-terrorism and homeland security. This book examines those issues and efforts to counter such propaganda.

There has been less attention focused on extremist propaganda that is homegrown in the U.S., even though that propaganda has had a severe impact on the security, sanity, and civility of the nation. This book also examines those issues and the source of that propaganda. It is depressing to recognize that much of the extremist propaganda in the U.S. has its origins where it should not and that is with high level elected officials and appointees in the U.S. Congress and even in the White House. It is also grown and disseminated from State Houses, places of worship, businesses, schools, and the very homes and families where people live. This weakens the strong foundation needed for sustainable homeland security.

This extremist propaganda is also spread through media of all sorts including broadcasts, print publications, websites, and ever increasingly through social media. The spread of and belief in extremist propaganda has become more dangerous because individuals, groups, organizations, and ethnicities can control their social media and other news feeds to the point where they are never exposed to any alternative narratives.

George Orwell, in the famous and timeless book *1984*, feared the rise of a dystopian society where the government and censors controlled what propaganda people are exposed to, thus creating a myopic intellectually and socially closed society. This has not happened yet. Instead, it was replaced with a blisstopian society where people customize their own propaganda feed and can live blissfully with the absence of any information that may contradict what they want to hear and what they want to believe.

One of the later chapters in this book is the result of several years of interviews and observations that revealed to me just how effective extremist propaganda can be in controlling people that have little if any exposure to an alternative narrative.

Michael Erbschloe

Acknowledgments

I thank Mark Listewnik of CRC Press/Taylor & Francis Group for his stewardship on seeing this book through from the proposal stage to publication. His insight and encouragement was a driving force in addressing this complex subject.

I also thank my close friend and colleague, John Vacca, for support and companionship over the last 30 years and my sister, Debra, for her support and her willingness to discuss and analyze the impact of propaganda.

Lastly, I thank the people that I observed and listened to over the last five years as they declared and occasionally explained feelings and beliefs that were born out of continued exposure to propaganda. They have no idea who they are.

Author

Michael Erbschloe worked for over 30 years performing analysis of the economics of information technology, public policy relating to technology, and utilizing technology in reengineering organization processes. He has authored several books on social and management issues of information technology, most of which covered some aspects of information or corporate security. Mr. Erbschloe has also taught at several universities and developed technology-related curriculums. His career has focused on several interrelated areas: technology strategy, analysis, and forecasting; teaching and curriculum development; writing books and articles; speaking at conferences and industry events; publishing and editing; and public policy analysis and program evaluation. He currently works as a consultant on technology and security issues.

Introduction

Propaganda is a systematic effort to spread opinions or beliefs, regardless of the accuracy of the information presented in the message. The effort to sway opinions and beliefs is age old and has often been associated with the rise of intolerance, extremism, and totalitarianism and has been deployed in a variety of mediums such as art, editorials, music, and movies. Now extremist propaganda has permeated social media of all types and is a threat to international security and homeland security in the U.S. as well as many countries around the world.

In the U.S., there is a constant struggle to protect and define First Amendment rights to free speech while addressing the issues of extremist propaganda. Although the First Amendment says "Congress shall make no law respecting an establishment of religion, or prohibiting the free exercise thereof; or abridging the freedom of speech, or of the press; or the right of the people peaceably to assemble, and to petition the Government for a redress of grievances," the Supreme Court has held that speakers are protected against all government agencies and officials: federal, state, and local, and legislative, executive, or judicial. The First Amendment does not protect speakers, however, against private individuals or organizations, such as private employers, private colleges, or private landowners. The First Amendment restrains only the government.

The Supreme Court has interpreted speech and press broadly as covering not only talking, writing, and printing, but also broadcasting, using the Internet, and other forms of expression. The freedom of speech also applies to symbolic expression, such as displaying flags, burning flags, wearing armbands, burning crosses, and the like. Freedom of speech includes the right:

- Not to speak (specifically, the right not to salute the flag). West Virginia Board of Education v. Barnette, 319 U.S. 624 (1943).
- Of students to wear black armbands to school to protest a war ("Students do not shed their constitutional rights at the schoolhouse gate."). Tinker v. Des Moines, 393 U.S. 503 (1969).
- To use certain offensive words and phrases to convey political messages. Cohen v. California, 403 U.S. 15 (1971).

- To contribute money (under certain circumstances) to political campaigns. Buckley v. Valeo, 424 U.S. 1 (1976).
- To advertise commercial products and professional services (with some restrictions). Virginia Board of Pharmacy v. Virginia Consumer Council, 425 U.S. 748 (1976); Bates v. State Bar of Arizona, 433 U.S. 350 (1977).
- To engage in symbolic speech (e.g., burning the flag in protest). Texas v. Johnson, 491 U.S. 397 (1989); United States v. Eichman, 496 U.S. 310 (1990).

Freedom of speech does not include the right:

- To incite actions that would harm others (e.g., "[S]hout[ing] 'fire' in a crowded theater."). Schenck v. United States, 249 U.S. 47 (1919).
- To make or distribute obscene materials. Roth v. United States, 354 U.S. 476 (1957).
- To burn draft cards as an anti-war protest. United States v. O'Brien, 391 U.S. 367 (1968).
- To permit students to print articles in a school newspaper over the objections of the school administration. Hazelwood School District v. Kuhlmeier, 484 U.S. 260 (1988).
- Of students to make an obscene speech at a school-sponsored event. Bethel School District #43 v. Fraser, 478 U.S. 675 (1986).
- Of students to advocate illegal drug use at a school-sponsored event. Morse v. Frederick, 551 U.S. 393 (2007) [1].

This book presents an analysis of the impact of social media on propaganda and the rise of extremism in mass society from both technological and social perspectives. In this analysis, blisstopian societies are seen to arise when the populace is complacent and have unquestioning acceptance of a social doctrine without challenge and introspection. The malleable populations in a blisstopian society self-select social media content and propaganda delivery mechanisms that motivate, reinforce, and contribute to their view of the world. This contributes to the rise of intolerance, extremism, and radicalization, which perpetuates racism, religious bigotry, violence, hate crimes, gender discrimination, and the continued oppression of individuals with non-traditional life styles. A contrived and manufactured bliss has fueled the rise and perpetuation of violent radical groups such as ISIS, neo-Nazis, white separatists, and white supremacist in the United States and has supported ethnic cleansing and racist actions around the world. This dynamic has created issues that homeland security, law enforcement, the military, and global organizations must deal with now and in the future.

The convergence of technology and society can be illustrated by how social media has infiltrated the daily lives of people from many walks of life and in many parts of the world. On one hand, social media has allowed people with common relations and interest to communicate and collaborate. On the other hand, social media technology has enabled individuals and groups to tailor and restrict the information and content of all types to which they are exposed. For example, a neo-Nazi can go through the day and never be exposed to anything that is not Nazi oriented.

Complacency and the unquestioning acceptance of a contrived social doctrine can be more easily achieved when individuals are not exposed to any content to oppose a doctrine. Such complacency results in individuals or groups happily accepting a doctrine and eventually defending and perpetuating that doctrine. Thus, those individuals become blissful and malleable and can be exposed to more extreme indoctrination as they filter out non-doctrine–related material and become radicalized to the point of antisocial behavior and violence. Complacency or bliss can be a first step to radicalization, and so many people have fallen into bliss and do not question the ideas to which they are exposed.

Examples for this book will include the 2016 presidential election in the United States, where millions of people followed candidates blissfully accepting lies as truth. In addition, neo-Nazi and white supremacist behavior has been reinforced and encouraged through social media during the last few years. This may yet lead to more extreme antisocial behavior as various right wing leaders and organizations support and predict extreme events such as civil war and revolution. The massive meddling in the United States elections through the dissemination of fake news and propaganda using social media, for which Russia has been charged, is also examined.

It may not take much more indoctrination to move millions of people from bliss and acceptance to mayhem and violence. Each chapter of the book examines how social media technology and applications can set the stage for and perpetuate extremisms and radicalization in various segments of society. This analysis serves to expand the homeland security perspective on dealing with intolerance, extremism, and radicalized groups and individuals as well as to learn how to better analyze organizational weaknesses and mitigation steps needed to protect against radicalized groups and individuals. The contents of the chapters are discussed in the following.

Chapter 1: A Framework to Analyze the Impact of Social Media Propaganda on Intolerance, Extremism, and Radicalization in Society: The convergence of media and information sources flowing through social media now permeates the daily lives of people. On one hand, social media has allowed people with common relations and interests to communicate and collaborate. On the other hand, social media technology has enabled individuals and groups to tailor and restrict the content to which they are exposed, regardless if it originated on television, in print sources, or from the White House, the pulpit, or hate groups. To analyze the potential impact of propaganda, it is important to have an understanding how people use their time in their daily lives and the time they spend exposed to social media. This chapter covers the forms propaganda is packaged into, practical methods for identifying propaganda, an understanding of extremists and extremism, radicalization resulting from propaganda, social media propaganda consumption, and violence on television as well as activities being undertaken to combat terrorist and extremist propaganda.

Chapter 2: Social Media Propaganda and the Political Electoral Process: Elections have always had a strong propaganda element, but the 2016 elections in the U.S. were 99% propaganda and 1% discussion of the issues. Social media helped to spread that propaganda, much of which was created by the candidates or various interest groups. The 2016 elections also had the added element of Russian meddling that involved the creation and dissemination of propaganda. This chapter examines the Intelligence Community Analysis of Russian campaign meddling, testimony of U.S. Congressional hearings on social media companies regarding the meddling, and the Honest Ads Act that is designed to promote greater transparency of social media posts that can impact the electoral process.

Chapter 3: Government Institutional Response to Social Media Propaganda, Extremism, and Radicalization: Governments have responded to social media propaganda, extremism, and radicalization by forming coalitions and partnerships to counter extremist social media propaganda and reduce the frequency of individuals and groups being radicalized toward violent extremism. This includes international coalitions, regional consortia, and local partnerships and programs. This process can be extremely challenging in free speech societies and can even face legal hurdles. This chapter examines programs established by the U.S. government—including those managed by the Department of Homeland Security (DHS) and the Department of Justice (DOJ)—to counter extremist propaganda and activities that lead to the radicalization of individuals and groups, along with the national initiatives that guide agency work and programs directed at dealing with extremist propaganda in social media.

Chapter 4: Military Response to Social Media Propaganda-Driven Extremism and Radicalization: The military faces several major challenges created by extremist propaganda. The emergence of organized groups like ISIL (ISIS) was largely driven by extremist propaganda that became a major military and political challenge. This propaganda has also radicalized local populations or individual citizens in Iraq and Afghanistan to do harm to coalition forces for which they worked or to which they were supposedly allied. The military also faces an insider threat as a result of members becoming radicalized to extremist views and violence. This chapter examines how the U.S. military is working to diminish the impact of extremist propaganda in social media.

Chapter 5: The Impact of Social Media Extremist Propaganda on Law Enforcement: Law enforcement personnel seem to have been in the middle of a variety of social conflicts for at least the last 100 years in the U.S. and social media perpetuates the turmoil for many individual police officers as well as the profession of law enforcement as a whole. Extremist propaganda that promotes violence is also a challenge for law enforcement because they are often the target of the violence, or the communities they police are targets. This chapter examines training for law enforcement on dealing with extremist propaganda, monitoring social media, the radicalization of law enforcement officers, and anti-cop versus pro-cop propaganda in social media.

Chapter 6: The Corporate Extremist Propaganda Machine: The extremist propaganda flowing from terrorist organizations and various hate groups is riddled with false and misleading statements designed to inspire, recruit, and radicalize followers. Such actions alarm the world. But those actions are not new and terrorists did not invent them. Capitalistic corporations have mastered the art of deception, lying, misinformation, and fraud, which has led to the deaths of millions of people worldwide. There are many more people who have suffered financial loss as well as disruption to and sometimes the destruction of their lives. This chapter examines the extremist propaganda being disseminated by corporations, with the primary case study being the tobacco industry in the U.S.

Chapter 7: Extremist Propaganda and Recruitment Targeting Youth: Youth in the U.S. are constantly exposed to violence, racism, and religious discrimination and are often ridiculed for their sexual orientation or chosen lifestyles. Extremists, including international and domestic groups, religious zealots, and even political parties, prey upon malleable youth in the human jungle we call society. The young people in the U.S. are ideal targets for recruitment by extremists seeking support for their radical ideologies because those groups sell appeal, inclusion, security, validation, and membership. There are a variety of recruiters targeting students ranging from neo-Nazis to anti-abortion organizations to ISIL. This chapter examines the teenagers as a recruitment target, the methods that groups use to recruit, teens' ongoing exposure to violence and bigotry, and some of the programs that have been established to mitigate the unwanted success of extremist groups indoctrinating and radicalizing young people.

Chapter 8: Electronic Aggression or Free Speech: Intolerance and hate in the U.S. have resulted in extremist electronic aggression permeating social media. Even though much of that aggressive expression is protected by the First Amendment, it is no less antagonistic or harmful to society. The extremists, be they alt-right activists or elected officials, bring an aggression that demonstrates a lack of emotional maturity and civic responsibility. They also set an encouraging tone for more hate and intolerance to spread. This chapter examines electronic aggression and how it is driven by nationalism, tribalism, clan conflict, and bigotry.

Chapter 9: Countering Extremist Anti-Science Propaganda: In the U.S., there is a growing anti-science movement entangled with an anti-intellectual sentiment among conservatives, which is fueling an anti-education attitude. People that have these intertwined attitudes and beliefs reject science and scientific methods, consider intellectuals an enemy of the conservative state, and disparage education. Many major party candidates for political office during the 2016 election took anti-science positions against evolution, climate change science, vaccines, stem cell research, and government funding for scientific research and development.

The anti-science movement is likely to continue. This chapter examines how the extremist propaganda in media and social media is being countered.

Chapter 10: Observations on the Distribution of Extremist Propaganda: There is not one single path that leads to extremism or radicalization and not everybody is swayed by extremist propaganda. The effectiveness of social media propaganda is, however, not random. The world is a whirlpool of propaganda emanating from numerous media sources and is spread and validated by interactions between individuals and groups. It should also be recognized that people with diminished mental capacity and those that are in closed social environments may be more readily influenced by extremist propaganda. This chapter examines the circumstances that can make the distribution and reception of extremist propaganda effective, including how it is distributed, group think, monoculturalism, and mental illness.

Chapter 11: Ten Reasons Why Propaganda Works: Extremist propaganda is a twenty-first century success story around the world and certainly in the U.S. There are numerous reasons why extremist propaganda has been so successful, ranging from people having a lack of knowledge to people succumbing to peer pressure. The author conducted a series of interviews to explore the reaction of people to propaganda and why they readily accept so much propaganda as truth. This chapter examines ten reasons why propaganda works so well, with anecdotal comments collected during the interviews along with casually observing individuals' acceptance and perpetuation of propaganda.

Course Activities

Each chapter in this book provides course activities that can help expand a student's perspective on propaganda and social media and its impact on society and homeland security. Social media is well populated with real-time examples of propaganda but poses a challenge to analyze because of the volume. The following web pages provide portals to a treasure trove of resources.

A historical document from the Dwight D. Eisenhower Presidential Library entitled "Propaganda, Information and Psychological Warfare: Cold War and Hot—A List of Holdings," compiled by David J. Haight in April 2008, provides a guide of a select bibliography of works that address various aspects of information (or propaganda). Students can consult these studies to gain a better understanding of information and propaganda activities (https://eisenhower.archives.gov/research/subject_guides/pdf/Propaganda_Psychological_Warfare.pdf).

The United States Holocaust Memorial Museum in Washington, DC, inspires citizens and leaders worldwide to confront hatred, prevent genocide, and promote human dignity. The museum's website has a section dedicated to exploring and explaining propaganda (https://www.ushmm.org/propaganda/). A subsection is dedicated to inciting genocide and there are several student activities provided. "State of Deception: The Power of Nazi Propaganda" is a traveling exhibition produced by the United States Holocaust Memorial Museum. It examines how the Nazis used propaganda to win broad voter support in Germany's young democracy after World War I, implement radical programs under the party's dictatorship in the 1930s, and justify war and mass murder.

The U.S. Air University provides a webpage on Influence Operations with links to numerous documents and operational units that focus on propaganda and counterpropaganda (http://www.au.af.mil/info-ops/influence.htm) and is worth exploring to learn more about the military challenges dealing with propaganda.

Suggested Reading and Viewing

There are numerous fiction books that have been recognized as providing insight on propaganda and how it can contribute to the emergence of dystopian societies. These books are globally popular and can provide a basis for discussion on the impact of propaganda on society, and several have been made into movies. They also continue to be re-released and the dates shown here do not reflect the original publication date.

- 1984 (1950) by George Orwell
- A Clockwork Orange (1995) by Anthony Burgess
- Brave New World (2006) by Aldous Huxley
- Fahrenheit 451 (2012) by Ray Bradbury
- It Can't Happen Here (2014) by Sinclair Lewis
- The Handmaid's Tale (1998) by Margaret Atwood

Reference

1. U.S. Federal Courts/What Does Free Speech Mean? Accessed December 18, 2017 http://www.uscourts.gov/about-federal-courts/educational-resources/about-educational-outreach/activity-resources/what-does.

Chapter 1

A Framework to Analyze the Impact of Social Media Propaganda on Intolerance, Extremism, and Radicalization in Society

1.1 Propaganda Comes in Many Forms

Propaganda is a systematic effort to spread opinions or beliefs regardless of their validity, accuracy or honesty. In many cases it may be easy to identify propaganda but the more likely people are to believe the message the less likely they are to understand that it is propaganda. The 2016 U.S. presidential election is an excellent example of people wanting to believe the message, and the more they wanted to believe the more preposterous the propaganda became.

In March 2016, Senate Bill 2692, the Countering Information Warfare Act of 2016, was introduced in the 114th U.S. Congress (2015–2016). The bill stated that it is the sense of Congress that

1. Foreign governments, including the Governments of the Russian Federation and the People's Republic of China, use disinformation and other propaganda tools to undermine the national security objectives of the United States and key allies and partners.
2. The Russian Federation, in particular, has conducted sophisticated and large-scale disinformation campaigns that have sought to have a destabilizing effect on United States allies and interests.
3. In the last decade disinformation has increasingly become a key feature of the Government of the Russian Federation's pursuit of political, economic, and military objectives in Ukraine, Moldova, Georgia, the Balkans, and throughout Central and Eastern Europe.
4. The challenge of countering disinformation extends beyond effective strategic communications and public diplomacy, requiring a whole-of-government approach leveraging all elements of national power.
5. The United States Government should develop a comprehensive strategy to counter foreign disinformation and propaganda and assert leadership in developing a fact-based strategic narrative.
6. An important element of this strategy should be to protect and promote a free, healthy, and independent press in countries vulnerable to foreign disinformation [1].

The Countering Foreign Propaganda and Disinformation Act was signed into law in December 2016 [2]. The bill demonstrated an understanding that propaganda is having an impact on countries around the world. One way to understand the process of propaganda is to examine the goals underlying a propaganda campaign or ongoing effort. Deception has been a major goal in propaganda as has creating confusion or uncertainty along with dividedness among individuals or groups. Offensive propaganda goals in social media are shown in Table 1.1 and defensive propaganda goals in social media are shown in Table 1.2.

There are several themes or messages that show up in social media propaganda and they are very similar to those used in business advertising campaigns. Bandwagon appeal, for example, conveys the message that our cause is so good that everyone is joining and you should too. Snob appeal is a reverse of the bandwagon appeal and messages suggest that joining our cause will make you better than everyone else since only special people are allowed to join. Other themes in social media propaganda include

◼ Appeals that target a specific group of people using social media content that attracts that audience. The various approaches include youth appeal, appeal to maturity, appeal to teenagers, young children, men, women, professionals, specific religious groups, or hate groups. Social media targeting specific audiences will use pictures, slang, music, and cultural content that appeals to the type of person targeted.

Table 1.1   Offensive Propaganda Goals in Social Media

Deception: False promises/invalid information
Confusion: Creating and perpetuating uncertainty
Dividedness: Instigating hatred and suspicion
Exposure: Unauthorized release of information
Nullify opponents: Efforts to discredit opponents

Source: Erbschloe, M., *Social Media Warfare: Equal Weapons for All*, CRC Press, Boca Raton, FL, 2017.

Table 1.2   Defensive Propaganda Goals in Social Media

Self validation: Assuring the world of the validity and legitimacy of a position or action
Influencing aligned entities: Convincing allies of the validity and legitimacy of a position or action
Reinforcing alliance partners: Showing support of an allies' position or action
Persuasion of non-aligned entities: Convincing non-allies of the validity and legitimacy of a position or action
Recruiting and indoctrination: Drawing people into a cause and teaching cause related doctrine
Nullifying opponents: Efforts to discredit opponents

Source: Erbschloe, M., *Social Media Warfare: Equal Weapons for All*, CRC Press, Boca Raton, FL, 2017.

■ Adoption of symbols, emblems, or tokens that represent a cause or depict a goal. The Swastika is probably the best known but animals such as lions and eagles have also been used in propaganda.

■ Use of statistics and numbers that depict a crisis or a need for action and motivate people to support or join a cause. None of the data need be accurate or properly presented to gain support. An example is making a claim that the United States has the highest taxes in the world when it clearly does not.

■ Sex appeal works in almost any campaign and attractive spokespeople help draw attention to a cause or campaign. The physical appearance and demeanor of the spokespeople need to be carefully chosen to match the desires of the target audience.

■ Card stacking presents positive aspects of a cause or a candidate while simultaneously pointing out negative aspects of the opposition to help reinforce an individual's decision to become a supporter. The information need not be accurate or true but does need to appeal to the perspective of the supporters.

■ Emotional appeals that play on people's fears, joys, and sadness work when they are unique but once the same appeal is packaged or played too many times the emotional response tends to diminish.

■ Generalities and catch phrases that are easy for people to remember and are easy to repeat such as "lock her up!"

■ Use of very snappy generalizations or connotations that prompt people to jump to the easiest, quickest, most obvious conclusion without evidence, data, or examples to support them.

■ Smoke screens are rhetoric used to avoid or hide an issue and are often used by political spokespeople who are trying not to answer a question or want to change topic; they were often used during the 2016 U.S. elections, during which the last thing people wanted to discuss were real issues so they kept bringing up Hillary Clinton's e-mail servers.

■ Stereotyping, labeling, falsely depicting a person or group of people or a cause in a class or category based on superficial qualities or prejudgments.

■ Fallacies, false analogies or deliberately incorrect or misleading comparisons that depict people or things in a negative or positive light with no real evidence of a relationship or characteristic.

■ Altered documents, photos, or recordings that represent events that did not occur or changed the meaning and context of actual events.

■ Use of figurative language, metaphors, simile, or personifications that enhance comparisons between a person, place, or thing that leads people to see them in a positive or negative light.

■ Using God or Bible quotations to justify a position or a negative action.

■ The use of false testimonials or endorsements from experts, famous people, or plain folks to make a message more appealing to a target population.

■ Disseminated misinformation that may be intentional or unintentional action to generate interest or *disinformation* primarily designed to distort and deceive [4].

Propaganda has long been everywhere in the broadcast and print media and now it is a dominate force in social media. Identifying propaganda requires an objective mind and unbiased thinking. One of the biggest threats to homeland security is that even those professionals working in the field have biases and predispositions towards different points of view. It is simple—most people believe what they want to believe and can be easily taken in by propaganda. The important thing to remember is that the goal of propaganda and hate messages is to influence opinions, emotions, attitudes or behavior of a target audience in order to further the agenda of the propaganda creator or disseminator.

The creation and dissemination of propaganda is becoming increasingly more sophisticated in a data driven world. Political parties, private corporations, governments, and nonprofit organizations use data to tailor propaganda messages to target audiences to influence perceptions and change behaviors. There are a variety of evolving approaches to using use data science methods to identify segments of a population that are receptive to specific content and ideas.

Terrorists, like every other multi-national organization, are using the Internet to grow their business and to connect with like-minded individuals. Al Qaeda in the Arabian Peninsula produced a full-color, English-language online magazine. They are not only sharing ideas, they are spreading *ideological conflict*, soliciting information and inviting recruits to join Al Qaeda. Al Shabaab—the Al Qaeda affiliate in Somalia—has had its own Twitter account. Al Shabaab uses it to taunt its enemies often in English and to encourage terrorist activity. Extremists are not merely making use of the Internet for propaganda and recruitment, they also use cyber space to conduct operations [5].

A top priority of the U.S. Federal Bureau of Investigation (FBI) is protecting the U.S. from terrorist attacks. From a threat perspective, the FBI has been concerned with three areas in particular: (1) Domestic fanatics and those who are inspired by the terrorists' propaganda and feel empowered to act out in support; (2) those who are enabled to act after gaining inspiration from extremist propaganda and communicating with members of foreign terrorist organizations who provide guidance on operational planning or targets; and (3) those who are directed by members of foreign terrorist organizations to commit specific, directed acts in support of the group's ideology or cause [6].

1.2 Practical Methods for Identifying Propaganda

Propaganda can be subtle or nuanced and may include any of the types of content identified earlier but can also be intermixed with misinformation and disinformation disseminated from official sources. To identify propaganda agencies and organizations, a person can employ a variety of methods ranging from simple straightforward fact checking to complex psychological analysis.

Propaganda campaigns use communication to alter a population's beliefs and views thus influencing their behavior. According to the U.S. Central Intelligence Agency (CIA) there are three types of propaganda: white, black, and grey. White propaganda openly identifies the source and uses gentle persuasion and public relations techniques to achieve a desired outcome. For example, during the Persian Gulf War, the CIA airdropped leaflets before some Allied bombing runs to allow civilians time to evacuate and encourage military units to surrender. Black propaganda, on the other hand, is misinformation that identifies itself with one side of a conflict, but is truly produced by the opposing side.

Grey propaganda is the most mysterious of all because the source of the propaganda is never identified [7].

There are several basic steps that can help analysts and agents identify and label propaganda so it can be sorted by threat level and tactics to counter the propaganda be developed. Key questions to ask when determining the level of propaganda in any content include

- Fact checking by verifying content with reliable knowledgeable sources
- Objective analysis by subject matter experts
- Subjective analysis by staff or consultants
- Source analysis by evaluating the creator or support of any material
- Target audience analysis by determining the demographics of the intended audience
- Media impact analysis by evaluating what type of media outlets gave attention to the content
- Context analysis by examining the environment and circumstance from which the content originated
- Response analysis by reviewing what type of response the content received in social media
- Behavioral effect analysis by determining what behaviors the content is trying to prompt or has caused in the past
- Cultural analysis by determining if the content appeals to a specific society, culture, or subculture
- *Sociocultural analysis* of propaganda disseminators that integrates concepts, knowledge, and understanding of societies, populations, and other groups of people, including their activities, relationships, and perspectives across time and space at varying scales

Large government agencies and advocacy organizations have considerable resources for analyzing propaganda. However, many smaller agencies are not so well equipped or staffed. There are resources that can be helpful in examining propaganda. Several organizations work to fight against hate, including the Southern Poverty Law Center (www.splcenter.org), which monitors hate groups and hate crimes and provides material that can be helpful in monitoring and analyzing propaganda.

In addition to the Southern Poverty Law Center there are numerous groups that monitor and fight against hate. These organizations can be helpful in identifying and providing information on sources of social media propaganda

- American-Arab Anti-Discrimination Committee
- American Association of University Women
- Anti-Defamation League
- Asian American Justice Center

- Hindu American Foundation
- Human Rights Campaign
- The Leadership Conference on Civil and Human Rights
- National Association for the Advancement of Colored People
- National Center for Transgender Equality
- National Council of Jewish Women
- National Disability Rights Network
- National Gay and Lesbian Task Force
- National Organization for Women
- Sikh American Legal Defense and Education Fund
- The Sikh Coalition [8]

1.3 Understanding Extremists and Extremism

Basic extremism is the holding of beliefs and attitudes that are discriminatory, prejudicial, racial biased, antisocial, or anti-government and establishment. The passive extremist mostly broods and talks. They may be unpleasant people but fortunately not violent. On the other hand, violent extremism is defined by the FBI as encouraging, condoning, justifying, or supporting the commission of a violent act to achieve political, ideological, religious, social, or economic goals.

Many extremists and *international fanatics* join groups, which can be a powerful way to bring people together to achieve common goals. Groupthink happens, however, when those in the group stop stating their opinions or using critical thinking because they wish to avoid conflict. This can result in extremely poor decision-making. Violent extremist organizations are highly vulnerable to groupthink. They are often headed or motivated by a strong leader who is rarely challenged. Differing beliefs or ideas are not accepted. Violent extremist groups often work in secret, not only because their activities and plans are illegal, but also because they want to keep out other opinions. They tailor their social media consumption to sources and content that perpetuate their extremist beliefs.

Violent extremists are driven by twisted beliefs and values or ideologies that are tied to political, religious, economic, or social goals. Many violent extremist ideologies are based on the hatred of another race, religion, ethnicity, gender, or country/government. Violent extremists often think that their beliefs or ways of life are under attack and that extreme violence is the only solution to their frustrations and problems. Despite what they sometimes say, violent extremists often do not believe in fundamental values like democracy, human rights, tolerance, and inclusion. They often twist religious teachings and other beliefs to support their own goals.

A hate crime is a traditional offense like murder, arson, or vandalism with an added element of bias. For the purposes of collecting statistics, the FBI has defined a hate crime as a criminal offense against a person or property motivated in whole or in part by an offender's bias against a race, religion, disability, sexual orientation, ethnicity, gender, or gender identity. Hate itself is not a crime and the FBI by law must be mindful of protecting freedom of speech and other civil liberties.

Hate crimes are a type of violent extremism. They are directed at a person or group of people because of their race, color, religion, gender, gender identity, sexual orientation, national origin, or disability. These crimes can take many forms such as burning down a religious building or threatening or injuring another person. Hate crimes can be carried out by a single person or by small groups inspired by hateful beliefs. In many cases, an individual may commit a hate crime because of peer pressure. Many violent extremists wrongly blame their hate crimes on their victims, claiming the victims provoked them or were somehow at fault. Violent extremists have many distorted beliefs that they use to justify violence and hateful attacks including:

■ White Supremacy Extremists believe that members of inferior races should be killed.
■ Environmental Extremists believe that destroying property and even harming people is needed to protect the environment.
■ Militia Extremists believe that the U.S. government is a threat to the people and should be opposed by force.
■ Religious Extremists believe that violent attacks are needed to protect our beliefs from the corrupting influence of certain people or countries.
■ Anarchist Extremists believe that society needs no government or laws and that violence is necessary to create such a society [9].

The Uniform Crime Reporting (UCR) Program collects data about both single-bias and multiple-bias hate crimes. For each offense type reported, law enforcement must indicate at least one bias motivation. A single-bias incident is defined as an incident in which one or more offense types are motivated by the same bias. As of 2013, a multiple-bias incident is defined as an incident in which one or more offense types are motivated by two or more biases.

In 2015, there were 5,818 single-bias incidents that involved 6,837 offenses, 7,121 victims, and 5,475 known offenders. The 32 multiple-bias incidents reported in 2015 involved 48 offenses, 52 victims, and 18 known offenders. Analysis of the 5,818 single-bias incidents reported in 2015 revealed that

■ 56.9% were motivated by a race/ethnicity/ancestry bias.
■ 21.4% were prompted by religious bias.
■ 18.1% resulted from sexual-orientation bias.
■ 2.0% were motivated by gender-identity bias.
■ 1.3% were prompted by disability bias.
■ 0.4% (23 incidents) were motivated by a gender bias.

In 2015, law enforcement agencies reported that 4,029 single-bias hate crime offenses were motivated by race/ethnicity/ancestry. Of these offenses:

■ 52.7% were motivated by anti-Black or African-American bias.
■ 18.2% stemmed from anti-White bias.
■ 9.4% were classified as anti-Hispanic or Latino bias.
■ 3.4% were motivated by anti-American Indian or Alaska Native bias.
■ 3.4% were a result of bias against groups of individuals consisting of more than one race (anti-multiple races, group).
■ 3.3% resulted from anti-Asian bias.
■ 1.2% were classified as anti-Arab bias.
■ 0.1% (6 offenses) were motivated by bias of anti-Native Hawaiian or other Pacific Islander.
■ 8.2% were the result of an anti-other Race/Ethnicity/Ancestry bias [10].

Protecting the U.S. from terrorist attacks is one of the FBI's top priorities, which requires a variety of disciplines to work closely with a range of partners to neutralize terrorist cells and operatives and dismantle extremist networks worldwide. This includes cutting off financing and other forms of support provided to foreign terrorist organizations by terrorist sympathizers.

International terrorism is perpetrated by individuals and/or groups inspired by or associated with designated foreign terrorist organizations or nations (state-sponsored). For example, the December 2, 2015, shooting in San Bernardino, CA, that killed 14 people and wounded 22 involved a married couple who radicalized for some time prior to the attack and were inspired by multiple extremist ideologies and foreign terrorist organizations.

Domestic terrorism is perpetrated by individuals and/or groups inspired by or associated with primarily U.S.-based movements that espouse extremist ideologies of a political, religious, social, racial, or environmental nature. For example, the June 8, 2014, Las Vegas shooting, during which two police officers inside a restaurant were killed in an ambush-style attack, was committed by a married couple who held anti-government views and who intended to use the shooting to start a revolution.

The threat landscape has expanded considerably, though it is important to note that the more traditional threat posed by Al Qaeda and its affiliates is still present and active. The threat of domestic terrorism also remains persistent overall, with actors crossing the line from First Amendment protected rights to committing crimes to further their political agenda. Three factors have contributed to the evolution of the terrorism threat landscape:

■ *The Internet*: International and domestic actors have developed an extensive presence on the Internet through messaging platforms and online images, videos, and publications, which facilitate the groups' ability to radicalize and recruit individuals receptive to extremist messaging. Such message is constantly available to people participating in social networks dedicated to various causes, particularly younger people comfortable with communicating in the social media environment.

■ *Use of social media*: In addition to using the Internet, social media has allowed both international and domestic terrorists to gain unprecedented, virtual access to people living in the U.S. in an effort to enable homeland attacks. ISIS, in particular, encourages sympathizers to carry out simple attacks where they are located against targets, soft targets in particular, or to travel to ISIS-held territory in Iraq and Syria and join its ranks as foreign fighters. This message has resonated with supporters in the U.S. and abroad, and several recent attackers have claimed to be acting on ISIS' behalf.

■ *Homegrown violent extremists* (*HVEs*): The FBI does not focus solely on the terrorist threat emanating from overseas; it also must identify those sympathizers who have radicalized and become HVEs within the U.S. and aspire to attack the nation from within. HVEs are defined by the Bureau as global-jihad-inspired individuals who are based in the U.S., have been radicalized primarily in the U.S., and are not directly collaborating with a foreign terrorist organization. Currently, the FBI is investigating suspected HVEs in every state [11].

1.4 Radicalization and Propaganda

In February 2015, Michael Steinbach, Assistant Director, Counterterrorism Division U.S. FBI, discussed the dynamic threat posed by foreign fighters traveling in support of the Islamic State of Iraq and the Levant (ISIL) and the continued threat to the U.S. posed by homegrown violent extremists with the U.S. House Judiciary Committee, Subcommittee on Crime, Terrorism, Homeland Security, and Investigations. He commented that upwards of 150 Americans had traveled or attempted to travel to Syria to join extremist groups. While this number is small in comparison to the number of European travelers, the FBI had to consider the influence groups like ISIL have on individuals located in the U.S. who can be inspired to commit acts of violence. It is this blending of homegrown violent extremism with the foreign fighter ideology that was the latest adaptation of the threat. The possibility of homegrown extremists becoming radicalized by information available on the Internet had become very real. ISIL's widespread reach through the Internet and social media was most concerning as the group had proven dangerously competent at employing such tools. ISIL had used widespread social media campaigns to propagate its extremist ideas through propaganda included various English language publications circulated via social media.

As a communications tool, the Internet remains a critical node for terror groups to exploit. The FBI was concerned about recent calls to action by ISIL and its supporters on violent extremist web forums that could potentially motivate home-grown extremists to conduct attacks in the U.S. In one case, an Ohio-based man was arrested after he stated his intent to conduct an attack on the U.S. Capitol building. The individual used a Twitter account to post statements, videos, and other content indicating support for ISIL. In another incident ISIL released a video via social media networking sites reiterating the group's support of lone offender attacks in Western countries, which specifically advocated attacks against soldiers, law enforcement, and intelligence members. After that there were several incidents in the U.S. and Europe that indicated this call to arms had resonated among ISIL supporters and sympathizers. Al Qaeda in the Arabian Peninsula (AQAP) had also promoted conducting attacks using simple and inexpensive methods and continues to pose a threat to the U.S. AQAP's online English magazine Inspire advocated for lone wolves to conduct attacks against the U.S. homeland and Western targets and once again highlighted some ways to do so in an edition released on December 24, 2014. As with the previous editions, the magazine encouraged homegrown violent extremists to carry out small arms attacks and provide detailed how-to instructions for constructing and deploying a successful bomb [12].

Other warnings that Congress received included that social media are a critical tool that terror groups can exploit. The FBI had observed that certain children and young adults were being drawn deeper into the ISIL narrative. These individuals are often comfortable with virtual communication platforms, specifically social media networks. Ultimately, many of these individuals are seeking a sense of belonging. Social media has allowed groups, such as ISIL, to use the Internet to spot and assess potential recruits. With the widespread distribution of social media, terrorists can identify vulnerable individuals of all ages in the U.S. and spot, assess, recruit, and radicalize them either to travel abroad to join ISIL or to conduct a homeland attack. The foreign terrorist now had gained direct access into the U.S. like never before [13].

There is no single path to radicalization. There is no single profile of those individuals and there is no easy way to reveal who might actually be ready to take action. These are not professionally trained operatives with careful educated plans. Far too often, they are unstable, erratic, and prone to acting quickly and unpredict-ably. They are shifting from large-scale weaponry and sophisticated bombs to easily acquired weapons including small arms, knives, and vehicles. They are crude, but nimble, and often very lethal. They are also striking at what some refer to as soft targets such as people at concerts, people in cafes and clubs, people just walking down the street.

The terrorists of this stripe present very different challenges for the law enforce-ment to identify and track. The same can be said for domestic extremists, who pose their own threat of violence and economic harm, often by chillingly lethal lone offenders. Unfortunately, with the additional factor of default encryption on devices and the apps used in our communications, it's even more difficult to ascer-tain where they are, who they're working with, and what they are planning to do, even with a court order [14].

As technology advances, so too does terrorists' use of technology to communicate both to inspire and recruit. The widespread use of technology propagates the persistent terrorist message to attack U.S. interests whether in the Homeland or abroad. Terrorists' use of social media is resonating with vulnerable populations. Media platforms like Twitter are used to spread their message and enable supporters to find one another [15].

1.5 Social Media and Propaganda Consumption

Propaganda disseminators can reach a massive audience through Internet websites, social media and other media, which certainly legitimizes the fear that people can be radicalized from a level of intolerance and mild extremism to violent extremism. However, it is important to realize that the reach is not universal and social media may not be as pervasive as it seems. It is also important to recognize that people spend a lot of time watching television. Watching TV was the leisure activity that occupied the most time (2.7 hours per day), accounting for just over half of leisure time, on average, for those age 15 and over. The amount of time people spent watching TV varied by age. Those ages 15–44 spent the least amount of time watching TV, averaging around 2.0 hours per day, and those ages 65 and over spent the most time watching TV, averaging over 4.0 hours per day [16].

The U.S. Census Bureau, 2016 American Community Survey 1-Year Estimates, shows that 10.7% of households in the U.S. do not have a computer and 18.1% do not have an Internet subscription. In addition, 43.4% of households with incomes under $20,000 per year do not have an Internet subscription and 19.8% of households with annual incomes between $20,000 and $74,999 do not have an Internet subscription. The results of the survey are shown in Table 1.3.

Internet use increased significantly among children and older Americans between 2013 and 2015. Children between the ages of 3 and 14 became substantially more likely to go online, as Internet use among this group increased from 56% in 2013 to 66% in 2015, and Internet use among those aged 65 or older increased from 51% to 56% during the same period. In contrast, usage remained largely unchanged among those who were previously most likely to go online, with 83% of Americans between the ages of 25 and 44 reporting Internet use in both 2013 and 2015.

Along with increased use among the oldest and youngest Americans, the latest data suggests a slowly shrinking digital divide among other demographic lines, including educational attainment. While Internet use among those Americans with at least some post-secondary education remained steady between 2013 and 2015, it increased significantly among those with education up to a high school diploma. Although those with lower levels of educational attainment are gradually increasing their online presence, the gap in Internet use based on education remains quite large, with 88% of college graduates going online in 2015, compared with 58% of those with no high school diploma.

Table 1.3   Types of Computers and Internet Subscriptions 2016

	Number	Percent (%)
Total U.S. households	118,860,065	
Types of Computer		
Has one or more types of computing devices:	106,118,106	89.3
Desktop or laptop	91,941,841	77.4
Desktop or laptop with no other type of computing device	9,843,608	8.3
Smartphone	90,893,712	76.5
Smartphone with no other type of computing device	8,445,396	7.1
Tablet or other portable wireless computer	68,649,291	57.8
Tablet or other portable wireless computer with no other type of computing device	1,269,379	1.1
Other computer	3,610,014	3.0
Other computer with no other type of computing device	32,654	0.0
No computer	12,741,959	10.7
Type of Internet Subscriptions		
With an Internet subscription:	97,307,412	81.9
Dial-up with no other type of Internet subscription	510,666	0.4
Broadband of any type	96,796,746	81.4
Cellular data plan	81,066,266	68.2
Cellular data plan with no other type of Internet subscription	12,405,627	10.4
Broadband such as cable, fiber optic or DSL	80,017,971	67.3
Satellite Internet service	7,450,939	6.3
Without an Internet subscription	21,552,653	18.1

(Continued)

Table 1.3 (*Continued*) Types of Computers and Internet Subscriptions 2016

	Number	Percent (%)
Household Income in the Past 12 months (in 2016 Inflation-Adjusted Dollars)		
Less than $20,000:	19,278,704	
With dial-up Internet subscription alone	99,663	0.5
With a broadband Internet subscription	10,809,508	56.1
Without an Internet subscription	8,369,533	43.4
$20,000–$74,999:	53,720,614	
With dial-up Internet subscription alone	304,103	0.6
With a broadband Internet subscription	42,753,345	79.6
Without an Internet subscription	10,663,166	19.8
$75,000 or more:	45,860,747	
With dial-up Internet subscription alone	106,900	0.2
With a broadband Internet subscription	43,233,893	94.3
Without an Internet subscription	2,519,954	5.5

Source: U.S. Census Bureau, 2016 American Community Survey 1-Year Estimates, https://factfinder.census.gov/faces/tableservices/jsf/pages/productview. xhtml?pid=ACS_16_1YR_S2801&prodType=table.

Internet use also grew more rapidly among African-Americans (to 68% in 2015 from 64% in 2013), Hispanics (66% from 61%), and American Indians and Alaska Natives (70% from 61%), compared with Whites (78% from 75%) and Asian Americans (77% from 75%).

In addition, 70% of adult Internet users are using online Social Networks and 90% visit websites. Of those households that do not have Internet access 23% report that Internet access is not affordable [18].

1.6 The Relationship between Television and Violence

As mentioned earlier, television has played a significant role in society far longer than social media and the Internet in general. In 1972, the U.S. National Institute of Mental Health published a report that surveyed the literature and discussed original research on television viewing habits, the presentation of violent incidents, and the relationship between viewing aggression and aggressive acting-out.

The experimental studies bearing on the effects of aggressive television entertainment content on children supported certain conclusions.

■ First, violence depicted on television can immediately or shortly thereafter induce mimicking or copying by children.
■ Second, under certain circumstances television violence can instigate an increase in aggressive acts.

The report stated that the accumulated evidence, however, does not warrant the conclusion that televised violence has a uniformly adverse effect or the conclusion that it has an adverse effect on the majority of children. It cannot even be said that the majority of the children in the various studies reviewed showed an increase in aggressive behavior in response to the violent fare to which they were exposed. The evidence did indicate that televised violence may lead to increased aggressive behavior in certain subgroups of children, who might constitute a small portion or a substantial proportion of the total population of young television viewers.

The experimental studies reviewed discuss the characteristics of those children who are most likely to display an increase in aggressive behavior after exposure to televised violence. There is evidence that among young children (ages four to six) those most responsive to television violence are those who are highly aggressive to start with and who are prone to engage in spontaneous aggressive actions against their playmates and, in the case of boys, who display pleasure in viewing violence being inflicted upon others. The very young have difficulty comprehending the contextual setting in which violent acts are depicted and do not grasp the meaning of cues or labels concerning the make-believe character of violence episodes in fictional programs.

For older children, one study had found that labeling violence on a television program as make-believe rather than as real reduces the incidence of induced aggressive behavior. Contextual cues to the motivation of the aggressor and to the consequences of acts of violence might also modify the impact of televised violence, but evidence on this topic is inconclusive [19].

In October of 1999, U.S. Federal Communications Commission (FCC) Commissioner Gloria Tristani testified before the U.S. Congress on television violence. She stated that according to the Department of Justice (DOJ), 19% of all arrests in 1997 were juveniles, including 14% of all murder arrests and 17% of all violent crime arrests. Just as alarming, the Center for Disease Control and Prevention reported that 5.9% of high school students carried a gun in the 30 days prior to the survey, and 8.5% of them carry some sort of weapon to school. Social problems like youth violence rarely have simple causes. Whenever the problem boils over, as it did in Columbine, it's probably some lethal cocktail of many things all going wrong at once.

Tristani said one contributing factor to the youth violence that's afflicting the nation was violence on television but not saying that violence on TV is the main problem, or that other root causes should be ignored. But while TV violence is not the whole problem, she did believe it is part of the problem. The more risk factors can be reduced for children, the fewer situations that will boil over into violence. Violence on TV has become so prevalent, that we have all become a bit numb. Children are exposed to 8,000 murders and 100,000 acts of violence on TV by the time they complete elementary school. A recent survey found that prime time TV viewers see a violent scene every four minutes. A recent study by Children Now found that almost three-fourths of children ages 10–17 describe males on TV as violent.

She further commented on what parents are up against today, now that we have hundreds of TV channels, video arcades, the Internet, VCRs, and portable stereos, each trying to outdo the others to capture kids' attention by being more lewd and outrageous than the next. Our information society has so many ways of getting into our children's heads that it's not realistic to expect parents to monitor them all but at a minimum, we should stop targeting our children with violence [20].

A report to the U.S. FCC In the Matter of Violent Television Programming and Its Impact on Children presented on April 6, 2007 discussed if it is in the public interest for the government to adopt a definition of excessively violent programming that is harmful to children, and could the government formulate and implement such a definition in a constitutional manner.

The report stated that there is deep concern among many American parents and health professionals regarding harm from viewing violence in media. The report also agreed with the views of the U.S. Surgeon General that there is strong evidence that exposure to violence in the media can increase aggressive behavior in children, at least in the short term. The report also recognized that violent content is a protected form of speech under the First Amendment. It was noted that the government interests at stake, such as protecting children from excessively violent television programming, are similar to those which have been found to justify other content-based regulations. The Commission asked questions concerning the adequacy of current program blocking technology and the effectiveness of the TV ratings system in helping parents control access to violent programming.

The report findings were that although the V-chip and TV ratings system appear useful in the abstract, they are not effective at protecting children from violent content for a number of reasons. In particular, it was determined that the TV ratings system has certain weaknesses that prevent parents from screening out much programming that they find objectionable.

There has been some dispute regarding the amount of research in the field of television violence and aggression. However, more than 3,500 research studies have examined the association between media violence and violent behavior; all but 18 had shown a positive relationship. Most of the discrepancies in the claims about how many studies have been conducted are the result of differing definitions of what constitutes a viable study. An important conclusion is that exposure to violent programming may desensitize the child's innate negative emotional response to violence, thus making aggressive acts easier to commit or tolerate [21].

The concern about the relationship between television violence, and now even video game violence, is that children exposed to excessive violence on television may be malleable to recruitment through social media propaganda when they become adults. Now the television industry has voluntary ratings for TV programs that appear in the corner of your television screen during the first 15 seconds of each television program. The ratings are also included in many magazines that give TV ratings and in the television listings of many newspapers. Ratings are given to all television programming except news, commercials, sports, and unedited movies on premium cable channels.

A 2013 Federal Trade Commission (FTC) undercover shopper survey found that video game retailers continue to enforce age-based ratings, while movie theaters have made marked improvement in box office enforcement. Only 13% of underage shoppers were able to purchase M-rated video games, while a historic low of 24% were able to purchase tickets to R-rated movies. In addition, for the first time since the FTC began its mystery shop program in 2000, music CD retailers turned away more than half of the undercover shoppers. Movie DVD retailers also demonstrated steady improvement, permitting less than one-third of child shoppers to purchase R-rated DVDs and unrated DVDs of movies that had been rated R for theaters.

The FTC arranged for 13- to 16-year-olds, unaccompanied by a parent, to attempt to buy R-rated movie tickets; R-rated DVDs; unrated DVDs that were R-rated when first released in theaters; music CDs carrying a Parental Advisory Label (PAL) that warns of explicit content; and video games rated M, which means they may be suitable for persons age 17 and older. Between April and June 2012, the teenagers attempted to buy these products, which are rated or labeled by self-regulatory bodies of the entertainment industry from national and regional chain stores and theaters across the U.S.

- *Movie tickets*: Ratings enforcement at the movie box office was at its highest level since the FTC began its mystery shopper program in 2000. Less than one-quarter of underage shoppers were able to buy a ticket to an R-rated movie, down from one-third in 2010.
- *Movie DVDs*: Retailers of R-rated and unrated DVDs continued their trend toward increased ratings enforcement. Thirty percent of shoppers were able to purchase R-rated DVDs compared to 38% in 2010, and 30% were able to buy unrated DVDs, down from 47% in 2010.
- *Music CDs*: Retailers of explicit-content music are increasingly turning away children attempting to purchase music CDs bearing the Parental Advisory Label. Less than half of underage shoppers (47%) were able to purchase CDs with this label, down from 64% in 2010 and 72% in 2009.
- *Video games*: Unchanged from 2010, 13% of underage teenage shoppers were able to buy M-rated video games—the highest level of compliance among the industries [22].

1.7 Countering Propaganda in Social Media

The Global Engagement Center is an interagency entity, housed at the U.S. State Department, charged with coordinating U.S. counterterrorism messaging to foreign audiences. The Center leads the coordination, integration, and synchronization of Government-wide communications activities directed at foreign audiences abroad in order to counter the messaging and diminish the influence of international terrorist organizations, such as ISIL. Designed to be an agile, innovative organization, the Center uses modern, cutting-edge technology and takes advantage of the best talent and tools throughout the private sector and government. The Global Engagement Center replaced the Center for Strategic Counterterrorism Communications. The new strategy seeks to be more effective in the information space and is focused on partner-driven messaging and data analytics.

The Global Engagement Center is led by the U.S. State Department, but has active senior level participation of the Department of Defense (DoD), the U.S. Agency for International Development (USAID), the Broadcasting Board of Governors, the Intelligence Community, and other relevant agencies. The Center develops, integrates, and synchronizes whole-of-government initiatives to expose and counter foreign disinformation operations enemies and proactively advance fact-based narratives that support U.S. allies and interests. The work of the Center is focused around four core areas:

- *Partnerships*: Including empowering and building the capacity of a global network of positive messengers against violent extremism. Operating at a local level, partners use *credible voices* to deliver messages that resonate with at-risk populations. Partners include NGOs, schools, young people, social and civil society leaders, religious leaders, governments, and others. They are supported through a variety of means including funding, technical assistance, capacity building, and conceiving and implementing joint projects.
- *Data analytics*: The Center is becoming an analytics-based organization and is using data analytics systems from both the public and private sectors to better understand radicalization dynamics online, to guide and inform messaging efforts, and to measure effectiveness. In addition to data analytics systems, data from proven polling operations, target audience studies, and academic research are also being used.
- *Content*: The Center is pursuing collaborative, thematic campaigns in coordination with counter-ISIL coalition nations and other global partners. The Center also develops and procures unbranded *counter-messaging* and *counter-narratives to radicalization* content and makes it available to the global network of partners. Direct engagement with violent extremists has been reduced in favor of partner-driven messaging and enhancing the content capabilities of partners.

■ *Interagency engagement*: The Center liaises daily with the interagency to coordinate day to day operations and campaign efforts among the many U.S. national security agencies that operate in the information space. The Center is staffed by detailees from several U.S. agencies, allowing the Center to effectively coordinate, integrate, and synchronize efforts across the interagency [23].

The center supports the development of *alternative master narratives* designed to replace violent extremist narratives and *alternative narratives* designed to replace radical or extremist narratives related to a specific context. The dissemination of the alternative narratives is assisted by *civil society leaders* who assist in developing a *community-targeted approach* to reduce vulnerability and among populations and thus build greater *community resilience* against radicalization to violent extremism.

1.8 Summary

To analyze the potential impact of propaganda it is important to have an understanding how people use their time in their daily lives and the time they spend exposed to social media. It is also important to have a common definition of who produces propaganda and who consumes propaganda. This chapter discusses social media propaganda creation, delivery, and consumption as well as how propaganda is being analyzed and combated. Key points covered include:

■ Propaganda is a systematic effort to spread opinions or beliefs regardless of their validity, accuracy or honesty.
■ Propaganda has long been everywhere in the broadcast and print media and now it is a dominant force in social media.
■ Governments of the Russian Federation and the People's Republic of China use disinformation and other propaganda tools to undermine the national security objectives of the U.S.
■ The Russian Federation, in particular, has conducted sophisticated and large-scale disinformation campaigns.
■ The creation and dissemination of propaganda is becoming increasingly more sophisticated in a data driven world.
■ There are several themes or messages that show up in social media propaganda and they are very similar to those used in business advertising campaigns.
■ Terrorists, like every other multi-national organization, are using the Internet to grow their business and to connect with like-minded individuals.
■ To identify propaganda agencies and organizations can require a variety of methods ranging from simple straightforward fact checking to complex psychological analysis.

- Violent extremism is defined by the FBI as encouraging, condoning, justifying, or supporting the commission of a violent act to achieve political, ideological, religious, social, or economic goals.
- Many violent extremist ideologies are based on the hatred of another race, religion, ethnicity, gender, or country/government.
- International terrorism is perpetrated by individuals and/or groups inspired by or associated with designated foreign terrorist organizations or nations (state-sponsored). Domestic terrorism is perpetrated by individuals and/or groups inspired by or associated with primarily U.S.-based movements that espouse extremist ideologies of a political, religious, social, racial, or environmental nature.
- There is no single path to radicalization. There is no single profile of those individuals and there is no easy way to reveal who might actually be ready to take action.
- Use of Social Media: In addition to using the Internet, social media has allowed both international and domestic terrorists to gain unprecedented, virtual access to people living in the U.S. in an effort to enable homeland attacks.
- With the widespread distribution of social media, terrorists can identify vulnerable individuals of all ages in the U.S. and spot, assess, recruit, and radicalize them either to travel abroad to join ISIL or to conduct a homeland attack.
- American parents and health professionals see harmful effects from viewing violence in media. Violence depicted on television can immediately or shortly thereafter induce mimicking or copying by children.
- The concern about the relationship between television violence, and now even video game violence is that children exposed to excessive violence on television may be malleable to recruitment through propaganda when they become adults.
- The Global Engagement Center is an interagency entity, housed at the U.S. State Department, is charged with coordinating U.S. counterterrorism messaging to foreign audiences.

1.9 Course Activities

Project number one: Identify three propaganda social media posts by using the propaganda analysis techniques in this chapter and explain why and how you determined they are propaganda. Compare your propaganda social media posts with other participants in the course.

Project number two: Analyze which propaganda technique described in his chapter is used in each of the three social media posts identified in project number one. Compare your analysis with those of other participants in the course.

Project number three: Create a social media propaganda post using the propaganda techniques identified in this chapter. Compare your social media propaganda post with those of other participants in the course.

Project number four: Discuss the propaganda present in the book 1984 by George Orwell.

Project number five: Discuss why the Nazi propaganda used in Germany before and during World War II was as effective as it was.

References

1. U.S. Senate. S.2692—114th Congress (2015–2016) Countering Information Warfare Act of 2016. Accessed November 18, 2017 https://www.congress.gov/bill/114th-congress/senate-bill/2692/text.
2. President Signs Portman-Murphy Counter-Propaganda Bill into Law. Press release from U.S. Senator Bob Portman, December 23, 2016. Accessed November 18, 2017 https://www.portman.senate.gov/public/index.cfm?p=press-releases&id=F973E46B-AA8C-4F3E-91B4-8EC0FC7F2F3E.
3. M. Erbschloe. *Social Media Warfare: Equal Weapons for All*, CRC Press, Boca Raton, FL, 2017.
4. U.S. National Park Service Manzanar National Historic Site. Propaganda and the Mass Media Glossary. Accessed November 18, 2017 https://www.nps.gov/manz/learn/education/propaganda-glossary.htm.
5. R. S. Mueller, III. *Federal Bureau of Investigation. Comments Delivered at the RSA Cyber Security Conference*, San Francisco, CA, March 1, 2012. Accessed November 18, 2017 https://archives.fbi.gov/archives/news/speeches/combating-threats-in-the-cyber-world-outsmarting-terrorists-hackers-and-spies.
6. J. B. Comey. *FBI. Statement Before the Senate Judiciary Committee*, Washington, DC, May 3, 2017. Accessed November 18, 2017 https://www.fbi.gov/news/testimony/oversight-of-the-federal-bureau-of-investigation-050317.
7. The Spymaster's Toolkit. U.S. CIA, February 14, 2016. Accessed November 18, 2017 https://www.cia.gov/news-information/featured-story-archive/2016-featured-story-archive/the-spymasters-toolkit.html.
8. Hate Crimes. *What We Investigate*. U.S. FBI. Accessed November 19, 2017 https://www.fbi.gov/investigate/civil-rights/hate-crimes.
9. U.S. FBI. *What is Violent Extremism?* Accessed November 19, 2017 https://www.fbi.gov/cve508/teen-website/what-is-violent-extremism.
10. U.S. FBI. *About Hate Crime Statistics, 2015 and Recent Developments*. Accessed November 19, 2017 https://ucr.fbi.gov/hate-crime/2015.
11. U.S. FBI. *Terrorism*. Accessed November 19, 2017 https://www.fbi.gov/investigate/terrorism.
12. M. Steinbach. Counterterrorism Division U.S. FBI. ISIL in America: Domestic terror and radicalization. *Statement Before the House Judiciary Committee, Subcommittee on Crime, Terrorism, Homeland Security, and Investigations*, Washington, DC, February 26, 2015. Accessed November 19, 2017 https://www.fbi.gov/news/testimony/isil-in-america-domestic-terror-and-radicalization.
13. M. Steinbach. National Security Branch U.S. FBI/ISIL online: Countering terrorist radicalization and recruitment on the Internet and social media. *Statement Before the Senate Committee on Homeland Security and Governmental Affairs*,

Permanent Subcommittee on Investigations, Washington, DC, July 6, 2016. Accessed November 19, 2017 https://www.fbi.gov/news/testimony/isil-online-countering-terrorist-radicalization-and-recruitment-on-the-internet-and-social-media-.

14. C. Wray. U.S. FBI. *Speaking at the Seventh Annual High-Value Detainee Interrogation Group (HIG) Research Symposium*, U.S. Institute of Peace, Washington, DC, October 16, 2017. Accessed November 19, 2017 https://www.fbi.gov/news/speeches/hig-using-science-and-research-to-combat-national-security-threats.

15. M. B. Steinbach. Counterterrorism Division U.S. FBI. Terrorism gone viral: The attack in Garland, Texas and beyond statement. *Before the House Homeland Security Committee*, Washington, DC, June 3, 2015. Accessed November 19, 2017 https://www.fbi.gov/news/testimony/terrorism-gone-viral-the-attack-in-garland-texas-and-beyond.

16. U.S. Bureau of Labor Statistics. *American Time Use Survey Summary*, June 27, 2017. Accessed November 19, 2017 https://www.bls.gov/news.release/atus.nr0.htm.

17. U.S. Census Bureau. 2016 *American Community Survey 1-Year Estimates.* https://factfinder.census.gov/faces/tableservices/jsf/pages/productview.xhtml?pid=ACS_16_1YR_S2801&prodType=table.

18. U.S. National Telecommunications and Information Administration. *First Look: Internet Use in 2015*, March 21, 2016. Accessed November 19, 2017 https://www.ntia.doc.gov/blog/2016/first-look-internet-use-2015.

19. U.S. Department of Health, Education, and Welfare. National Institute of Mental Health. *Television and Growing Up—The Impact of Televised Violence—Report to the Surgeon General, U.S. Public Health Service from the Surgeon General's Scientific Advisory Committee on Television and Social Behavior*, 1972. Accessed November 20, 2017 https://www.ncjrs.gov/App/publications/Abstract.aspx?id=18009.

20. Wrestling for Our Children's Future. *Remarks of U.S. FCC Commissioner Gloria Tristani before the U.S. Congress on Television Violence of Puerto Rico*, October 12, 1999. Accessed November 20, 2017 https://www.fcc.gov/Speeches/Tristani/spgt916.html.

21. Violent Television Programming and its impact on children. Report to the U.S. FCC, April 6, 2007. Accessed November 20, 2017 https://apps.fcc.gov/edocs_public/attachmatch/FCC-07-50A1.pdf.

22. U.S. FTC. FTC undercover shopper survey on entertainment ratings enforcement finds compliance highest among video game sellers and movie theaters, March 25, 2013. Accessed November 20, 2017 https://www.ftc.gov/news-events/press-releases/2013/03/ftc-undercover-shopper-survey-entertainment-ratings-enforcement.

23. U.S. Department of State. *Fact Sheet: The Global Engagement Center*, July 6, 2016. Accessed November 20, 2017 https://geneva.usmission.gov/2016/07/07/fact-sheet-the-global-engagement-center/.

Chapter 2

Social Media Propaganda and the Political Electoral Process

2.1 Russian Propaganda Activities in the 2016 U.S. Elections

During the Cold War, the Soviet Union used intelligence officers, influence agents, forgeries, and press placements to disparage candidates perceived as hostile to the Kremlin, according to a former KGB archivist. Since the Cold War, Russian intelligence efforts related to U.S. elections have primarily focused on foreign intelligence collection. For decades, Russian and Soviet intelligence services have sought to collect insider information from U.S. political parties that could help Russian leaders understand a new U.S. administration's plans and priorities.

In January 2017, the U.S. Intelligence Community Assessment entitled *Assessing Russian Activities and Intentions in Recent US Elections* was released and was rather immediately discounted and dismissed by President Trump. The report stated that Russian intelligence obtained and maintained access to elements of multiple U.S. state or local electoral boards. DHS assesses that the types of systems Russian actors targeted or compromised were not involved in vote tallying. In addition, The Russian state-run propaganda machine contributed to the influence campaign by serving as a platform for Kremlin messaging to Russian and international audiences.

The report concluded with high confidence that Russian President Vladimir Putin ordered an influence campaign in 2016 aimed at the U.S. presidential election, the consistent goals of which were to undermine public faith in the U.S.

democratic process, denigrate Secretary Clinton, and harm her electability and potential presidency. In addition, Putin and the Russian government developed a clear preference for President Trump. When it appeared to Moscow that Secretary Clinton was likely to win the election, the Russian influence campaign then focused on undermining her expected presidency and publicly contrasting her unfavorably to him.

Putin most likely wanted to discredit Secretary Clinton because he has publicly blamed her since 2011 for inciting mass protests against his regime in late 2011 and early 2012 and because he holds a grudge for comments he almost certainly saw as disparaging him. Beginning in June 2016, Putin's public comments about the U.S. presidential race avoided directly praising President Trump, probably because Kremlin officials thought that any praise from Putin personally would backfire in the U.S.

Nonetheless, Putin publicly indicated a preference for Trump's stated policy to work with Russia, and pro-Kremlin figures spoke highly about what they saw as his Russia-friendly positions on Syria and Ukraine. Putin publicly contrasted Trump's approach to Russia with Secretary Clinton's aggressive rhetoric. Putin has had many positive experiences working with Western political leaders whose business interests made them more disposed to deal with Russia, such as former Italian Prime Minister Silvio Berlusconi and former German Chancellor Gerhard Schroeder.

Before the election, Russian diplomats had publicly denounced the U.S. electoral process and were prepared to publicly call into question the validity of the results. Putin, Russian officials, and other pro-Kremlin pundits stopped publicly criticizing the U.S. election process as unfair almost immediately after the election because Moscow probably assessed it would be counterproductive to building positive relations.

Kremlin bloggers had prepared a Twitter campaign, #DemocracyRIP, on election night in anticipation of Secretary Clinton's victory, judging from their social media activity. Moscow's use of disclosures during the U.S. election was unprecedented, but its influence campaign otherwise followed a longstanding Russian messaging strategy that blends covert intelligence operations such as cyber activity with overt efforts by Russian government agencies, state-funded media, third-party intermediaries, and paid social media users or trolls.

Moscow's campaign aimed at the U.S. election reflected years of investment in its capabilities, which Moscow has honed in the former Soviet states. By their nature, Russian influence campaigns are multifaceted and designed to be deniable because they use a mix of agents of influence, cutouts, front organizations, and false-flag operations. Moscow demonstrated this during the Ukraine crisis in 2014, when Russia deployed forces and advisers to eastern Ukraine and denied it publicly.

Russia's intelligence services conducted cyber operations against targets associated with the 2016 U.S. presidential election, including targets associated with both major U.S. political parties. Russian intelligence services collected data against the

U.S. primary campaigns, think tanks, and lobbying groups they viewed as likely to shape future U.S. policies. In July 2015, Russian intelligence gained access to Democratic National Committee (DNC) networks and maintained that access until at least June 2016.

The General Staff Main Intelligence Directorate (GRU) probably began cyber operations aimed at the U.S. election by March 2016. The GRU operations resulted in the compromise of the personal e-mail accounts of Democratic Party officials and political figures. By May, the GRU had exfiltrated large volumes of data from the DNC. The GRU used the Guccifer 2.0 persona, DCLeaks.com, and WikiLeaks to release U.S. victim data obtained in cyber operations publicly and in exclusives to media outlets. Guccifer 2.0, who claimed to be an independent Romanian hacker, made multiple contradictory statements and false claims about his likely Russian identity throughout the election. Press reporting suggests more than one person claiming to be Guccifer 2.0 interacted with journalists.

Content that was taken from e-mail accounts targeted by the GRU in March 2016 appeared on DCLeaks.com starting in June. The GRU relayed material it acquired from the DNC and senior Democratic officials to WikiLeaks. Moscow most likely chose WikiLeaks because of its self-proclaimed reputation for authenticity. Disclosures through WikiLeaks did not contain any evident forgeries. In early September, Putin said publicly it was important the DNC data was exposed to WikiLeaks, calling the search for the source of the leaks a distraction and denying Russian state-level involvement.

The Kremlin's principal international propaganda outlet RT (formerly Russia Today) has actively collaborated with WikiLeaks. RT's editor-in-chief visited WikiLeaks founder Julian Assange at the Ecuadorian Embassy in London in August 2013, where they discussed renewing his broadcast contract with RT, according to Russian and Western media. Russian media subsequently announced that RT had become the only Russian media company to partner with WikiLeaks and had received access to new leaks of secret information. RT routinely gives Assange sympathetic coverage and provides him a platform to denounce the U.S.

On 6 August, RT published an English language video called *Julian Assange Special: Do WikiLeaks Have the E-mail That'll Put Clinton in Prison?* and an exclusive interview with Assange entitled *Clinton and ISIS Funded by the Same Money*. RT's most popular video on Secretary Clinton, *How 100% of the Clintons' "Charity" Went to...Themselves*, had more than 9 million views on social media platforms. RT's most popular English language video about President Trump, called *Trump Will Not Be Permitted to Win*, featured Assange and had 2.2 million views.

Russia used social media trolls as well as RT as part of its influence efforts to denigrate Secretary Clinton. This effort amplified stories on scandals about Secretary Clinton and the role of WikiLeaks in the election campaign. The likely financier of the so-called Internet Research Agency (IRA) of professional trolls located in Saint Petersburg is a close Putin ally with ties to Russian intelligence. A journalist who is a leading expert on the IRA claimed that some social media accounts that appear to be tied to Russia's professional trolls—because they previously were devoted to supporting Russian actions in Ukraine—started to advocate for President Trump as early as December 2015 [1].

In June 2017, Congressman French Hill spoke to a Congressional Hearing, contending that even though witness after witness has traipsed through the House and Senate to testify on the subject of Russian meddling in U.S. elections and questions persist as to whether Trump associates wittingly or unwittingly colluded to aid Russia in its goals, there is little indication of a plan to act despite all the bipartisan indignation. The long faces of lawmakers from both parties as intelligence experts have warned that Russia used active measures to sow doubt, helped spread fake stories that would harm Hillary Clinton, and stolen voter data have not inspired a call to arms [2].

In June 2017, Senator Sheldon Whitehouse made a written statement for a Congressional hearing on Transparency, Corruption, and Russian Meddling. He contended that the U.S. suffered an unprecedented intrusion into the Presidential elections and referred to the January 2017 intelligence agencies report that stated agents of Russia, on the orders of President Vladimir Putin, engaged in a massive election influence campaign throughout 2016 and that Congress had to act against such interference decisively. The strengthening of economic sanctions against the Russian gangster state hit them where it hurts, right in the oligarch. However, even though Russia was interfering, there has been little sign of consequences so far from the Trump White House.

Michael Flynn, as adviser to the President-elect, had illicit communications with the Russian Ambassador, about which he then lied. Trump appointees at the State Department alarmed career officials with their rush to craft a pro-Russia program. President Trump held an unprecedented, cozy meeting with Russian envoys, a meeting for which Putin says he has a transcript. In Europe, Trump, dropping the assurances about Article 5 protections from his NATO speech, gave the Russians joy. The Trump administration has been reportedly trying to return two compounds used by Russian intelligence here in the United States to Russian control. Former FBI Director James Comey told the Senate during the previous week that President Trump never spoke to him, not even once, about defending against Russia's acts of aggression.

Senators Whitehouse and Graham held hearings in the Judiciary Subcommittee on Crime and Terrorism, exploring the Russian toolbox for interference in democracies across the globe and how Russia exploits the dark shadows of other countries' political and economic systems. One tool is campaign money. Russia is reported to have funneled money to French far-right party Presidential candidate, Marine Le Pen, for instance, as part of a reward for her support of Russia's actions in Crimea. Ken Wainstein, Homeland Security Advisor to George W. Bush, cited Russia as a threat of that kind of foreign financial infiltration in the U.S.

The U.S. election system permits the free flow of dark money. Since the Citizens United decision, there has been unprecedented dark money flow into the elections from anonymous dark money organizations, groups that can hide the identities of their big donors. It is not known who is behind that dark money or what they are demanding in return.

The Kremlin's Trojan Horses is a study of Russian influence in Western Europe done by the Atlantic Council. Russia takes advantage of nontransparency in campaign financing and financial transactions, the report says, to build political alliances with ideologically friendly political groups and individuals, as well as to establish pro-Russian organizations in civil society, creating a shadowy web of political networks that help to propagate the regime's point of view.

Senator Whitehouse further contended that electoral rules should be amended, so that publicly funded political groups, primarily political parties, should at the very least be required to report the sources of their funding. The Kremlin's blatant attempts to influence and disrupt the U.S. Presidential election should serve as an inspiration for a democratic pushback. Where Russia can work in darkness, Russian agents systematically exploit democratic institutions to acquire influence over politicians and political systems using corruption. Russia has done this in the former Soviet Union and in Europe for decades. Part of the Kremlin's playbook is to use shell corporations and other devices to establish illicit financial relationships with prominent local figures. The shell entities allow Russian money to flow anonymously into crooked deals. The crooked deals give rise to corrupt relationships, and these corrupt relationships give Russia leverage, either through the carrot of continued bribery of the prominent local figure or the stick of threatened disclosure of the crooked deal imperiling the prominent local figure. The answer to the problem of shell corporations is simple: Have each state track the actual owners of companies they charter and make that information available to federal, state, and local law enforcement agencies through proper process [3].

2.2 Google Testifies before U.S. Congress

In November 2017, representatives from the social media companies Google®, Facebook®, and Twitter® testified before the U.S. Congress at the Hearing before the U.S. House of Representatives Permanent Select Committee on Intelligence regarding Russian meddling in the U.S. 2016 elections. Kent Walker, Google's lead of Legal, Policy, Trust and Safety, and Philanthropy teams and a former Assistant U.S. Attorney at the Department of Justice (DOJ) focusing on technology crimes, made the Google presentation.

He indicated that Google believes that it has a responsibility to prevent the misuse of the Google platforms and the abuse of the tools and platforms Google provides is antithetical to that mission. Google is committed to working with Congress, law enforcement, others in the industry, and the NGO community to strengthen protections around elections and ensure the security of users, and help combat disinformation. However, Google is dealing with difficult questions that balance free expression issues, unprecedented access to information, and the need to provide high quality content to users. Other points he made include:

■ Disinformation and propaganda campaigns are not new, and have involved many different types of media and publications. When it comes to online platforms, for many years nation states and criminals attempt to breach firewalls, game search results, and interfere with platforms. These attempts range from large-scale threats, such as distributed denial of service attacks, all the way down to small-scale, extremely targeted attacks, such as attempts to gain access to e-mail accounts of high-profile individuals.

■ Google tools detect and prevent artificially boosting content, spam, and other attempts to manipulate systems. On Google News, for example, links are label so users can see if the content is locally sourced, an OpEd, or an in-depth piece.

■ For Google Search, the quality guidelines have been updated and evaluations help identify misleading information, helping surface more authoritative content from the web. Google has updated advertising guidelines to prohibit ads on sites that misrepresent themselves. On YouTube, there is a sophisticated spam and security-breach detection system to detect anomalous behavior and catch people trying to inflate view counts of videos or numbers of subscribers.

■ While Google did find activity associated with suspected government-backed accounts, that activity appears to have been limited. Relevant information was provided to the Committee and issued in a public summary of the results of the review.

■ Google found two accounts that appear to be associated with this effort. These accounts spent approximately $4,700 dollars in connection with the 2016 presidential election, representing less than 0.0002% of the total amount spent on that race.

■ On YouTube, 18 channels—with roughly 1,100 videos, a total of 43 hours of content—were found that were uploaded by individuals who we suspect are associated with this effort and which contained political content. These videos generally had very low view counts; only around 3% had more than 5,000 views. The videos were not targeted to any particular sector of the U.S. population as that's not feasible on YouTube.

■ In addition, it was found that a limited number of Gmail accounts appear to have been primarily used to set up accounts on social media platforms.

■ In 2018, Google will release a transparency report for election ads, sharing data about who is buying election ads on the platforms and how much money is being spent. The transparency report will be paired with a database of election ad creatives from across ads products and the database will be available for public research.

■ Google will continue enhancing existing safeguards to ensure that only U.S. nationals can buy U.S. election ads. Moving forward, Google will go further by verifying the identity of anyone who wants to run an election ad or use political-interest-based tools and confirming that person is permitted to run that advertisement.

▪ Google has supported significant outreach to increase security for candidates and campaigns across the U.S., France, Germany, and other countries. Google has offered in-person briefings and introduced a suite of digital tools designed to help election websites and political campaigns protect themselves from phishing, unauthorized account access, and other digital attacks.

▪ Google has partnered with the National Cyber Security Alliance to fund and advise on security training programs that focus specifically on elected officials, campaigns, and staff members. Google is also increasing a long-standing support for the bipartisan Defending Digital Democracy Project at the Belfer Center for Science and International Affairs at Harvard Kennedy School [4].

2.3 Facebook Testifies before U.S. Congress

Also, in November 2017, before The U.S. House of Representatives Permanent Select Committee on Intelligence, Colin Stretch, General Counsel of Facebook, provided comments and information about Russian meddling in the 2016 presidential election. He indicated that Facebook believes it has an important role to play in the democratic process and that foreign actors, hiding behind fake accounts, abused the platform and other Internet services to try to sow division and discord and to try to undermine the election process, which is an assault on democracy that also violates Facebook values.

He reported that in the continuing investigation it was found that these actors used fake accounts to place ads on Facebook and Instagram® that reached millions of Americans over a two-year period, and that those ads were used to promote *pages*, which in turn posted more content. People shared these posts, spreading them further. Many of these ads and posts are inflammatory. (See Table 2.1 for text of some of the ads Facebook submitted to the Committee.) Some are downright offensive. All of these accounts and pages violated Facebook policies, and they have been removed. Other points covered include:

▪ Going forward, Facebook is making some very significant investments and are hiring more ad reviewers, doubling or more security engineering efforts, putting in place tighter ad content restrictions, launching new tools to improve ad transparency, and requiring documentation from political ad buyers.

▪ The goal of *News Feed* is to show people the stories that are most relevant to them. The average person has thousands of things on any given day that they could read in their News Feed, so a personalized ranking determines the order of stories they are shown making each person's News Feed unique. It is shaped by the friends they add; the people, topics, and news sources they follow; the groups they join; and other signals like their past interactions.

- On average, a person in the U.S. is served roughly 220 stories in News Feed each day. From 2015 to 2017, Americans using Facebook were exposed to, or served, a total of over 33 trillion stories in their News Feeds.
- The News Feed is also a place where people see ads on Facebook. To advertise in News Feed, a person must first set up a Facebook account using their real identity and creating a Facebook page. These pages represent a wide range of people, places, and things, including causes that people are interested in. Any user may create a page to express support for or interest in a topic, but only official representatives can create a page on behalf of an organization, business, brand, or public figure. It is against Facebook terms for pages to contain false, misleading, fraudulent, or deceptive claims or content.
- Facebook marks some official pages such as for a public figure, media company, or brand with a verified badge to let people know they are authentic. All pages must comply with Community Standards and ensure that all the stories they post or share respect policies prohibiting hate speech, violence, and sexual content, among other restrictions. People can like or follow a page to get updates, such as posts, photos, or videos, in their News Feed. The average person in the U.S. likes 178 pages.
- It is easy for people to override Facebook recommendations by giving them additional controls over whether they see a page's updates higher in their News Feed or not at all. For context, from 2015 to 2017, people in the U.S. saw 11.1 trillion posts from pages on Facebook.
- Page administrators can create ads to promote their page and show their posts to more people. The vast majority of advertisers are small- and medium-sized businesses that use self-service tools to create ads to reach their customers. Advertisers choose the audience they want to reach based on demographics, interests, behaviors or contact information. They can choose from different ad formats, upload images or video, and write the text they want people to see.
- Advertisers can serve ads on the platform for as little as $0.50 per day using a credit card or other payment method. By using these tools, advertisers agree to Self-Serve Ad Terms. Before ads appear on Facebook or Instagram, they go through an ad review process that includes automated checks of an ad's images, text, targeting and positioning, in addition to the content on the ad's landing page. People on Facebook can also report ads, find more information about why they are being shown a particular ad, and update their ad preferences to influence the type of ads they see.
- Fake accounts undermine this objective, and are closely related to the creation and spread of inauthentic communication such as spam as well as used to carry out disinformation campaigns like the one associated with the Internet Research Agency (IRA), a Russian company located in St. Petersburg.
- Each day, millions of fake accounts are blocked at registration. The systems examine thousands of account attributes and focus on detecting behaviors that are very difficult for bad actors to fake, including their connections to others on Facebook.

- For years, Facebook had been aware of other types of activity that appeared to come from Russian sources and which have been traditional security threats such as attacking people's accounts or using social media platforms to spread stolen information.
- In several instances before November 8, 2016, a security team detected and mitigated threats from actors with ties to Russia and reported them to U.S. law enforcement officials. This included activity from a cluster of accounts assessed to belong to a group (APT28) that the U.S. government has publicly linked to Russian military intelligence services. This activity, which was aimed at employees of major U.S. political parties, fell into the normal categories of offensive cyber activities being monitored. Facebook warned the targets who were at highest risk, and were later in contact with law enforcement authorities on this activity.
- Later in the summer we also started to see a new kind of behavior from APT28-related accounts, namely, the creation of fake personas that were then used to seed stolen information to journalists. These fake personas were organized under the banner of an organization that called itself DC Leaks. This activity violated Facebook policies, and the DC Leaks accounts were removed.
- After the election, when the public discussion of fake news rapidly accelerated, Facebook continued to investigate and learn more about the new threat of using fake accounts to amplify divisive material and deceptively influence civic discourse. Facebook shared what was learned with government officials and others in the tech industry. In April 2017, Facebook shared findings with the public by publishing a white paper that described the activity detected and the initial techniques used to combat it.
- In October 2016, for example, Facebook disabled about 5.8 million fake accounts in the U.S. Facebook disabled more than 30,000 accounts in advance of the French election and technology helped disable tens of thousands more accounts before the German elections in September.
- Facebook found that fake accounts associated with the IRA spent approximately $100,000 on more than 3,000 Facebook and Instagram ads between June 2015 and August 2017. Analysis also showed that these accounts used these ads to promote the roughly 120 Facebook pages they had set up, which in turn posted more than 80,000 pieces of content between January 2015 and August 2017.
- The Facebook accounts that appeared tied to the IRA violated policies because they came from a set of coordinated, inauthentic accounts. Facebook shut these accounts down and began trying to understand how they misused our platform.
- The suspect ads had 44% of total ad impressions before the U.S. election on November 8, 2016 and 56% of total ad impressions were after the election. Facebook estimates that 11.4 million people in the U.S. saw at least one of these ads between 2015 and 2017.

- The amount spent on the ads varied. For 50% of the ads, less than $3 was spent. For 99% of the ads, less than $1,000 was spent. Many of the ads were paid for in Russian currency, though currency alone is a weak signal for suspicious activity.
- Most of the ads appear to focus on divisive social and political messages across the ideological spectrum, touching on topics from LGBTQ matters to race issues to immigration to gun rights. A number of the ads encourage people to follow pages on these issues, which in turn produced posts on similarly charged subjects.
- Facebook estimates that roughly 29 million people were served content in their News Feeds directly from the IRA's 80,000 posts over the two years. Posts from these pages were also shared, liked, and followed by people on Facebook, and as a result, three times more people may have been exposed to a story that originated from the Russian operation.
- Facebook's best estimate is that approximately 126 million people may have been served content from a page associated with the IRA at some point during the two-year period. This equals about four-thousandths of 1% (0.004%) of content in News Feed, or approximately 1 out of 23,000 pieces of content.
- Facebook also deleted roughly 170 Instagram accounts that posted about 120,000 pieces of content.

Colin Stretch reported that Facebook is taking steps to enhance trust in the authenticity of activity on the platform, including increasing ads transparency, implementing a more robust ads review process, imposing tighter content restrictions, and exploring how to add additional authenticity safeguards.

Table 2.1 Text of Facebook Ads Submitted to U.S. House of Representatives Permanent Select Committee on Intelligence in November 2017

Religious face coverings are putting American people at huge risk! We must not sacrifice national security to satisfy the demands of minorities. All face covering should be banned in every state across America!
Who is behind this mask? A man? A woman? A terrorist? Burqa is a security risk and it should be banned on U.S. soil.
Hillary Clinton is the co-author of Obama's anti-police and anti-Constitutional propaganda. Down with Hillary!
The community of 2nd Amendment supporters, guns lovers and patriots. Defend the 2nd.
We call for disqualification and removal of Hillary Clinton from the presidential ballot as dynastic succession of the Clinton family in American politics breaches the core democratic principles laid out by our Founding Fathers. Sign the petition!

Source: HPSCI minority open hearing exhibits, https://democrats-intelligence. house.gov/hpsci-11-1/hpsci-minority-open-hearing-exhibits.htm.

1. *Promoting authenticity and preventing fake accounts*: Facebook maintains a calendar of upcoming elections and uses internal and external resources to best predict the threat level to each. They take preventative measures based on their information, including working with election officials where appropriate. Within this framework, they set up direct communication channels to escalate issues quickly. These efforts complement civic engagement work, which includes voter education. In October 2017, for example, Facebook launched a Canadian Election Integrity Initiative to help candidates guard against hackers and help educate voters on how to spot false news.

2. Going forward, Facebook will also be requiring political advertisers to provide more documentation to verify their identities and disclose when they're running election ads. Potential advertisers will have to confirm the business or organization they represent before they can buy ads. Their accounts and their ads will be marked as political, and they will have to show details, including who paid for the ads.

3. For political advertisers that don't proactively identify themselves, Facebook is building machine learning tools that will help find them and require them to verify their identity. Authenticity is important for pages as well as ads. Facebook will soon test ways for people to verify that the people and organizations behind political and issue-based pages are who they say they are.

4. Facebook has been working with many others in the technology industry, including with Google and Twitter, on a range of elements related to this investigation. Facebook is also reaching out to leaders in their industry and governments around the world to share information on bad actors and threats so that they can make sure they stay off all platforms.

5. To provide even greater transparency for people and accountability for advertisers, Facebook is now building new tools that will allow you to see the other ads a page is running as well as ads that aren't targeted to you directly. Hopefully that will establish a new standard for our industry in ad transparency.

6. Facebook relies on both automated and manual ad review, and is now taking steps to strengthen both. Reviewing ads means assessing not just what's in an ad but also the context in which it was bought and the intended audience, so they are changing the ads review system to pay more attention to these signals. Facebook is also adding more than 1,000 people to the global ads review teams over the next year and investing more in machine learning to better understand when to flag and take down ads.

7. Facebook ads policies already prohibit shocking content, direct threats and the promotion of the sale or use of weapons. Going forward, they are expanding these policies to prevent ads that use even more subtle expressions of violence [6].

2.4 Twitter Testifies before U.S. Congress

Also, in November 2017 at the same Hearing before The U.S. House of Representatives Permanent Select Committee on Intelligence in November 2017, Sean J. Edgett, Acting General Counsel for Twitter, Inc. provided testimony. He commented that the events underlying this hearing have been deeply concerning to our company and the broader Twitter community. Twitter is familiar with problems of spam and automation, including how they can be used to amplify messages. The abuse of those methods by sophisticated foreign actors to attempt state-sponsored manipulation of elections is a new challenge for us and one that we are determined to meet. Today, we intend to demonstrate the seriousness of our commitment to addressing this new threat, both through the effort that we are devoting to uncovering what happened in 2016 and by taking steps to prevent it from happening again. While Twitter's open and real-time environment is a powerful antidote to the abusive spreading of false information, we do not rest on user interaction alone. We are taking active steps to stop malicious accounts and tweets from spreading, and we are determined that our strategies will keep ahead of the tactics of bad actors. Other key points included:

■ Twitter has 330 million monthly active users around the world, 67 million of which are located in the United States. Users engage with our platform in a variety of ways. Users choose what content they primarily see by following (and unfollowing) other user accounts. Users generate content on the platform by tweeting original content, including text, *hashtags*, photos, GIFs, and videos. They may also reply to tweets, retweet content already posted on the platform, and like tweets and retweets.

■ An important concept on the Twitter platform is trends. *Trends* are words, phrases, or hashtags that may relate to an event or other topic (e.g., #CommitteeHearing). Twitter detects trends through an advanced algorithm that picks up on topics about which activity is growing quickly and thus showing a new or heightened interest among Twitter users. Trends thus do not measure the aggregate popularity of a topic, but rather the velocity of tweets with related content. The trends that a user sees may depend on a number of factors, including their location and their interests. If a user clicks on a trend, the user can see tweets that contain that hashtag.

■ Automation is a process that generates user activity such as tweets, likes, or following behavior without ongoing human input. Automated activity may be designed to occur on a schedule, or it may be designed to respond to certain signals or events. Accounts that rely on automation are sometimes also referred to as bots.

■ Automation can also be used for malicious purposes, most notably in generating spam or unwanted content consisting of multiple postings either from the same account or from multiple coordinated accounts. While spam is frequently viewed as having a commercial element, since it is a typical vector for spreading advertising, Twitter's rules take an expansive view of spam because it negatively impacts the user experience.

- Examples of spam violations on Twitter include automatically retweeting content to reach as many users as possible, automatically tweeting about topics on Twitter in an attempt to manipulate trends, generating multiple tweets with hashtags unrelated to the topics of those hashtags, repeatedly *following* and *unfollowing* accounts to tempt other users to follow reciprocally, tweeting duplicate replies and mentions, and generating large volumes of unsolicited mentions.
- We have the capability to detect suspicious activity at the tweet level and, if certain criteria are met, to internally tag that tweet as spam, automated, or otherwise suspicious. Tweets that have been assigned those designations are hidden from searches, do not count toward generating trends, and generally will not appear in feeds unless a user follows that account. Typically, users whose tweets are designated as spam are also put through the challenges described earlier and are suspended if they cannot pass.
- We have a number of enforcement options. For example, we can stop the spread of malicious content by categorizing a tweet as restricted pending deletion, which requires a user to delete the tweet before the user is permitted to continue using the account. More serious violations, such as posting child sexual exploitation or promoting terrorism, result in immediate suspension and may prompt interaction with law enforcement.
- Advertising on Twitter generally takes the form of *promoted tweets*, which advertisers purchase to reach new groups of users or spark engagement from their existing followers. Promoted tweets are clearly labeled as promoted when an advertiser pays for their placement on Twitter. In every other respect, promoted tweets look and act just like regular tweets and can be *retweeted*, replied to, and liked.
- Because promoted tweets are presented to our users from accounts they have not yet chosen to follow, Twitter applies to those tweets a robust set of policies that prohibit, among other things, ads for illegal goods and services, ads making misleading or deceptive claims, ads for drugs or drug paraphernalia, ads containing hate content, sensitive topics, and violence, and ads containing offensive or inflammatory content.
- In the period preceding the 2016 election we observed new ways in which accounts were abusing automation to propagate misinformation on our platform. Among other things, we noticed accounts that tweeted false information about voting in the 2016 election, automated accounts that tweeted about trending hashtags and users who abused their access to the platform we provide developers. At the time, we understood these to be isolated incidents, rather than manifestations of a larger, coordinated effort at misinformation on our platform. Once we understood the systemic nature of the problem in the aftermath of the election, we launched a dedicated initiative to research and combat that new threat.
- We detected examples of automated activity and deliberate misinformation in 2016, including in the run-up to the 2016 election, that in retrospect

appear to be signals of the broader automation problem that came into focus after the election had concluded. On December 2, 2016, for example, we learned of @PatrioticPepe, an account that automatically replied to all tweets from @realDonaldTrump with spam content. Those automatic replies were enabled through an application that had been created using our Application Programming Interface (API). Twitter provides access to the API for developers who want to design Twitter-compatible applications and to innovate the process of using Twitter data.

■ We noticed an upward swing in such activity during the period leading up to the election, and @PatrioticPepe was one such example. On the same day we identified @PatrioticPepe, we suspended the API credentials associated with that user for violation of our automation rules. On average, we take similar actions against violative applications more than 7,000 times per week.

■ Another example of aberrant activity we identified and addressed during this period involved voter suppression efforts. In particular, Twitter identified, and has since provided to the Committee, examples of tweets with images in English and Spanish that encouraged Clinton supporters to vote online, vote by phone, or vote by text. In response to the attempted vote-by-text effort and similar voter suppression attempts, Twitter restricted as inaccessible, pending deletion, 918 tweets from 529 users who proliferated that content.

■ Twitter also permanently suspended 106 accounts that were collectively responsible for 734 vote-by-text tweets. Twitter identified, but did not take action against, an additional 286 tweets of the relevant content from 239 Twitter accounts, because we determined that those accounts were seeking to refute the text-to-vote message and alert other users that the information was false and misleading. Notably, those refuting retweets generated significantly greater engagement across the platform compared to the tweets spreading the misinformation: eight times as many impressions, engagement by 10 times as many users, and twice as many replies.

■ Before the election, we also detected and took action on activity relating to hashtags that have since been reported as manifestations of efforts to interfere with the 2016 election. For example, our automated spam detection systems helped mitigate the impact of automated tweets promoting the #PodestaEmails hashtag, which originated with WikiLeaks' publication of thousands of e-mails from the Clinton campaign chairman John Podesta's Gmail account. The core of the hashtag was propagated by WikiLeaks, whose account sent out a series of 118 original tweets containing variants on the hashtag #PodestaEmails referencing the daily installments of the e-mails released on the WikiLeaks website.

■ In the 2 months preceding the election, around 57,000 users posted approximately 426,000 unique tweets containing variations of the #PodestaEmails hashtag. Approximately one quarter (25%) of those tweets received internal tags from our automation detection systems that hid them from searches.

As described in greater detail in the following, our systems detected and hid just under half (48%) of the tweets relating to variants of another notable hashtag, #DNCLeak, which concerned the disclosure of leaked e-mails from the Democratic National Committee. These steps were part of our general efforts at the time to fight automation and spam on our platform across all areas.

■ Since the 2016 election, we have made significant improvements to reduce external attempts to manipulate *content visibility*. These improvements were driven by investments into methods to detect malicious automation through abuse of our API, limit the ability of malicious actors to create new accounts in bulk, detect coordinated malicious activity across clusters of accounts, and better enforce policies against abusive third-party applications.

■ Our efforts have produced clear results in terms of our ability to detect and block such content. With our current capabilities, we detect and block approximately 450,000 suspicious logins each day that we believe to be generated through automation. In October 2017, our systems identified and challenged an average of 4 million suspicious accounts globally per week, including over three million challenged upon signup, before they ever had an impact on the platform, which was more than double our rate of detection at this time last year.

■ We also recognized the need to address more systematically spam generated by third party applications, and we have invested in the technology and human resources required to do so. Our efforts have been successful. Since June 2017, we have suspended more than 117,000 malicious applications for abusing our API. Those applications are collectively responsible for more than 1.5 billion tweets posted in 2017.

■ Because there is no single characteristic that reliably determines geographic origin or affiliation, we relied on a number of criteria, including whether the account was created in Russia, whether the user registered the account with a Russian phone carrier or a Russian e-mail address, whether the user's display name contains Cyrillic characters, whether the user frequently tweets in Russian, and whether the user has logged in from any Russian IP address, even a single time. We considered an account to be Russian-linked if it had even one of the relevant criteria.

■ We observed that a high concentration of *automated engagement* and content originated from data centers and users accessing Twitter via Virtual Private Networks (VPNs) and proxy servers. In fact, nearly 12% of tweets created during the election originated with accounts that had an indeterminate location. Use of such facilities obscures the actual origin of traffic. Although our conclusions are thus necessarily contingent on the limitations we face, and although we recognize that there may be other methods for analyzing the data, we believe our approach is the most effective way to capture an accurate understanding of activity on our system.

- We identified 36,746 accounts that generated automated, election-related content and had at least one of the characteristics we used to associate an account with Russia. During the relevant period, those accounts generated approximately 1.4 million automated, election-related tweets, which collectively received approximately 288 million impressions.

- The 36,746 automated accounts that we identified as Russian-linked and tweeting election-related content represent approximately one one-hundredth of a percent (0.012%) of the total accounts on Twitter at the time. The 1.4 million election-related tweets that we identified through our retrospective review as generated by Russian-linked, automated accounts constituted less than three quarters of a percent (0.74%) of the overall election-related tweets on Twitter at the time.

- Based on our analysis of the data, we determined that the number of accounts we could link to Russia and that were tweeting *election-related content* was small in comparison to the total number of accounts on our platform during the relevant time period. Similarly, the volume of automated, election-related tweets that originated from those accounts was small in comparison to the overall volume of election-related activity on our platform. Furthermore, those tweets generated significantly fewer impressions as compared to a typical election-related tweet.

- In an effort to better understand the impact of Russian-linked accounts on broader conversations on Twitter, we examined those accounts' volume of engagements with election-related content. We first reviewed the accounts' engagement with tweets from @HillaryClinton and @realDonaldTrump. Our data showed that, during the relevant time period, a total of 1,625 @HillaryClinton tweets were retweeted approximately 8.3 million times. Of those retweets, 32,254 or 0.39% were from Russian-linked automated accounts. Tweets from @HillaryClinton received approximately 18 million likes during this period; 111,326 or 0.62% were from Russian-linked automated accounts. The volume of engagements with @realDonaldTrump tweets from Russian-linked automated accounts was higher, but still relatively small. The 851 tweets from the @realDonaldTrump account during this period were retweeted more than 11 million times; 416,632 or 3.66% of those retweets were from Russian-linked, automated accounts. Those tweets received approximately 27 million likes across our platform; 480,346 or 1.8% of those likes came from Russian-linked *automated accounts*.

- We also reviewed engagement between automated or Russia-linked accounts and the @WikiLeaks, @DCLeaks, and @GUCCIFER_2 accounts. The amount of automated engagement with these accounts ranged from 47% to 72% of retweets and 36% to 63% of likes during this time—substantially higher than the average level of automated engagement, including with other high-profile accounts. The volume of automated engagements from Russian-linked accounts was lower overall. Our data show that, during the relevant time period, a total of 1,010 @WikiLeaks tweets were retweeted approximately

5.1 million times. Of these retweets, 155,933 or 2.98% were from Russian-linked automated accounts. The 27 tweets from @DCLeaks during this time period were retweeted approximately 4,700 times, of which 1.38% were from Russian-linked automated accounts. The 23 tweets from @GUCCIFER_2 during this time period were retweeted approximately 18,000 times, of which 1.57% were from Russia-linked automated accounts.

■ We next examined activity surrounding hashtags that have been reported as potentially connected to Russian interference efforts. We noted earlier that, with respect to two such hashtags, PodestaEmails and #DNCLeak. Automated systems detected, labeled, and hid a portion of related tweets at the time they were created. The insights from our retrospective review have allowed us to draw additional conclusions about the activity around those hashtags. We found that slightly under 4% of tweets containing #PodestaEmails came from accounts with potential links to Russia, and that those tweets accounted for less than 20% of impressions within the first seven days of posting. Approximately 75% of impressions on the trending topic were views by U.S.-based users. A significant portion of these impressions, however, are attributable to a handful of high-profile accounts, primarily @WikiLeaks. At least one heavily-retweeted tweet came from another potentially Russia-linked account that showed signs of automation.

■ With respect to #DNCLeak, approximately 23,000 users posted around 140,000 unique tweets with that hashtag in the relevant period. Of those tweets, roughly 2% were from potentially Russian-linked accounts. As noted earlier, our automated systems at the time detected, labeled, and hid just under half (48%) of all the original tweets with #DNCLeak. Of the total tweets with the hashtag, 0.84% were hidden and also originated from accounts that met at least one of the criteria for a Russian-linked account. Those tweets received 0.21% of overall tweet impressions. We learned that a small number of tweets from several large accounts were principally responsible for the propagation of this trend. In fact, two of the ten most-viewed tweets with #DNCLeak were posted by @Wikileaks, an account with millions of followers.

■ We separately analyzed the accounts that we have thus far identified through information obtained from third-party sources as linked to the Internet Research Agency (IRA). We have so far identified 2,752 such accounts. Those 2,752 accounts include the 201 accounts that we previously identified to the Committee. In responding to the Committee and through our cooperation with its requests, we have since linked the 201 accounts to other efforts to locate IRA-linked accounts from third-party information. We discovered that we had found some of the 201 accounts as early as 2015, and many had already been suspended as part of these previous efforts. Our retrospective work, guided by information provided by investigators and others, has thus allowed us to connect the 201 accounts to broader Russian election-focused efforts, including the full set of accounts that we now believe at this point are associated with the IRA.

■ The 2,752 IRA-linked accounts exhibited a range of behaviors, including automation. Of the roughly 131,000 tweets posted by those accounts during the relevant time period, approximately 9% were election-related, and many of their tweets over 47% were automated.

■ IRA-linked accounts exhibited non-automated patterns of activity that attempted more overt forms of broadcasting their message. Some of those accounts represented themselves as news outlets, members of activist organizations, or politically-engaged Americans. We have seen evidence of the accounts actively reaching out to journalists and prominent individuals (without the use of automation) through mentions. Some of the accounts appear to have attempted to organize rallies and demonstrations, and several engaged in abusive behavior and harassment. All 2,752 accounts have been suspended, and we have taken steps to block future registrations related to these accounts.

■ We identified nine accounts that had at least one of the criteria for a Russian-linked account and promoted election-related content tweets that, based on our manual review, violated existing or recently implemented ads policies, such as those prohibiting inflammatory or low-quality content. Two of those accounts were @RT_COM and @RT_America. Those two accounts represented the vast majority of the promoted tweets, spend and impressions for the suspect group identified in our review. Together, the two accounts spent $516,900 in advertising in 2016, with $234,600 of that amount devoted to ads that were served to users in the U.S. During that period, the two accounts promoted 1,912 tweets and generated approximately 192 million impressions across all ad campaigns, with approximately 53.5 million representing impressions generated by U.S.-based users. On Thursday, October 26, 2017, Twitter announced that it would no longer accept advertisements from RT and will donate the $1.9 million that RT had spent globally on advertising on Twitter to academic research into elections and civil engagement.

■ The remaining seven accounts that our review identified represented small, apparently unconnected actors. Those accounts spent a combined total of $2,282 on advertising through Twitter in 2016, with $1,184 of this amount spent on ads that were served to users in the U.S. Our available impressions data indicates that in 2016, those accounts ran 404 promoted tweets and generated a total of 2.29 million impressions across all ad campaigns. Approximately 222,000 of those impressions were generated by U.S.-based users. We have since off-boarded these advertisers.

■ While Russian, election-related malicious activity on our platform appears to have been small in comparison to overall activity, we find any such activity unacceptable. Our review has prompted us to commit ourselves to further enhancing our policies and to tightening our systems to make them as safe as possible. Over the coming months, we will be focusing on a series of improvements both to our user safety rules and our advertising policies that we believe will advance the progress we have already made this year.

Sean J. Edgett, Acting General Counsel, Twitter also reported that in 2017, Twitter prioritized work to promote safety and fight abuse across much of the platform. Twitter engineering, product, policy, and user operations teams worked with urgency to make important and overdue changes designed to shift the burden of reporting online abuse away from the victim and to enable Twitter proactively to identify and act on such content. As a result of that focus, Twitter has:

- Improved Twitter's detection of new accounts created by users who have been permanently banned.
- Introduced safer search, which is activated by default and limits potentially sensitive and abusive content from search results.
- Limited the visibility and reach of abusive and low-quality tweets.
- Provided additional user controls both to limit notifications from accounts without verified e-mail or phone numbers and/or profile photos and to allow more options to block and mute.
- Launched new forms of enforcement to interrupt abuse while it is happening.
- On October 19, 2017, Twitter published a calendar of our immediate plans. That calendar identifies dates for upcoming changes to the Twitter Rules that will enhance the ability to remove non-consensual nudity, glorification of acts of violence, use of hate symbols in account profiles, and various changes to user-reported Twitter Rules violations. See https://blog.twitter.com/official/en_us/topics/company/2017/safetycalendar.html.
- Enhancements to the Twitter advertising policy were made to increase transparency and provide the public with more detail than ever before about social media and online advertisers. The enhancements include the ability to see what advertisements are currently running on Twitter, how long the advertisements have been running, and all creative pieces associated with electioneering advertisements that clearly identify a candidate or party associated with a candidate for any elected office [7].

2.5 The Honest Ads Act

H.R.4077 was introduced in the U.S. House of Representatives on October 19, 2017 in the 115th Congress, 1st Session. The U.S. Senate introduced similar legislation. The goal of the act was to enhance transparency and accountability for online political advertisements by requiring those who purchase and publish such ads to disclose information about the advertisements to the public, and for other purposes. This Act was to be cited as the Honest Ads Act.

The purpose of this Act was to enhance the integrity of American democracy and national security by improving disclosure requirements for online political advertisements in order to uphold the U.S. Supreme Court's well-established standard that the electorate bears the right to be fully informed. Congress made the following findings:

1. On January 6, 2017, the Office of the Director of National Intelligence published a report titled "Assessing Russian Activities and Intentions in Recent U.S. Elections," noting that "Russian President Vladimir Putin ordered an influence campaign in 2016 aimed at the U.S. Presidential election …". Moscow's influence campaign followed a Russian messaging strategy that blends covert intelligence operation—such as cyber activity—with overt efforts by Russian government agencies, state-funded media, third-party intermediaries, and paid social media users or *trolls*.

2. On November 24, 2016, the Washington Post reported findings from two teams of independent researchers that concluded Russians "exploited American-made technology platforms to attack U.S. democracy at a particularly vulnerable moment … as part of a broadly effective strategy of sowing distrust in U.S. democracy and its leaders."

3. Findings from a 2017 study on the manipulation of public opinion through social media conducted by the Computational Propaganda Research Project at the Oxford Internet Institute found that the Kremlin is using pro-Russian bots to manipulate public discourse to a highly targeted audience. With a sample of nearly 1,300,000 tweets, researchers found that in the 2016 election's three decisive states, propaganda constituted 40% of the sampled election-related tweets that went to Pennsylvanians, 34% to Michigan voters, and 30% to those in Wisconsin. In other swing states, the figure reached 42% in Missouri, 41% in Florida, 40% in North Carolina, 38% in Colorado, and 35% in Ohio.

4. On September 6, 2017, the nation's largest social media platform disclosed that between June 2015 and May 2017, Russian entities purchased $100,000 in political advertisements, publishing roughly 3,000 ads linked to fake accounts associated with the Internet Research Agency, a pro-Kremlin organization. According to the company, the ads purchased focused "on amplifying divisive social and political messages…".

5. In 2002, the Bipartisan Campaign Reform Act became law, establishing disclosure requirements for political advertisements distributed from a television or radio broadcast station or provider of cable or satellite television. In 2003, the Supreme Court upheld regulations on electioneering communications established under the Act, noting that such requirements "provide the electorate with information and insure that the voters are fully informed about the person or group who is speaking."

6. According to a study from Borrell Associates, in 2016, $1,415,000,000 was spent on online advertising, more than quadruple the amount in 2012.

7. The reach of a few large Internet platforms—larger than any broadcast, satellite, or cable provider—has greatly facilitated the scope and effectiveness of disinformation campaigns. For instance, the largest platform has over 210,000,000 American users—over 160,000,000 of them on a daily basis. By contrast, the largest cable television provider has 22,430,000 subscribers, while the largest satellite television provider has 21,000,000 subscribers. The most-watched television broadcast in U.S. history had 118,000,000 viewers.

8. The public nature of broadcast television, radio, and satellite ensures a level of publicity for any political advertisement. These communications are accessible to the press, fact-checkers, and political opponents; this creates strong disincentives for a candidate to disseminate materially false, inflammatory, or contradictory messages to the public. Social media platforms, in contrast, can target portions of the electorate with direct, ephemeral advertisements often on the basis of private information the platform has on individuals, enabling political advertisements that are contradictory, racially or socially inflammatory, or materially false.

9. According to comScore, 2 companies own 8 of the 10 most popular smartphone applications as of June 2017, including the most popular social media and e-mail services—which deliver information and news to users without requiring proactivity by the user. Those same two companies accounted for 99% of revenue growth from digital advertising in 2016, including 77% of gross spending. Seventy-nine percent of online Americans—representing 68% of all Americans—use the single largest social network, while 66% of these users are most likely to get their news from that site.

10. In its 2006 rulemaking, the Federal Election Commission noted that only 18% of all Americans cited the Internet as their leading source of news about the 2004 Presidential election; by contrast, the Pew Research Center found that 65% of Americans identified an Internet-based source as their leading source of information for the 2016 election.

11. The Federal Election Commission, the independent federal agency charged with protecting the integrity of the federal campaign finance process by providing transparency and administering campaign finance laws, has failed to take action to address online political advertisements.

12. In testimony before the Senate Select Committee on Intelligence titled, "Disinformation: A Primer in Russian Active Measures and Influence Campaigns," multiple expert witnesses testified that while the disinformation tactics of foreign adversaries have not necessarily changed, social media services now provide "platform[s] practically purpose-built for active measures[.]" Similarly, as Gen. (RET) Keith B. Alexander, the former Director of the National Security Agency, testified, during the Cold War, "If the Soviet

Union sought to manipulate information flow, it would have to do so principally through its own propaganda outlets or through active measures that would generate specific news: planting of leaflets, inciting of violence, creation of other false materials and narratives. But the news itself was hard to manipulate because it would have required actual control of the organs of media, which took long-term efforts to penetrate. Today, however, because the clear majority of the information on social media sites is uncurated and there is a rapid proliferation of information sources and other sites that can reinforce information, there is an increasing likelihood that the information available to average consumers may be inaccurate (whether intentionally or otherwise) and may be more easily manipulable than in prior eras."

13. Current regulations on political advertisements do not provide sufficient transparency to uphold the public's right to be fully informed about political advertisements made online.

The proposed legislation stated that it is the sense of Congress that:

1. The dramatic increase in digital political advertisements, and the growing centrality of online platforms in the lives of Americans, requires the Congress and the Federal Election Commission to take meaningful action to ensure that laws and regulations provide the accountability and transparency that is fundamental to our democracy.
2. Free and fair elections require both transparency and accountability, which give the public a right to know the true sources of funding for political advertisements in order to make informed political choices and hold elected officials accountable.
3. Transparency of funding for political advertisements is essential to enforce other campaign finance laws, including the prohibition on campaign spending by foreign nationals.

The legislation expanded the definition of public communication to be inclusive of all types of communication satellite, paid Internet, or paid digital communication, electioneering communication as well as any public communication that would take into account methods that had not yet been invented or placed on the market. It also called for a clear and conspicuous manner requirement that revealed the source of such communication, stated the name of the person who paid for the communication, and provided a means for the recipient of the communication to obtain the remainder of the information required under this section with minimal effort and without receiving or viewing any additional material other than such required information.

In addition, an online platform shall maintain, and make available for online public inspection in machine readable format, a complete record of any request to purchase on such online platform a qualified political advertisement that is made by a person whose aggregate requests to purchase qualified political advertisements on such online platform during the calendar year exceeds $500. Any person who requests to purchase a qualified political advertisement on an online platform shall provide the online platform with such information as is necessary for the online platform to comply with the requirements of subparagraph.

The term *qualified political advertisement* was to mean any advertisement (including search engine marketing, display advertisements, video advertisements, native advertisements, and sponsorships) that is made by or on behalf of a candidate; or communicates a message relating to any political matter of national importance, including a candidate; any election to federal office; or a national legislative issue of public importance. Such information shall be made available as soon as possible and shall be retained by the online platform for a period of not less than four years. Each television or radio broadcast station, provider of cable or satellite television, or online platform was to make reasonable efforts to ensure that communications were not purchased by a foreign national, directly or indirectly [8].

2.6 Summary

Elections have always had a strong propaganda element but the 2016 elections in the U.S. were 99% propaganda and 1% discussion of the issues. The 2016 elections also had the added element of Russian meddling, which involved the creation and dissemination of propaganda. This chapter examines the Intelligence Community Analysis of Russian campaign meddling, testimony before U.S. Congressional hearings of social media companies regarding the meddling, and the Honest Ads Act, which is designed to promote greater transparency of social media posts that can impact the electrical process. Key points covered include:

- ▪ In January 2017, the U.S. Intelligence Community Assessment entitled *Assessing Russian Activities and Intentions in Recent US Elections* was released and was rather immediately discounted and dismissed by President Trump.
- ▪ The Kremlin's principal international propaganda outlet RT (formerly Russia Today) has actively collaborated with WikiLeaks. RT's editor-in-chief visited WikiLeaks founder Julian Assange at the Ecuadorian Embassy in London in August 2013, where they discussed renewing his broadcast contract with RT, according to Russian and Western media.
- ▪ Russia used social media trolls as well as RT as part of its influence efforts to denigrate Secretary Clinton. This effort amplified stories on scandals about Secretary Clinton and the role of WikiLeaks in the election campaign.
- ▪ In November 2017, representatives from the social media companies Google®, Facebook®, and Twitter® testified before the U.S. Congress at the Hearing before the U.S. House of Representatives Permanent Select Committee on Intelligence regarding Russian meddling in the U.S. 2016 elections.

- During the hearings Kent Walker, Google's lead of Legal, Policy, Trust and Safety, and Philanthropy teams, indicated that Google believes that it has a responsibility to prevent the misuse of the Google platforms, and the abuse of the tools and platforms Google provides is antithetical to that mission. Google is committed to working with Congress, law enforcement, others in the industry, and the NGO community to strengthen protections around elections and ensure the security of users, and help combat disinformation.
- Also, in November 2017 before The U.S. House of Representatives Permanent Select Committee on Intelligence, Colin Stretch, General Counsel of Facebook, provided comments and information about Russian meddling in the 2016 presidential election. He indicated that Facebook believes it has an important role to play in the democratic process and that foreign actors, hiding behind fake accounts, abused the platform and other Internet services to try to sow division and discord and to try to undermine the election process, which is an assault on democracy that also violates Facebook values.
- Also, in November 2017 at the same Hearing before The U.S. Houses of Representatives Permanent Select Committee on Intelligence in November 2017, Sean J. Edgett, Acting General Counsel for Twitter, Inc., provided testimony. He commented that the events underlying this hearing have been deeply concerning to our company and the broader Twitter community. Twitter is familiar with problems of spam and automation, including how they can be used to amplify messages. The abuse of those methods by sophisticated foreign actors to attempt state-sponsored manipulation of elections is a new challenge for us and one that we are determined to meet.
- H.R.4077 was introduced in the U.S. House of Representatives on October 19, 2017, and the U.S. Senate introduced similar legislation. The goal of the act was to enhance transparency and accountability for online political advertisements by requiring those who purchase and publish such ads to disclose information about the advertisements to the public, and for other purposes. This Act was to be cited as the Honest Ads Act.

2.7 Course Activities

Course project number one: Develop a five-to-ten question questionnaire to survey people on if and how social media impacted their voting choices in the 2016 elections in the U.S. or any country in which the student may be residing. Share the questionnaires with other class members and compare the questions.

Course project number two: Using the questionnaire developed in course project number one, interview five to ten people about the impact of social media on their voting choices in the 2016 elections in the U.S. or any country in which they may have resided at the time.

Course project number three: Tally the results of the surveys for all class members and create a PowerPoint presentation of those results for viewing and discussion during a class meeting.

Course project number four: Read and discuss one of the suggested readings listed in the Introduction.

References

1. Office of the Director of National Intelligence. *National Intelligence Council, Assessing Russian Activities and Intentions in Recent U.S. Elections*, January 6, 2017. Accessed November 23, 2017 https://www.dni.gov/files/documents/ICA_2017_01.pdf.
2. Congress Must Stop Russia's Meddling in Our Elections. U.S. Congressman French Hill. *Comments to Congressional Hearing*, June 26, 2017. Accessed November 23, 2017 https://hill.house.gov/media-center/in-the-news/congress-must-stop-russias-meddling-our-elections.
3. Transparency, corruption, and Russian meddling. *Senator Sheldon Whitehouse Comments to Congressional hearing*, June 14, 2017. Accessed November 23, 2017 https://www.white-house.senate.gov/news/speeches/transparency-corruption-and-russian-meddling-.
4. Written Testimony of Kent Walker. House Permanent Select Committee on Intelligence. *Hearing on Russia Investigative Task Force Hearing with Social Media Companies*, November 1, 2017. Accessed November 23, 2017 https://intelligence.house.gov/uploadedfiles/prepared_testimony_of_kent_walker_from_google.pdf#page=1&zoom=auto,-14,79.
5. *HPSCI Minority Open Hearing Exhibits.* https://democrats-intelligence.house.gov/hpsci-11-1/hpsci-minority-open-hearing-exhibits.htm.
6. C. Stretch. *Hearing Before the United States House of Representatives Permanent Select Committee on Intelligence*, November 1, 2017. Accessed November 23, 2017 https://intelligence.house.gov/uploadedfiles/prepared_testimony_of_colin_stretch_from_facebook.pdf.
7. S. J. Edgett. *Hearing Before the United States House of Representatives Permanent Select Committee on Intelligence*, November 1, 2017. Accessed November 23, 2017 https://intelligence.house.gov/uploadedfiles/prepared_testimony_of_sean_j._edgett_from_twitter.pdf.
8. U.S. House of Representatives. *H.R.4077—Honest Ads Act.* Accessed January 15, 2018 https://congress.gov/bill/115th-congress/house-bill/4077.

Chapter 3

Government Institutional Response to Social Media Propaganda, Extremism, and Radicalization

3.1 Mobilizing to Combat Violent Extremism

Throughout history, violent extremist individuals who support or commit *ideologically-motivated violence* to further political goals have promoted messages of divisiveness and justified the killing of innocents. The U.S. Constitution recognizes freedom of expression, even for individuals who espouse unpopular or even hateful views. But when individuals or groups choose to further their grievances or ideologies through violence, by engaging in violence themselves or by recruiting and encouraging others to do so, it becomes the collective responsibility of governments and civil society to take a stand against extremists. In recent history several countries have faced plots by neo-Nazis and other anti-Semitic hate groups, racial supremacists, and international and domestic terrorist. Supporters of these groups and their associated ideologies come from different socioeconomic backgrounds, ethnic and religious communities, and diverse regions of many countries, making it difficult to predict where violent extremist narratives will resonate. As history has shown, the prevalence of particular violent extremist ideologies changes over time, and new threats will undoubtedly arise in the future.

Countering radicalization to violence is frequently attempted by engaging and empowering individuals and groups at the local level to build resilience against radicalization with *positive message promotional activities*. Law enforcement plays an essential role but so too does engagement and partnership with communities. How radicalization to violence is defined can help to guide the development of partnerships and programs to continually enhance our understanding of the threat posed by violent extremism and the ways in which individuals or groups seek to recruit and radicalize new members. This requires closely monitoring and understanding their tactics, both online and offline. It is also helpful to have nonviolent means for addressing policy concerns, safeguarding equal and fair treatment, and making it more difficult for violent extremists to divide communities by empowering local partners prevent violent extremism [1].

The strategy to prevent violent extremism in the U.S. outlines how the government will support and help empower communities and their local partners in grassroots efforts to prevent violent extremism and the *recruiting and indoctrination* of community members by extremist groups. This strategy commits the U.S. government to improving support to communities, including sharing more information about the threat of radicalization; strengthening cooperation with local law enforcement, who work with these communities every day; and helping communities to better understand and protect themselves against violent extremist propaganda, especially online in *publicly available social media*.

Protecting communities from Al Qaeda's hateful ideology, for example, is not the work of government alone. Communities, especially Muslim communities whose children, families, and neighbors are being targeted for recruitment by Al-Qaeda, are often best positioned to take the lead because they know their communities best. Indeed, Muslim communities have categorically condemned terrorism, worked with law enforcement to help prevent terrorist attacks, and forged creative programs to protect their sons and daughters from Al Qaeda's murderous ideology. There are three broad areas of action where the U.S. government provides value to supporting partnerships at the local level and countering violent extremism (CVE):

- Enhancing federal engagement with and support to local communities that may be targeted by violent extremists. Engagement is essential for community-based efforts to prevent violent extremism because it allows government and communities to share information, concerns, and potential solutions.
- Building government and law enforcement expertise for preventing violent extremism. Government agencies must be vigilant in identifying, predicting, and preempting new developments. This necessitates ongoing research and analysis, as well as exchanges with individuals, communities, and government officials who work on the frontlines to counter threats.
- Countering violent extremist social media propaganda while promoting positive rhetoric and ideals with a *social media presence* is a process of actively and

aggressively countering the range of ideologies violent extremists employ to radicalize and recruit individuals by challenging justifications for violence and by actively promoting the unifying and inclusive vision of American ideals [2].

Building resistance to extremist propaganda and countering terrorist use of the Internet is vital to *counter extremist content*, which has become more prevalent online. The Global Counter ISIS Coalition Communications Working Group (led by the UAE, UK, and U.S.) regularly convenes over 30 member countries with media and technology companies to share information and strategies to counter violent extremist messages online and present positive alternative narratives. The Communications Working Group also supports a network of messaging centers that monitor *media convergence* and expose, refute, and combat online terrorist propaganda. These centers harness the creativity and expertise of local actors to generate positive content that challenges the vision of groups like ISIS and its supporters. The Counter-ISIS Communications Cell in London and the Sawab Center in Abu Dhabi lead the Coalition's efforts to tackle ISIS propaganda.

The Global Engagement Center, an interagency entity within the U.S. State Department, uses online technology to target potential recruits of terrorist organizations and redirect them to counter extremist content. In addition, videos developed by partners across the Coalition for a campaign targeting vulnerable audiences in Tunisia, Morocco, and Saudi Arabia have been watched more than 14 million times. The effort has expanded to other nations, including Libya, Jordan, and France. Twitter has suspended more than 635,000 ISIS-related or affiliated accounts that have been shown to abuse their platforms since the middle of 2015. This is making it increasingly difficult for ISIS and other such organizations to spread their ideology among vulnerable audiences.

Global Coalition Twitter accounts in Arabic, French, and English continue to increase their number of followers. The Coalition Communications Cell in London is staffed from 10 countries, guiding the public global messaging through daily media packs that are distributed to 850 government officials in 60 countries worldwide.

Since the Strategy to Empower Local Partners to Prevent Violent Extremism in the U.S. was issued in 2011, many federal, state, local and tribal governments have contributed meaningfully to the CVE effort. However, the efforts of ISIL and other groups to radicalize American citizens has required the U.S. government to update the efforts that began several years ago. Beginning in the summer of 2015, representatives from 11 departments and agencies reviewed the current structure, strategy and programs and made concrete recommendations for improvement. The review validated the objectives of the 2011 strategy but identified gaps in its implementation. The new task force was to coordinate government efforts and partnerships to prevent violent extremism in the U.S. [3].

3.2 Research and Analysis to Countering Violent Extremism

As U.S. policy and programs evolved it became apparent that efforts to countering violent extremism (CVE) should be guided by a rigorous, evidence-based approach to research and analysis that addresses all forms of violent extremism. Partners in this effort should include academic researchers, analysts, and program implementers, inside and outside government. Departments and agencies thus began to pursue a research and analysis agenda to build expertise on topics such as recruitment narratives and tactics, radicalization to violence, the role of the Internet in the radicalization process, youth radicalization and recruitment, behaviors commonly undertaken during mobilization to violence, and what motivates individuals to travel to conflict zones and join violent extremist groups. This has helped to improve development and coordination of analytic materials that have enhanced government and nongovernmental capabilities to prepare for observing indications of violence, including behaviors or precursor activities. Research has also improved understanding of community and individual resilience, benchmarks for successful local program models, and disengagement from violent extremist groups. The agenda called for future, open-source datasets to encourage better and broader understanding of the behaviors, operations, locations, networks, and activities of violent extremists domestically and abroad. Research into protective factors and warning signs to enable intervention efforts was also pursued.

A top priority was to map existing CVE-relevant research and analysis, identify gaps, and coordinate future projects. The breadth of federally sponsored research requires efforts to be synchronized across the U.S. government to ensure efficient use of resources and responsiveness to the needs identified by program implementers, public safety officials, local communities, and other stakeholders. To this end, Department of Homeland Security (DHS) catalogued existing federally-sponsored research meant to guide CVE efforts [4].

International stakeholders launched the Researching Solutions to Violent Extremism (RESOLVE) Network in September 2015 during a summit held on the sidelines of the United Nations General Assembly in New York. The primary goal of the Network is to generate, facilitate, aggregate, and synthesize methodologically sound, locally informed research on the drivers of vulnerability and sources of resilience to violent social movements and extremism. The mission is to connect, capture, curate, and catalyze locally informed research on violent extremism to promote effective policy and practice.

The U.S. Institute of Peace hosts the RESOLVE Network Secretariat at its headquarters in Washington, DC. The Network is primarily supported by its Steering Committee, Secretariat, Strategic Network Partners, and Honorary Partners. To learn more about RESOLVE partnerships and how to become a member of the Network, see http://www.resolvenet.org/global-network/. The RESOLVE website provides a database of research for extremist activities in countries around the world. The objectives of the network are to

- Catalyze collaboration between organizations and individuals around the world to leverage locally informed research to identify effective responses to violent extremism.
- Support the aggregation and synthesis of data, analysis, best practices and tools to address violent extremism through the establishment of a shared Knowledge Platform.
- Grow the cadre of local researchers and expand their capacity to leverage methodologically sound analysis to influence policy and practice and to connect and train future generations of researchers, practitioners, and thought leaders.
- Facilitate comprehensive identification of knowledge gaps on the dynamics of violent extremism.
- Enhance the understanding of indicators and drivers of violent extremism.
- Facilitate the development of a shared research agenda in response to policymakers' and practitioners' needs to address the problem of violent extremism.
- Connect people working on common themes to create a community of practice that will help support local research and link that research to policymakers and practitioners.
- Support the development of quality, evidence-based local research and program evaluation and practice evaluation.
- Disseminate analysis and research findings to policymakers and practitioners at all levels, from the local to the international [5].

Drawing on CVE research and analysis developed inside and outside government, DHS and the Department of Justice (DOJ) was required to broadly disseminate findings to stakeholders and create feedback mechanisms to enhance the utility and quality of future research and analysis. This meant that research would be synthesized and shared with stakeholders. DHS and DOJ were to develop a library of summaries tailored to particular stakeholder groups including state and local government and law enforcement, public health professionals, educators, parents, and community leaders. DOJ and DHS, in coordination with the CVE Task Force, will widely distribute these summaries and full research and analysis products when appropriate to ensure they inform the development and implementation of CVE programs and are incorporated into practice.

To increase the applicability of CVE research and analysis, DHS and DOJ developed feedback mechanisms to gather input from program implementers and incorporate it into specific projects as well as the overall research agenda. This will encourage partnership between researchers and stakeholders to ensure research and analysis can be used to inform program development. The research catalogue and summaries library created easily accessible resources to support the development of training materials. The CVE Task Force established a process for coordinating and evaluating CVE training curricula to ensure they are based on the latest research and analysis.

Benchmarks and measures of performance and effectiveness are to be included in all federally sponsored CVE efforts and will be tailored to each specific initiative before programs are launched. DHS, DOJ, U.S. Agency for International Development (USAID), and others have conducted assessments relevant to CVE programs. Building on this work, the CVE Task Force is coordinating and disseminating guidelines that departments and agencies can use at all stages of domestic CVE program design, implementation, and evaluation [6].

Community outreach and engagement programs are intended to enhance trust between government and communities as well as foster cooperation and partnerships to advance a range of local interests. Sustained dialogue draws attention to concerns from the public and can help communities understand the reasons behind actions by government entities. These are not to be singular events, but consistent and regular engagements on topics such as civil rights and civil liberties, education, economic stability, and other issues important to communities.

Violent extremism is one of many issues important to local stakeholders and must be addressed. Discussions about violent extremism should inform the public, build trust between government and local communities, and facilitate partnership among stakeholders. As with many other local challenges, such dialogue and partnerships will likely result in new ideas and initiatives that address specific needs related to preventing recruitment and radicalization to violence in a given location. Technical assistance may be provided to inform and enable the resulting ideas and initiatives.

Violent extremist narratives, often perpetuated under an *online alias*, espouse a rigid division of us and them that often promotes an individual's exclusion and isolation from his or her community and broader society and encourages a hostile relationship with government and other defined groups. Public discourse can also sometimes reinforce us versus them narratives. This can obscure the actual threat and contribute to perceptions of alienation and persecution among individuals who may already feel marginalized. Federal outreach and engagement activities should aim to decrease exclusion and isolation, avoid stigmatization, encourage civic engagement, and empower potential partners to demonstrate how a thriving, inclusive community is the strongest front against violent extremism.

Thus, the goal is to engage communities on all relevant issues and ensure responsiveness to local priorities. Officials specializing in civil rights and civil liberties, immigration, transportation security, law enforcement, and other professionals from the DOJ and DHS regularly conduct roundtables and outreach efforts to better understand the challenges facing their jurisdictions. U.S. Attorneys are generally the lead for these types of federal engagements given their unique, long-term understanding of local needs and their permanent presence in districts throughout the country. In addition, in many districts the DHS Office for Civil Rights and Civil Liberties (CRCL) also plays a prominent role in community engagement through a series of quarterly roundtables. These engagements often identify ways the federal government can better serve local communities with respect to civil rights and civil liberties, religious and other discrimination, public safety, and security measures, among other issues. These engagements are also opportunities to inform audiences about government structure and policies as well as programs available to them. It is also important to coordinate CVE engagements in regions throughout the country and around the world.

Many U.S. Attorneys' offices rely on staffs that are responsible for engagement across multiple issues, making full-time focus on support to CVE framework development and implementation difficult. DHS provides full-time staffs in selected regions across the country that are specifically responsible for CVE efforts and serve as a connection between national and local programs. The CVE Task Force coordinates a review of available resources for field support and, depending on the availability of funding, works with DOJ and DHS to identify priority jurisdictions to receive additional staff.

Connecting promising local initiatives to one another is also critical. Many ongoing, locally-led CVE efforts throughout the country benefit from improved access to information and relationships with stakeholders in other jurisdictions. The CVE Task Force identifies and builds awareness of promising programs to support the expansion of effective local CVE initiatives around the nation. The Task Force, in partnership with the Department of State (DOS), connects interested jurisdictions to relevant international initiatives including the Strong Cities Network, which aims to build the capacity of local governments to prevent violent extremism by establishing links between and among cities pursuing CVE programs.

Sustaining CVE efforts in the long term requires leveraging existing resources and grant programs as well as identifying new funding opportunities for CVE programming. Additionally, national programs should be flexible enough to be tailored to the specific needs of local stakeholders. In recent years, several metropolitan areas have begun implementing locally driven, partnership-dependent, multidisciplinary CVE frameworks. Where appropriate, DHS and DOJ focus and coordinate support for implementation of these frameworks. In addition, the CVE Task Force coordinates federal support to jurisdictions that have not yet adopted CVE frameworks, including by identifying promising practices and relevant subject matter experts.

Departments and agencies are to use training and presentations to build awareness, develop the expertise and skills of program implementers, and increase the number of proficient stakeholders who are able to carry out CVE initiatives. Depending on the need, training and presentations may include descriptions of the types of violent extremism and recruitment narratives used by violent extremist groups, factors that are often found in cases of radicalization to violent extremism, intervention methods, and ways to prevent recruitment and build resilience. They may also include information on specific resources, such as how to deliver the Community Awareness Briefing or facilitate a Community Resilience Exercise, both of which are tools used to foster dialogue, address grievances, and enhance relationships between law enforcement and local communities. Trainings and presentations will be based on sound, peer-reviewed research or analysis, as required by existing CVE training guidelines.

Several organizations have developed relevant training that can be utilized and built upon, including the Federal Law Enforcement Training Center, International Association of Chiefs of Police, and Federal Emergency Management Agency (FEMA). The Task Force, in coordination with departments and agencies, will compile existing relevant programs, identify gaps, and make recommendations for streamlining or developing new training. Departments and agencies will seek ways to combine CVE training and presentations with other public safety topics, when possible.

The scope of resources available to support CVE was expanded in order to ensure community stakeholders are able to create, implement, and sustain effective initiatives. Resources include direct government grants and financial assistance, expertise from other disciplines that can inform CVE efforts, and networks that connect communities to each other and to nongovernmental and private sector organizations. There are a number of non-CVE-specific DHS and DOJ grant programs that can be leveraged for local CVE work. These include the DHS State Homeland Security Program and the Urban Area Security Initiative as well as DOJ's Community Oriented Policing Services program. Additionally, DHS created a CVE-specific competitive grant program in 2016. The CVE Task Force was to provide consolidated funding information to stakeholders and seek opportunities to connect them with applicable national resources [6].

3.3 Department of Homeland Security Grant Opportunities

The DHS CVE grant program is designed to develop and expand efforts at the community level to counter violent extremist recruitment and radicalization to violence. The program provides funding for activities that enhance the resilience of communities being targeted by violent extremists, provide alternatives to individuals who have started down a road to violent extremism, and create or amplify alternative messages to terrorist/violent extremist recruitment and radicalization efforts. It also seeks to develop and support efforts that counter violent extremists' online recruitment efforts.

As appropriated by Section 543 of the Department of Homeland Security Appropriations Act 2016, (Pub. L. 114-113) and authorized by the same and Section 102(b)(2) of the Homeland Security Act of 2002, as amended (Pub. L. No. 107-296), the fiscal year 2016 CVE grant program provided resources to support programs, projects, and activities that prevent recruitment or radicalization to violence by interrupting those efforts, building community-level resilience, identifying the early signs of radicalization to violence, and providing appropriate interventions through civic organizations, law enforcement or other entities.

The 2014 Quadrennial Homeland Security Review reflected the importance of CVE by identifying it as a priority area of emphasis within DHS's focus areas. The fiscal year 2016 CVE grant program organized eligible activities into five focus areas that research had shown are likely to be most effective in countering violent extremism, which are shown in Table 3.1.

States, local governments, tribal governments, non-profit institutions, and institutes of higher education in all 56 states and territories were eligible to apply for fiscal year 2016 funds in specific CVE focus areas. Applicants representing state government agencies, local government agencies, tribal government agencies, and non-profit organizations were invited to apply for funding to implement programs for developing resilience, training and engaging with community members, and managing intervention activities. Applicants representing non-profit organizations and institutions of higher education were invited to apply for funding to implement programs for challenging the narrative and building capacity of community-level non-profit organizations active in CVE.

Proposed programs, projects or activities were required to not infringe on individual privacy, civil rights, and civil liberties. Applications described any potential impacts to privacy, civil rights, and civil liberties and ways in which applicants will protect against or mitigate those impacts and administer their program(s) in a nondiscriminatory manner.

In all cases, applicants must have either an existing CVE program or demonstrable expertise to create and administer a program, project or activity that falls within one of the five identified focus areas. Applications that do not describe an organization with appropriate expertise will be deemed ineligible for funding. Guidance regarding eligibility can be found in the Notice of Funding Opportunity (NOFO) at Grants.gov. For fiscal year 2016, a total of $10,000,000 was available to be awarded to a projected 60 grantees through a competitive, panel-reviewed application process.

DHS assesses funded projects for promising practices and makes them available in a replicable form for other communities or sectors. DHS is seeking to fund activities in geographically diverse communities across the country and present a

Table 3.1 CVE Grant Focus Areas

Grant Focus Areas	FY 2016 Funding
Developing resilience	$3,000,000
Training and engaging with community members	$2,000,000
Managing intervention activities	$2,000,000
Challenging the narrative	$2,000,000
Building capacity of community-level non-profit organizations active in CVE	$1,000,000

mix of awards to the different eligible applicant types. The period of performance is generally 24 months.

There is no maintenance of effort (MOE), cost match, or share match required under this program. Recipients can use grant funds only for the purpose set forth, and must be consistent with the statutory authority for the award. Recipients cannot use grant funds for matching funds for other federal grants/cooperative agreements, lobbying, or intervention in federal regulatory or adjudicatory proceedings. In addition, recipients cannot use federal funds to sue the federal government or any other government entity. It is likely that these terms will remain in place in future years.

Evaluation criteria include technical merit, needs analysis, community partnerships, cost effectiveness/sustainability, innovation, outcomes, and budget. Senior leadership from the DHS Office for Community Partnerships, FEMA, the DHS Office for Civil Rights and Civil Liberties, and the CVE Task Force reviews all scoring results and makes recommendations on which projects, or portions of projects, to fund in order to maximize the total impact of the available funding. The results are presented to the Director, Office for Community Partnerships and the Assistant Administrator, FEMA Grant Programs Directorate, who jointly approve/disapprove the recommended selection of recipients for this program. Final funding determinations are made by the Secretary of Homeland Security, who retains the discretion to consider other factors and information in addition to those included in the recommendations.

Because fiscal year 2016 was the inaugural year of the grant program, DHS developed a set of program performance metrics that measure the degree to which the CVE Grant Program enhances resilience to violent extremist recruitment and radicalization. Community resilience in the CVE context means fostering an environment where violent extremists routinely meet disinterest and opposition, recruitment attempts routinely fail, and communities know what tools and support are available to assist individuals that may be on a path towards violence [7].

3.4 Homeland Security Academic Advisory Council

The Homeland Security Academic Advisory Council (HSAAC) provides advice and recommendations to the DHS Secretary and senior leadership on matters related to homeland security. The HSAAC met in Washington DC on June 5, 2017 for the 12th time in its history. During the meeting, the HSAAC Academic Subcommittee on Countering Violent Extremism presented its report to the Council. The report offered several recommendations, developed jointly by academic leaders and subject matter experts. To date, the Council had provided more than 120 recommendations to DHS across its seven subcommittees. Subcommittees of the HSAAC are shown in Table 3.2.

Table 3.2 HSAAC Subcommittees

Student and recent graduate recruitment
Homeland security academic programs
Academic research and faculty exchange
International students
Campus resilience
Cybersecurity

Under the Secretary's authority in Title 6, United States Code, Section 451, this charter establishes the HSAAC as a discretionary committee expected to meet two times each year and the meetings are open to the public. The duties of the HSAAC are solely advisory in nature. The estimated annual operating cost of the HSAAC is $160,000, which includes 1.4 staff years of support.

The HSAAC is composed of up to 23 members who are appointed by and serve at the pleasure of the Secretary of DHS. To ensure a diverse, balanced membership, members are to represent institutions of higher education, community colleges, school systems and/or partnership groups with up to 14 members representing state colleges and universities, community colleges, government universities, international education, women's colleges and universities, Historically Black Colleges and Universities, Tribal Colleges and Universities, Hispanic Serving Institutions, Minority Serving Institutions or the DHS Centers of Excellence with one-fourth of members' terms of office expiring each year. HSAAC recommendations related to the topics in this book include:

■ DHS should leverage the Intergovernmental Personnel Act Mobility Program to formally establish an Academic Exchange Program that consists of the following three components: (1) Academic Speakers Bureau, (2) Guest Lecturer Series, and (3) Faculty Exchange Program.

■ The DHS Academic Exchange Program should include the following programmatic elements: (1) targeted outreach to institutions of higher education to enhance visibility; (2) appropriate titles for program participants (i.e., Senior Fellows, Junior Fellows, etc.); and (3) when possible, a cost-sharing mechanism between DHS and participating institutions of higher education.

■ DHS should implement virtual faculty exchanges within the Academic Exchange Program to allow institution of higher education faculty and staff to participate in faculty exchange opportunities on a short-term basis and to increase program flexibility.

■ DHS should insert guidance specific to institutions of higher education into grants program guides and outreach materials, where appropriate, to clarify their ability to participate in these programs, and identify additional opportunities and uses for funding.

■ DHS should consider expanding the use of its existing resilience-related resources, where appropriate, to specifically include and be adapted to the higher education community (e.g., the "If You See Something, Say Something™" campaign).

■ DHS should, in cooperation with its partner agencies, develop a reporting mechanism that provides senior leadership with the aggregate funding made available to higher education (directly and indirectly) for campus resilience programs.

■ DHS should increase the marketing efforts and visibility of the Federal Law Enforcement Training Center at institutions of higher education, through methods such as direct outreach, attendance at conferences, and information on DHS.gov.

■ DHS should organize and deploy national tabletop exercises and simulations specific to institutions of higher education and campus communities. These exercises will ensure better preparedness for natural and man-made incidents, and enhance campus resilience.

■ DHS should establish a campus resilience program with corresponding funding, technical assistance, and training to work with campus officials in assessing their preparedness, developing and implementing related plans, and monitoring campus readiness over time. An online clearinghouse and inventory of available resources should be included as part of this program.

■ DHS should continue to support its Campus Resilience Pilot Program as funding allows.

■ DHS should partner with the Department of Justice's National Center to promote campus resilience as well as offer the Campus Resilience Enhancement System as a resource to the broader higher education community.

■ FEMA's Region 1 should be recognized as a DHS best practice for engagement with the higher education community on campus preparedness and resilience efforts.

■ DHS should explore situational awareness and information sharing resources and tools such as DHS's Virtual USA and commercial solutions that enable institutions of higher education to better share best practices and coordinate on campus resilience, preparedness and response issues.

■ DHS should develop a comprehensive package for university and college presidents and chancellors to include potential risk management areas and corresponding resources to address risk factors.

■ DHS should coordinate with academic organizations and associations to incorporate the topic of engaging senior leadership in campus resilience into workshops for new university and college presidents and chancellors [8].

3.5 The U.S. Department of Justice Fighting Terrorism for Decades

On October 14, 2015, Assistant Attorney General John P. Carlin delivered remarks on domestic terrorism at an event co-sponsored by the Southern Poverty Law Center (SPLC) and the George Washington University Center for Cyber and Homeland Security's Program on Extremism. He noted that the partnership between SPLC and GW serves as a reminder that violent extremism is neither a new phenomenon nor one that is limited to any single population, region or ideology. Since its creation in 1971, SPLC has been an important voice on the wide range of extremist groups throughout this country. Over the past four decades, the existence of hate, violence and extremism has remained unfortunately all too constant. Major points covered in the presentation include:

■ Much attention has focused on those inspired by Al Qaeda and the Islamic State of Iraq and the Levant's (ISIL) message of hate and violence spreading worldwide and reaching homes here in America through the group's unprecedented social media recruitment efforts. However, the U.S. must deal with *Western-based extremists* and Americans attacking Americans based on U.S.-based extremist ideologies. Violent extremism in the U.S. ranges from individuals motivated by anti-government animus, to eco-radicalism, to racism, as it has for decades.

■ The range of national security threats is staggeringly broad ranging from ISIL, Al Qaeda, AQAP and other terrorist groups; the threats posed by foreign terrorist fighters intent on waging jihad abroad; and the threat of fighters who may seek to return home, trained and willing to die for their extremist cause.

■ Terror and extremism do not always originate elsewhere or take place outside our borders. Homegrown violent extremists can be motivated by any viewpoint on the full spectrum of hate: anti-government views, racism, bigotry, anarchy and other despicable beliefs. When it comes to hate and intolerance, no single ideology governs. In America, harboring extremist views is not itself a crime, nor is the expression of even a hateful ideology or association with a hateful group.

■ Incidents have included plots and attacks on government buildings, synagogues and mosques, businesses and public infrastructure; assassinations and planned assassinations of police officers, judges, civil rights figures, doctors and others; stockpiles of illegal weapons, explosives and biological and chemical weapons; and killing sprees that have terrorized local communities. According to at least one study more people died in the U.S. in attacks by domestic extremists than attacks associated with international terrorist groups over the last, say, 5–6 years.

■ Among domestic extremist movements active in the U.S., white supremacists are the most violent. The Charleston shooter, who had a manifesto laying out a racist worldview, is just one example. His actions followed earlier deadly shooting sprees by white supremacists in Kansas, Wisconsin and elsewhere. In August 2012, Wade Michael Page, who also espoused white supremacist and neo-Nazi views, fatally shot six people and wounded four others, including a responding police officer, at a Sikh temple in Wisconsin. He acted alone and died in the course of the attacks from a self-inflicted gunshot wound.

■ More broadly, law enforcement agencies nationwide are concerned about the growth of the *sovereign citizen* movement. According to one 2014 study, state, local and tribal law enforcement officials considered sovereign citizens to be the top concern of law enforcement, ranking above ISIL and Al Qaeda-inspired extremists. Adherents to the sovereign citizen ideology believe they don't have to answer to any government authority, including courts, taxing entities or law enforcement. Although most sovereign citizens peacefully espouse these views, some sovereign citizen extremists resort to violence.

■ Terry Nichols, convicted accomplice in the Oklahoma City bombing, may have viewed himself as a member of the sovereign citizen movement. In 2010, Jerry and Joseph Kane, a father and son who identified with the sovereign citizen movement, killed two police officers and were themselves killed in the ensuing shootout with police after a routine traffic stop. In June 2014, Jerad and Amanda Miller, likely motivated by the sovereign citizen anti-government ideology, killed two Las Vegas Metropolitan Police Department officers at a restaurant in Las Vegas. Then they went to a nearby Walmart and killed another innocent person. During their attacks, they declared the beginning of a so-called revolution.

■ Across the spectrum of extremist ideologies, two related traits emerge: first, the prevalence of lone offender attacks that do not require a terrorist network and second, the increasing number of disaffected people inspired to violence who communicate their hate-filled views over the Internet and through social media.

■ Whether you label it domestic terrorism, hate crime or plain murder as was the case with McVeigh and Nichols and the Charleston shooter, lone offenders or small groups often plan and carry out attacks on their own or with limited assistance. In these cases, few others know of their violent plans, making their plotting more difficult to disrupt.

■ Across the spectrum of extremist ideologies, an alarming new trend is the increasing number of disaffected people linked together in their adherence to violence over the Internet and through social media.

■ As the ISIL threat reveals, new communications technologies, including social media and the widespread use of encryption, pose tremendous challenges to public safety and national security and these are challenges everyone with a stake in the matter must continue to work together to address.

■ The same is true for domestic terrorism and extremism. Sovereign citizens continue to communicate and recruit through the use of YouTube and Twitter.

White supremacists post to social media, and studies now posit that mass killings are contagious. Violence begets violence, and through the power of the Internet, a meeting hall is no longer needed. Formal organizational structures are unnecessary. Connections are made, and messages spread, through the push of a button.

- DOJ does not investigate people for exercising their First Amendment rights, but is obligated to investigate extremist groups and individuals when there is a reason to believe they may be involved in the commission of a federal crime, including threatening violence.
- With the explosive use of social media and encrypted communications between those inspired to violence by messages of hate, we run the risk that we will see less as the bad guys see more. Social media can create for an extreme segment of society a sort of radicalization echo chamber where followers reinforce for each other extremist propaganda and calls for violence through *active deception* and propaganda.
- Internet and social media service providers must take responsibility for how their services can be abused. Responsible providers understand what the threats are and take action to prevent terrorist groups from abusing their services to induce recruits to commit terrorist acts.
- In the wake of the Oklahoma City bombing, Congress passed the Antiterrorism and Effective Death Penalty Act of 1996, or AEDPA. That legislation is critical to the U.S. government's efforts to protect the nation against international and domestic terrorism.
- On the domestic front, the code book defines domestic terrorism as illegal activities that are dangerous to human life that take place primarily in the U.S. and appear to be intended to intimidate or coerce a civilian population, influence the policy of a government by intimidation or coercion, or affect the conduct of a government.
- Although law enforcement is a powerful tool, it is not the only tool. We must also reach individuals early on their path towards radicalization. Programs like those associated with GW and SPLC will be particularly valuable on this front.
- Community members see things that law enforcement agencies do not. Here in the U.S., one study found that in more than 80% of violent extremist cases with a connection to international terrorism, third-party bystanders observed activities or behaviors suggesting radicalization or violent intent. However, more than half of the witnesses discounted or downplayed their observations.
- Similar evidence exists regarding bystanders in other cases of crime and extremism. So, community members are not only best positioned to intervene with those on a path towards violent extremism, they also may be the first to see potential steps towards radicalization to violence.
- DOJ is exploring options to intervene with would-be violent extremists before violence occurs, and to address disengagement and rehabilitation, including off ramps on the path of radicalization to violence [9].

Nationwide, DOJ and its U.S. Attorney's Offices (USAOs) have prosecuted many terrorism cases in recent years. In 2014, Human Rights First published a comprehensive study on prosecuting terrorism in federal court from 9/11 through the end of 2007. The study, entitled: *In Pursuit of Justice: Prosecuting Terrorism Cases in the Federal Court*, found that federal prosecutors achieved a conviction rate of more than 90% in the set of terrorism cases examined by the report's authors. The study examined a specific set of 257 defendants charged with terrorism-related violations in the United States between 9/11 and the end of 2007. Of the 160 defendants from this group who had their cases resolved, 145 were convicted of at least one count, either by a verdict of guilty after trial or by a guilty plea [10].

3.6 General Accountability Office Evaluation of U.S. Government Countering Violent Extremism Efforts

The U.S. General Accountability Office (GAO) evaluated the CVE program in 2012. Since then, several improvements have been made in the way the federal agencies are managing their responsibilities. DHS and DOJ have responsibility for training state and local law enforcement and community members on how to defend against violent extremism and ideologically motivated violence to further political goals. Community members and advocacy organizations have raised concerns about the quality of some CVE-related training that DOJ and DHS provide or fund. As requested, GAO examined (1) the extent to which DHS and DOJ have identified and communicated topics that CVE-related training should address to their components and state and local partners, (2) any concerns raised by state and local partners who have participated in CVE-related training provided or funded by DHS or DOJ, and (3) actions DHS and DOJ have taken to determine *best practices* and applying a *lessons learned process* to improve the quality of CVE-related training. GAO reviewed relevant documents, such as training participant feedback forms and DHS and DOJ guidance, and interviewed relevant officials from DHS and DOJ components.

The GAO found, for example, that DHS had identified and was communicating to its components and state and local partners topics that the training on CVE it provides or funds should cover. In contrast, the DOJ had not identified what topics should be covered in its CVE-related training. According to a DHS official who leads DHS's CVE efforts, identifying topics has helped to provide a logical structure for DHS's CVE-related training efforts. According to DOJ officials, even though they had not specifically identified what topics should be covered in CVE-related training, they understood internally which of the department's training is CVE-related and contributes either directly or indirectly to the department's training responsibilities under the CVE national strategy.

However, over the course of the review, the DOJ generally relied upon the framework GAO developed for potential CVE-related training topics to determine which of its existing training was CVE-related. Further, because DOJ had not identified CVE-related training topics, DOJ components have had challenges in determining the extent to which their training efforts contribute to DOJ's responsibilities under the CVE national strategy. In addition, officials who participated in an interagency working group focusing on ensuring CVE-related training quality stated that the group found it challenging to catalogue federal CVE-related training because agencies' views differed as to what CVE-related training includes.

The majority of state and local participant feedback on training that DHS or DOJ provided or funded and that GAO identified as CVE-related was positive or neutral, but a minority of participants raised concerns about biased, inaccurate, or offensive material. DHS and DOJ collected feedback from 8,424 state and local participants in CVE-related training during fiscal years 2010 and 2011, and 77 (less than 1%) provided comments that expressed such concerns. According to DHS and DOJ officials, agencies used the feedback to make changes where appropriate.

The FBI and other components generally solicit feedback for more formal, curriculum-based training, but the FBI does not require this for activities such as presentations by guest speakers because the FBI does not consider this to be training. Similarly, DOJ's USAOs did not require feedback on presentations and similar efforts. Nevertheless, FBI field offices and USAOs covered about 39% (approximately 9,900) of all participants in DOJ CVE-related training during fiscal years 2010 and 2011 through these less formal methods, yet only 4 of 21 FBI field offices and 15 of 39 USAOs chose to solicit feedback on such methods. GAO has previously reported that agencies need to develop systematic evaluation processes in order to obtain accurate information about the benefits of their training. Soliciting feedback for less formal efforts on a more consistent basis could help these agencies ensure their quality.

DOJ and DHS have undertaken reviews and developed guidance to help improve the quality of CVE-related training. For example, in September 2011, the DOJ Deputy Attorney General directed all DOJ components and USAOs to review all of their training materials, including those related to CVE, to ensure they are consistent with DOJ standards. In addition, in October 2011, DHS issued guidance that covers best practices for CVE-related training and informs recipients of DHS grants who use the funding for training involving CVE on how to ensure high-quality training. Since the departments' reviews and efforts to implement the guidance they have developed are relatively new, it is too soon to determine their effectiveness.

The GAO recommended that DOJ identify and communicate principal CVE-related training topics and FBI field offices and USAOs consider soliciting feedback more consistently. DOJ agreed that it should more consistently solicit feedback, but disagreed that it should identify CVE training topics because DOJ does not have primary responsibility for CVE-related training, among other things. GAO believed this recommendation remains valid as discussed further in the report [11].

In July 2015, the GAO reported that the Department of State's (DOS) Bureau of Counterterrorism had an annual increase in authorized full-time equivalent

(FTE) positions since fiscal year 2011 and has recently undertaken efforts to reduce a persistent staffing gap. The bureau's authorized FTEs increased from 66 in fiscal year 2011 to 96 in fiscal year 2015, and over the same period, FTE vacancies ranged from 17% to 23%. The vacancies included both staff and management positions. Bureau officials said they postponed filling some positions until the Coordinator for Counterterrorism had sufficient time to assess the bureau's needs and priorities. A senior Bureau of Counterterrorism official testified before Congress in June 2015 that the bureau was making progress and that it had 11 vacancies. However, the GAO had not been able to verify that four of the reportedly filled positions have been filled because DOS did not provide sufficient documentation.

While the bureau had undertaken efforts to assess its progress, it had not yet evaluated its priority CVE program and had not established time frames for addressing recommendations from program evaluations. Specifically, the bureau established indicators and targets for its foreign assistance related goals and reported results achieved toward each indicator. The bureau had also completed four evaluations covering three of its six programs that resulted in 60 recommendations. The bureau reported having implemented about half of the recommendations (28 of 60) as of June 2015 but had not established time frames for addressing the remaining recommendations. Without specific time frames, it will be difficult for the bureau to ensure timely implementation of programmatic improvements. In addition, despite identifying its CVE program as a priority and acknowledging the benefit of evaluating it, the bureau has postponed evaluating it each fiscal year since 2012.

The bureau's coordination on two programs GAO reviewed, CVE and Counterterrorism Finance, generally reflects key practices for effective collaboration. For example, GAO identified efforts to define outcomes and accountability, bridge organizational cultures, and establish written guidance and agreements, all key practices of effective collaboration [12].

In April of 2017, the GAO reported that as of December 2016, DHS, DOJ, FBI, and the National Counterterrorism Center had implemented 19 of the 44 domestically-focused tasks identified in the 2011 Strategic Implementation Plan (SIP) for CVE in the U.S. Twenty-three tasks were in progress and no action had yet been taken on two tasks. The 44 tasks aim to address three core CVE objectives: community outreach, research and training, and capacity building. Implemented tasks included, for example, DOJ conducting CVE outreach meetings to communities targeted by violent extremism and DHS integrating CVE content into law enforcement counterterrorism training. Tasks in progress included, for example, DHS building relationships with the social media industry and increasing training available to communities to counter violent extremists online. Tasks that had not yet been addressed include implementing CVE activities in prisons and learning from former violent extremists. Federal CVE efforts aim to educate and prevent radicalization before a crime or terrorist act transpires, and differ from counterterrorism efforts such as collecting evidence and making arrests before an event has occurred [13].

3.7 Summary

Governments have responded to social media propaganda, extremism, and radicalization by forming coalitions and partnerships to counter extremist social media propaganda and reduce the frequency of individuals and groups being radicalized toward violent extremism. This chapter examines programs established by the U.S. government to counter extremist propaganda and activities that lead to the radicalization of individuals and groups, including those managed by DHS and DOJ along with the national initiatives that guide agency work and programs directed at dealing with extremist propaganda in social media. Key points covered include:

■ In recent history, several countries have faced plots by neo-Nazis and other anti-Semitic hate groups, racial supremacists, and international and domestic terrorists. Supporters of these groups and their associated ideologies come from different socioeconomic backgrounds, ethnic and religious communities, and areas of many countries, making it difficult to predict where violent extremist narratives will resonate.

■ There are three broad areas of action where the U.S. government provides value to supporting partnerships at the local level and countering violent extremism (CVE): enhancing federal engagement with and support to local communities, building government and law enforcement expertise for preventing violent extremism, and countering violent extremist social media.

■ As U.S. policy and programs evolved it became apparent that efforts to countering violent extremism (CVE) should be guided by a rigorous, evidence-based approach to research and analysis that addresses all forms of violent extremism.

■ Drawing on CVE research and analysis developed inside and outside government, DHS and DOJ were required to broadly disseminate findings to stakeholders and create feedback mechanisms to enhance the utility and quality of future research and analysis.

■ The CVE grant program is designed to develop and expand efforts at the community level to counter violent extremist recruitment and radicalization to violence; it provides funding for activities that enhance the resilience of communities being targeted by violent extremists, provide alternatives to individuals who have started down a road to violent extremism, and create or amplify alternative messages to terrorist/violent extremist recruitment and radicalization efforts.

■ The Homeland Security Academic Advisory Council (HSAAC) provides advice and recommendations to the DHS Secretary and senior leadership on matters related to homeland security. To date, the Council had provided more than 120 recommendations to DHS across its seven subcommittees.

■ Much attention has focused on those inspired by Al Qaeda and the Islamic State of Iraq and the Levant's (ISIL) message of hate and violence spreading worldwide and reaching homes here in America through the group's unprecedented social media recruitment efforts. However, the U.S. must deal with *Western-based extremists* and Americans attacking Americans based on U.S.-based extremist ideologies. Violent extremism in the U.S. ranges from individuals motivated by anti-government animus, to eco-radicalism, to racism, as it has for decades.

■ Law enforcement agencies in the U.S. are concerned about the growth of the *sovereign citizen* movement. According to one 2014 study, state, local and tribal law enforcement officials considered sovereign citizens to be the top concern of law enforcement, ranking above ISIL and Al Qaeda-inspired extremists.

■ Sovereign citizens continue to communicate and recruit through the use of YouTube and Twitter. White supremacists post to social media, and studies now posit that mass killings are contagious. Violence begets violence, and through the power of the Internet, a meeting hall is no longer needed. Formal organizational structures are unnecessary. Connections are made, and messages spread, through the push of a button.

■ DOJ is exploring options to intervene with would-be violent extremists before violence occurs, and to address disengagement and rehabilitation, including off ramps on the path of radicalization to violence.

3.8 Course Activities

Course project number one: Research what federally funded CVE activities or programs have been launched in your community and share the findings with others in the class.

Course project number two: Interview local law enforcement staff or community leaders that have been involved in federally funded CVE programs to determine what they think and feel about the programs. Share your findings with others in the class.

Course project number three: If you found that federally funded CVE activities or programs have not occurred in your community, interview local law enforcement or administrative staff and try to determine why they have not occurred. Share the findings with others in the class.

References

1. The Whitehouse. *Empowering Local Partners to Prevent Violent Extremism in the United States*, August 2011. Accessed November 27, 2017 https://www.dhs.gov/sites/default/files/publications/empowering_local_partners.pdf.

2. Office of the Director of National Intelligence, National Counterterrorism Center. *Methods & Tactics: Radicalization: Preventing Violent Extremism.* Accessed November 27, 2017 https://www.dni.gov/nctc/methods.html#sarin.
3. U.S. Department of State. Undersecretary for Public Diplomacy and Public Affairs, Bureau of Public Affairs Office of Press Relations, *The Global Coalition—Working to Defeat ISIS,* March 22, 2017. Accessed November 27, 2017 https://www.state.gov/r/pa/prs/ps/2017/03/268609.htm.
4. Executive Office of the President of the U.S. *Strategic Implementation Plan for Empowering Local Partners to Prevent Violent Extremism in the U.S. October 2016.* Accessed November 27, 2017 https://www.dhs.gov/sites/default/files/publications/2016_strategic_implementation_plan_empowering_local_partners_prev.pdf.
5. The RESOLVE Network. *Researching Solutions to Violent Extremism.* Accessed November 27, 2017 https://www.usip.org/programs/resolve-network-researching-solutions-violent-extremism.
6. U.S. DHS. *Countering Violent Extremism Task Force.* Accessed November 27, 2017 https://www.dhs.gov/cve/task-force.
7. U.S. DHS. *Fact Sheet: FY 2016 Countering Violent Extremism (CVE) Grants,* January 24, 2017. Accessed November 27, 2017 https://www.dhs.gov/news/2016/07/06/fy-2016-countering-violent-extremism-cve-grants.
8. U.S. DHS. *Homeland Security Academic Advisory Council (HSAAC),* September 1, 2017. Accessed November 28, 2017 https://www.dhs.gov/homeland-security-academic-advisory-council-hsaac.
9. Assistant Attorney General John P. Carlin Delivers Remarks on Domestic Terrorism at an Event Co-Sponsored by the Southern Poverty Law Center and the George Washington University Center for Cyber and Homeland Security's Program on Extremism. Washington, DC, October 14, 2015. Accessed November 28, 2017 https://www.justice.gov/opa/speech/assistant-attorney-general-john-p-carlin-delivers-remarks-domestic-terrorism-event-co.
10. U.S. DOJ. *Press Release Fact Sheet: Prosecuting and Detaining Terror Suspects in the U.S. Criminal Justice System,* June 9, 2009. Accessed November 28, 2017 https://www.justice.gov/opa/pr/fact-sheet-prosecuting-and-detaining-terror-suspects-us-criminal-justice-system.
11. U.S. GAO. *Countering Violent Extremism: Additional Actions Could Strengthen Training Efforts GAO-13-79,* October 18, 2012. Accessed November 28, 2017 http://www.gao.gov/products/GAO-13-79/.
12. U.S. GAO. *State Should Evaluate Its Countering Violent Extremism Program and Set Time Frames for Addressing Evaluation Recommendations.* GAO-15-684, July 22, 2015. Accessed November 28, 2017 http://www.gao.gov/products/GAO-15-684.
13. *Actions Needed to Define Strategy and Assess Progress of Federal Efforts.* GAO-17-300, April 6, 2017. Accessed November 28, 2017 http://www.gao.gov/products/GAO-17-300.

Chapter 4

Military Response to Social Media Propaganda-Driven Extremism and Radicalization

4.1 Addressing the Threat of Insider Radicalization

Cyber *deception operations* target people within a society, influencing their beliefs as well as behaviors, and diminishing trust in the government and the military. U.S. adversaries seek to control and exploit the trend mechanism on social media to harm U.S. interests, discredit public and private institutions, and sow domestic strife. Thus, instead of attacking the military or economic infrastructure, state and non-state actors outside the U.S. can access regular streams of online information via social media to influence networked groups and *chat groups*. Using existing online networks in conjunction with automatic bot accounts, foreign agents can insert *deception* into propaganda and into a social media platform, create a trend, and rapidly disseminate a message faster and cheaper than through any other medium [1].

The military and intelligence community encountered a rather sophisticated and effective cyber propaganda operation during the effort to defeat ISIL over the last several years. Much of that effectiveness was because of the power of visual images. This was a demonstration of the sophistication with which a variety of extremist and terrorist groups have adapted to the online environment, particularly through the use of powerful visual images. The strategic point is that weaker forces use visual materials to great effect and to even greater effect when countermeasures are not deployed. Compared to text or words heard over an audio track, images are remembered better, over a longer period of time, and with greater emotional power, having gained more attention initially. Domestic and international extremist groups have access to technologies that allow them develop *information operations* to produce and distribute, with virtually no special training and at very low cost, materials of a quality and sophistication that only a few years ago would have been out of reach of any but professional media labs. Any images available on the web can be repurposed and re-contextualized to serve their purpose. In a digital world, the need to respond quickly and effectively is going to be an ever more dominant aspect of any operating environment [2].

In addition, Islamic radicalization has also occurred within the U.S. Army, which is demonstrated by several cases of insider misconduct such as the terrorist massacre at Fort Hood; Ali Mohammed, an Egyptian-born Islamic fundamentalist who trained with the U.S. military and provided sensitive military documents to terrorists; and Louay Safi, the director of the extremist group known as the Islamic Society of North America Leadership Center, who visited Fort Hood to instruct soldiers about Islam not long after the massacre of soldiers there. The U.S. military does recognize the potential for an insider threat. The U.S. Army has published a list of indicators of a potential insider threat and may indicate that the individual is at risk of becoming an insider threat. Members of the military are encouraged report these behaviors immediately to their chain of command and Army Counterintelligence [3]. The behaviors are shown in Table 4.1.

The Army's Insider Threat Program spans all operating environments and the full spectrum of threats, from unauthorized disclosures regarding *intelligence operations* to acts of physical violence. The recent attacks against Army installations by homegrown violent extremists make it imperative that the military remain a step ahead of the threat. For example, a prospective terrorist attack at Fort Dix, New Jersey in 2007 involving six men, later referred to as the Fort Dix Six, conspired to attack and kill soldiers on the post. They selected Fort Dix from other installations in the area mostly based upon reconnaissance and accessibility. The group recorded their preparations and sent the video to an electronics store for duplication. An alert store employee notified the FBI, who then tracked and arrested the group before they could execute their plan. The members of the group were convicted and sent to prison all because of an alert and aware citizen [4].

The Army's Insider Threat Program is a system composed of seven lines of effort that include both established and emerging processes. The seven interconnected lines of effort depend on one another in order to maximize the system's capability to deter, detect, and mitigate insider threats. Table 4.2 shows the Army's process steps to deter, detect, and mitigate insider threats [5].

Terrorism is an enduring, persistent, worldwide threat to U.S. military forces. Extremist ideologies and separatist movements continue to have an anti-western and anti-U.S. orientation that threatens the nation. The integration of terrorist

Table 4.1   Indicators of a Potential Insider Threat

Encouraging disruptive behavior or disobedience to lawful orders
Expressing hatred or intolerance of American society or culture
Expressing sympathy for organizations that promote violence
Expressing extreme anxiety about or refusing a deployment
Associating with or expressing loyalty or support for terrorists
Browsing websites that promote or advocate violence against the U.S., or distributing terrorist literature or propaganda via the Internet
Expressing extreme outrage against U.S. Military operations
Advocating violence to achieve political/religious/ideological goals
Providing financial or other materiel support to a terrorist organization
Seeking spiritual sanctioning for or voicing an obligation to engage in violence in support of a radical or extremist organization or cause
Membership in a violent, extremist, or terrorist group, or adopting an ideology that advocates violence, extremism, or radicalism
Purchasing bomb making materials or obtaining information on bomb construction and use
Engaging in paramilitary training with radical or extremist organizations, either home or abroad
Having ties to known or suspected international terrorists, extremists, radicals, or their supporters
An employee released from or not selected for employment, promotion, or bonus who exhibits severe signs of PTSD, and who appears disgruntled and violent

threat assessments, analysis, and indications and warnings into the operations and intelligence process ensures commanders and units at all levels apply knowledge and understanding of the threat to enhance their overall protection posture. Given the persistent threat of terrorist attack, the entire Army community must prepare for, respond to, and recover from terrorist acts.

Army leaders help by coordinating and synchronizing insider threat efforts within existing organizational and command protection forums (e.g., Protection Executive Committee); ensure compliance with Army information assurance, security, and threat awareness training requirements; ensure compliance with Army

Table 4.2 Steps to Deter, Detect, and Mitigate Insider Threats

Screen the army: Determine a person's suitability for employment

Clear the army: Determine a person's eligibility for access to classified information

Protect the networks: Monitor network user activity for indications of malicious activity

Secure the installations: Vet personnel entering installations

Share information: Gather, aggregate, and disseminate a common operating picture of the threat

Establish and operate the insider threat hub: Implement an integrated analytical and response capability, in accordance with National Insider Threat Policy

Train, report, and respond: Ensure awareness training, reporting, and response to insider threats

policies for incident reporting (e.g., AR 380-67 and DA Form 5248-R, AR 190-45 and DA Form 4833, and AR 25-2); and assess insider threat response and mitigation policies and procedures within protection elements of command inspection programs.

Deterring the threat occurs when nefarious actors are prevented access to Army information, personnel, and facilities and by safeguarding Army information through OPSEC, protecting facilities through the Army Physical Security program and protecting personnel through the Army Antiterrorism program. Force protection consists of those actions to prevent or mitigate hostile actions against Department of Defense (DoD) personnel and includes family members, resources, facilities, and critical information. In the war on terrorism, the area of operations extends from Afghanistan to the East Coast and across the U.S. Force Protection and Antiterrorism measures have increased across Army installations in the Continental U.S. (CONUS) and overseas. Soldiers, Active and Reserve, are heavily engaged in force protection and antiterrorism missions. Soldiers guard military installations, nuclear power plants, dams and power generation facilities; tunnels, bridges, and rail stations; and emergency operations centers.

Army directives to restrict access to installations have all led to thorough assessments by the Department of the Army Inspector General, the Deputy Chief of Staff for Operations, and commanders. Efforts focus on improving force protection policy and doctrine; more rigorous training and exercises; improved threat reporting and coordination with national intelligence and law enforcement agencies; enhanced detection and deterrence capabilities for Chemical, Biological, Radiological, Nuclear, and Explosive (CBRNE) threats; increased capabilities and protection for access control; and expanded assessments of Major Commands (MACOM) and installation force protection programs. Both operational and installation environments rely upon secure, networked information infrastructure to execute daily enterprise-wide processes and decision-making, so the parameters of force protection include contemporary and evolving cyber threats, as well.

The Army's Information Systems Security Program (ISSP) secures The Army's portion of the Global Information Grid (GIG), secures the digitized force, and supports information superiority and network security defense-in-depth initiatives. ISSP provides the capability to detect system intrusions and alterations and react to information warfare attacks in a measured and coordinated manner. To the greatest extent possible, it protects warfighters' secure communications from the sustaining base to the foxhole [6].

4.2 Military Anti-Terrorism Activities beyond the Insider Threat

The Army continues to implement an anti-terrorism strategy and supporting communication plan to instill Army-wide heightened awareness and vigilance to protect the Army community and critical resources from terrorist activities. The anti-terrorism communication plan establishes four broad themes: constant vigilance, timely threat reporting, knowledge of anti-terrorism concepts and principles, and leadership emphasis [7].

The Pentagon Force Protection Agency (PFPA) was established in 1971 as a result of a growing number of disruptive incidents throughout the U.S. In response to the mass demonstrations, bombings and bomb threats of the era, the Federal Protective Service was established to provide comprehensive protection of the Pentagon and its personnel rather than the previous policy of concentration on property. On May 3, 2002, in response to the terrorist attack against the Pentagon on September 11, 2001, and the subsequent anthrax incidents, Deputy Secretary of Defense Paul Wolfowitz established the Pentagon Force Protection Agency as a DoD agency under the cognizance of the Director of Administration and Management, under the Office of the Secretary of Defense. Since its creation, PFPA has expanded its mission and provides force protection against a full spectrum of potential threats. While law enforcement is still a major portion of its mission, the agency also handles operations security, building surveillance, crisis prevention, consequence management, counterintelligence, antiterrorism, Hazmat and explosives, protection of high ranking DoD officials, information technology and administrative issues. PFPA continues to evolve, making it one of the nation's premier federal law enforcement organizations; it defends the Pentagon's personnel, facilities, and infrastructure against numerous, mounting threats [8].

4.3 Military Efforts to Counter Extremist Propaganda

The U.S. military is also facing an unprecedented challenge in countering the propaganda of adversaries who recruit and easily spread misinformation through the Internet. The military has a critical role to play in countering adversarial messages and is a contributor of unique capabilities and a partner to the whole-of-government effort led by the U.S. State Department, which is discussed in previous chapters. The U.S. Special Operations Command's Military Information Support Operations (MISO) force provides a critical capability in supporting the needs of the military as well as the overall strategic messaging effort of the State Department. Preparing the MISO forces for current and future conflict is an important role for the U.S. Special Operations Command and manning, training and equipping is especially critical. To address capability gaps, U.S. Special Operations Command is expanding MISO training into social media use, online advertising, web design and other areas.

MISO forces are currently deployed to 21 U.S. embassies, working with country teams and interagency partners to challenge adversary information, support broader U.S. government goals and build and disseminate *positive narratives*. The military information forces use existing web and social media platforms such as Facebook, Twitter and YouTube to support military objectives by shaping perceptions while highlighting ISIL atrocities, coalition responses to ISIL activities, and coalition successes. MISO personnel have the training and cultural understanding to assess enemy propaganda activities and propose unique solutions that support U.S. military objectives. MISO efforts in the Central Command area of responsibility are focused on challenging violent extremists [9].

From 2014 through 2017, Central Command ran two separate programs in the information war against ISIL. Through the command's Digital Engagement Team (DET), and separately through its web operations cell, military, civilian and contract employees worked to combat ISIL propaganda in the cyber domain. The 11-member DET included native-born speakers of Arabic, Urdu, Russian, Farsi, Dari and Pashto. Their job was to represent Central Command (CENTCOM) in those languages and tailor their messaging to regional news cycles: Arabic in Arabic-speaking countries, Dari and Pashto for Afghanistan, Farsi for Iran, Russian for the Central Asian states, and Urdu for Pakistan.

ISIL's dominance in the cyber realm diminished since the group came to prominence in 2014. CENTCOM officials said the main hub of ISIL's information campaign was still Twitter, but the group's reach has been diminished as both Twitter and Facebook had been pretty aggressive in taking down the accounts that they can recognize or that would get reported to them. ISIL's response was to have supporters create dozens of dormant accounts to fall back on as active accounts were cancelled.

The Iraqi on the street was the audience the DET sought to reach in its counter-ISIL efforts, officials said, and they reported that a groundswell of Iraqis took to Twitter in late May 2016, right around the time Iraqi security forces began the campaign to retake Fallujah. The DET amplified a popular meme that translated to Iraqis tweeting in Iraqi, which started kind of a meme throughout the region. They took the space back. Combined Joint Task Force Operation Inherent Resolve also weakened ISIL's hold in the cyber domain by destroying some of the facilities the group used to produce its propaganda products for *recruiting and indoctrination.*

CENTCOM'S other counter-ISIL social media-based effort went by the name of Web Ops, an effort involving military information support to operations that used to be known as psychological operations. Web Ops involved about 120 people. The group coordinated with the DET, coalition partners and the State Department to ensure themes and messages were consistent. Since 2014, a combination of aggressive suspensions from social media companies, attrition and decrease in morale in ISIL's own ranks, and a third element of counter-efforts from both governmental and nongovernmental entities gradually degraded ISIL's footprint, and thus ISIL's ability to quickly and easily reach the masses. ISIL defectors revealed how ISIL had staged a lot of their supposed demonstrations of power including everything from raids on enemy strongholds to food in the marketplace, and how everything about ISIL's public persona was being micromanaged by media spinners.

To locate ISIL adversaries and target audiences, DET used mostly commercial off-the-shelf searches to identify keywords associated with the adversary's narrative, along with obviously manual analyst target-audience analysis. For at-risk users it was a similar process: identify common terms that are publicly searchable that indicate an individual is sympathetic to the adversary's narrative [10].

The combined joint task force and the coalition made significant strides in countering ISIS's propaganda operations in the summer of 2017. The coalition had targeted and killed numerous senior ISIS propagandists and facilitators in Iraq and Syria. ISIS's online supporters dwindled, with counter-ISIS content outnumbering pro-ISIS content across the world. In spring of 2017, there was a 92% decrease in global shares of ISIS video content on Twitter and propaganda production dropped to its lowest point in more than six months, a 75% reduction in ISIS's monthly output in 2016. The global coalition also launched a campaign named #takedaeshdown to inform social media users of how to report ISIS extremist content to platform owners and add pressure on them to remove the content [11].

The U.S. military is in a constant research, observation, and learning process for dealing with extremist social media propaganda and how to counter that propaganda and deter and prevent radicalization of military troops as well as civilian populations. Policies and operating procedures are developed in a very systematic manner. Typical phases of the development and implementation of intervention and prevention programs are shown in Table 4.3.

Table 4.3 Typical Phases of the Development of Prevention Programs

Activity Areas
Collect information, observations, professional opinions, activity reports, and case studies
Aggregate and analyze information
Validate analysis
Develop strategies, tactics, and operating procedures
Develop training courses or modules for multiple delivery mechanisms
Deliver training and collect and analyze training evaluations from participants
Audit or otherwise evaluate the effectiveness of policies and operating procedures
Use evaluation results to help guide future projects

4.4 Summary

The military has been challenged with countering or eliminating extremist propaganda in social media. Such propaganda has radicalized local populations or individual citizens to commit acts of violence and support others who move to violence. This chapter examines several ways the U.S. military has worked to address extremist propaganda in social media. Key points include:

- Domestic and international extremist have access to technologies to support information operations that produce and distribute propaganda in several media types.
- The military and intelligence community encountered a rather sophisticated and effective cyber propaganda operation during the effort to defeat ISIL over the last several years. Much of that effectiveness was because of the power of visual images.
- Islamic radicalization has also occurred within the U.S. Army, which is demonstrated by several cases of insider misconduct such as the terrorist massacre at Fort Hood.
- The U.S. Army's Insider Threat Program spans all operating environments and the full spectrum of threats, from unauthorized disclosures regarding *intelligence operations* to acts of physical violence.

- The U.S. Army's anti-terrorism communication plan establishes four broad themes: constant vigilance, timely threat reporting, knowledge of anti-terrorism concepts and principles, and leadership emphasis.
- The U.S. military has a critical role to play in countering adversarial messages and is a contributor of unique capabilities and a partner to the whole-of-government effort led by the State Department.
- Through the command's Digital Engagement Team, or DET, and separately through its web operations cell, military, civilian and contract employees worked to combat ISIL propaganda in the cyber domain.
- In the summer of 2017, the coalition had targeted and killed numerous senior ISIS propagandists and facilitators in Iraq and Syria, severely damaging their propaganda abilities and activities.

4.5 Course Activities

Course project number one: Interview a member of the military and explore their views of extremist propaganda. Write a one-page summary of the interview and compare the results with those of other members of the class.

Course project number two: Review local media content in your community (newspapers, television news, and locally focused websites) to determine if there is any information or news that illustrates the U.S. military efforts to counter extremist propaganda. Write a one-page summary of the interview and compare the results with those of other members of the class.

Course project number three: Analyze the material gained through the interviews in course project number one and two and summarize what you believe would be the helpful counter message to extremist propaganda.

References

1. Lt Col Jarred Prier, USAF. Commanding the trend: Social media as information warfare. *Strategic Studies Quarterly*, Winter 2017. Accessed November 30, 2017 http://www.airuniversity.af.mil/Portals/10/SSQ/documents/Volume-11_Issue-4/Prier.pdf.
2. C. K. Winkler and C. E. Dauber. Army War College Carlisle Barracks Pennsylvania, Strategic Studies Institute. *Visual Propaganda and Extremism in the Online Environment*, July 2014. Accessed November 30, 2017 http://oai.dtic.mil/oai/oai?verb=getRecord&metadataPrefix=html&identifier=ADA607970.
3. U.S. Army Combined Arms Center. *Insider Threat & Terrorism Indicators of a Potential Insider Threat*, August 18, 2017. Accessed November 30, 2017 http://usacac.army.mil/organizations/902d-military-intelligence-group/insider-threat-and-terrorism.
4. U.S. Army. Jim Pasierb. *Army Unveils New Antiterrorism Strategic Plan*, July 24, 2009. Accessed November 30, 2017 https://www.army.mil/article/24922/army_unveils_new_antiterrorism_strategic_plan.

5. U.S. Army. 8th Theater Sustainment Command Public Affairs Office. *Antiterrorism Awareness Quarterly Theme—Insider Threat*, June 30, 2016. Accessed November 30, 2017 https://www.army.mil/article/170836/antiterrorism_awareness_quarterly_theme_insider_threat.

6. U.S. Army. Posture Statement. *Force Protection and Antiterrorism*. Accessed November 30, 2017 https://www.army.mil/aps/2003/realizing/readiness/force.html.

7. U.S. Army. *Army Worldwide Anti-terrorism Conference*, February 1, 2016. Accessed November 30, 2017 https://www.army.mil/standto/archive_2016-02-01/.

8. Pentagon Force Protection Agency (PFPA). *The History of PFPA*. Accessed December 1, 2017 http://www.pfpa.mil/history.html.

9. DoD News, Defense Media Activity. *Lisa Ferdinando. 'Unprecedented' Challenge in Countering Adversarial Propaganda, Official Says*, October 23, 2015. Accessed December 1, 2017 https://www.defense.gov/News/Article/Article/625750/unprecedented-challenge-in-countering-adversarial-propaganda-official-says/.

10. DoD News, Defense Media Activity. *Karen Parrish. Centcom Counters ISIL Propaganda*, July 6, 2016. Accessed December 1, 2017 https://www.defense.gov/News/Article/Article/827761/centcom-counters-isil-propaganda/.

11. DoD News, Defense Media Activity. *Terri Moon Cronk. Syrian Democratic Forces Make Gains in Raqqa Against ISIS*, July 27, 2017. Accessed December 1, 2017 https://www.defense.gov/News/Article/Article/1260394/syrian-democratic-forces-make-gains-in-raqqa-against-isis/.

Chapter 5

The Impact of Social Media Extremist Propaganda on Law Enforcement

5.1 Training for Collecting and Examining Extremist Propaganda

Through research sponsored by the National Institute of Justice (NIJ), homegrown terrorism in the U.S. has been linked to a global terrorist movement that relies on modern communication technologies, media, and a globalized social consciousness to push its belief system into every corner of the world. Jihadist recruitment has reached into small and mid-sized cities in every state of the U.S. and attracted followers from some 40 different ethnicities and every race in America.

Given the diversity of American homegrown terrorism offenders, there is no common denominator, no common grievances, not even common motivations, that can predict who may opt to join groups espousing violent jihad. Researchers conducted an analysis that compared the network structure of American terrorism offenders inspired by Hezbollah, Sunni extremist groups aligned with Al Qaeda, and ISIL. The analysis included the networks and organizations that mobilize and direct Americans for jihadist action or that raise money in the country for Hamas and Hezbollah.

According to the researchers, radicalization to violent political extremism is more likely to occur in a group setting where the adoption of extremist ideas is reinforced by shared emotions, particularly if the process is accompanied by positive external reinforcements. Watching online extremist videos and chatting with online avatars from the Islamic State is not sufficient to make someone take a life-changing decision to join a terrorist group. With the added effect of group reinforcement and a deepening involvement with the extremist networks, however, both off-line and online, becoming a terrorist can come to seem a desirable course of action for an individual.

Social media bridges the gap between home and the new life, the researchers noted. Young men and women have joined the Islamic State in patterns similar to chain migration, following in the footsteps of others from their town or neighborhood and settling with friends and family or newfound peers. Most American Islamist extremists have been connected to a core network of jihadist organizations and recruiters based abroad, either through travel or direct personal relationships with middle-men acting for the terrorist organization. The contemporary network configuration may be described as local, but globally connected and inspired and taking shape locally in peer groups and small cells [1].

This dynamic pressures law enforcement organizations to develop skills in monitoring, collecting, and analyzing social media propaganda and other Internet content. Chapter 1 provides background on analyzing propaganda. This section examines collecting digital evidence for analysis.

Digital evidence includes information on computers, audio files, video recordings, and images. This evidence is essential in computer and Internet crimes, but is also valuable for facial recognition, crime scene photos, and surveillance tapes. Digital evidence is information stored or transmitted in binary form that may be relied on in court. It can be found on a computer hard drive, a mobile phone, a personal digital assistant (PDA), a CD, and a flash card in a digital camera, among other places. Digital evidence is commonly associated with electronic crime, or e-crime, such as child pornography or credit card fraud. However, digital evidence is now used to prosecute all types of crimes, not just e-crime.

In an effort to fight e-crime and to collect relevant digital evidence for all crimes, law enforcement agencies are incorporating the collection and analysis of digital evidence, also known as computer forensics, into their infrastructure. Law enforcement agencies are challenged by the need to train officers to collect digital evidence and keep up with rapidly evolving technologies such as computer operating systems [2]. National Institute of Standards and Technology (NIST) researchers are developing tools, measurement methods, standards, and data to support forensic analysis of digital evidence. Table 5.1 shows NIST publications that help law enforcement personnel manage digital evidence [3].

The National Initiative for Cybersecurity Education (NICE) website (www. nist.gov/itl/applied-cybersecurity/nice) explains that the mission of NICE is to energize and promote a robust network and an ecosystem of cybersecurity education, training, and workforce development. There are a variety of interesting

Table 5.1 NIST Publications on Electronic Forensics

Guidelines on Mobile Device Forensics
Guidelines on Cell Phone Forensics
Guidelines on PDA Forensics, Recommendations of the National Institute of Standards and Technology
An Overview and Analysis of PDA Forensic Tools
Cell Phone Forensics Tools: An Overview and Analysis
Cell Phone Forensic Tools: An Overview and Analysis Update

Source: NIST National Institute of Standards and Technology, Digital & multimedia evidence, www.nist.gov/topics/digital-multimedia-evidence, Accessed December 2, 2017.

tools including the NICE Cybersecurity Workforce Framework Work Role Capability Indicators. This helps determine what qualities or accomplishments indicate that someone is suitable to perform a particular job or activity including many of the skills that criminal investigators need to properly collect forensic digital evidence. This is far more efficient than surfing the web looking for information.

There are two relevant job classifications, The Cyber Crime Investigator IN-INV-001, which identifies, collects, examines, and preserves evidence using controlled and documented analytical and investigative techniques, and the Digital Forensics (FOR) Law Enforcement/Counterintelligence Forensics Analyst IN-FOR-001, which conducts detailed investigations on computer-based crimes establishing documentary or physical evidence, to include digital media and logs associated with cyber intrusion incidents.

NICE, led by NIST in the U.S. Department of Commerce, is a partnership between government, academia, and the private sector focused on cybersecurity education, training, and workforce development. Located in the Information Technology Laboratory at NIST, the NICE Program Office operates under the Applied Cybersecurity Division, positioning the program to support the country's ability to address current and future cybersecurity challenges through standards and best practices. NICE fulfills its mission by coordinating with government, academic, and industry partners to build on existing successful programs, facilitate change and innovation, and bring leadership and vision to increase the number of skilled cybersecurity professionals helping to keep the nation secure [4].

Federal Law Enforcement Training Centers offer an Internet Investigations Training Program. The Internet Investigations course focuses on the examination of historical Internet data such as e-mails and website postings to identify the author or originator of the Internet activity by looking at system artifacts and attributes. The Online Investigations course focuses on the live and active interrogation of online data, such as investigating websites and attempting to determine their physical location [5]. Forensics Training is also hosted and sponsored by the National Institute of Justice (NIJ). In addition, there are many colleges and universities across the U.S. that provide cybersecurity education including digital forensics. This is a constantly evolving environment and interested parties should check with local institutions.

The Scientific Working Group on Digital Evidence (SWGDE) was established in February 1998 through a collaborative effort of the Federal Crime Laboratory Directors. SWGDE, as the U.S.-based component of standardization efforts conducted by the International Organization on Computer Evidence (IOCE), was charged with the development of cross-disciplinary guidelines and standards for the recovery, preservation, and examination of digital evidence, including audio, imaging, and electronic devices.

Acquisition of digital evidence begins when information and/or physical items are collected or stored for examination purposes. The term evidence implies that the collector of evidence is recognized by the courts. The process of collecting is also assumed to be a legal process and appropriate for rules of evidence in that locality. A data object or physical item only becomes evidence when so deemed by a law enforcement official or designee.

In order to ensure that digital evidence is collected, preserved, examined, or transferred in a manner safeguarding the accuracy and reliability of the evidence, law enforcement and forensic organizations work to establish and maintain an effective quality system. Standard Operating Procedures (SOPs) are documented quality-control guidelines that must be supported by proper case records and use broadly accepted procedures, equipment, and materials. Rapid technological changes are the hallmark of digital evidence, with the types, formats, and methods for seizing and examining digital evidence changing quickly. In order to ensure that personnel, training, equipment, and procedures continue to be appropriate and effective, management should review and update SOP documents at least annually.

Procedures used must be generally accepted in the field or supported by data gathered and recorded in a scientific manner. Because a variety of scientific procedures may validly be applied to a given problem, standards and criteria for assessing procedures need to remain flexible. The validity of a procedure may be established by demonstrating the accuracy and reliability of specific techniques. In the digital evidence area, peer review of SOPs by other agencies may be useful.

Although many acceptable procedures may be used to perform a task, considerable variation among cases requires that personnel have the flexibility to exercise judgment in selecting a method appropriate to the problem. Hardware used in the seizure and/or examination of digital evidence should be in good operating condition and be tested to ensure that it operates correctly. Software must be tested to ensure that it produces reliable results for use in seizure and/or examination purposes.

All activity relating to the seizure, storage, examination, or transfer of digital evidence must be recorded in writing and be available for review and testimony. In general, documentation to support conclusions must be such that, in the absence of the originator, another competent person could evaluate what was done, interpret the data, and arrive at the same conclusions as the originator.

The requirement for evidence reliability necessitates a *chain of custody* for all items of evidence. Chain-of-custody documentation must be maintained for all digital evidence. Case notes and records of observations must be of a permanent nature. Handwritten notes and observations must be in ink, not pencil, although pencil (including color) may be appropriate for diagrams or making tracings. Any corrections to notes must be made by an initialed, single strikeout; nothing in the handwritten information should be obliterated or erased. Notes and records should be authenticated by handwritten signatures, initials, digital signatures, or other marking systems.

Any action that has the potential to alter, damage, or destroy any aspect of original evidence must be performed by qualified persons in a forensically sound manner. Evidence has value only if it can be shown to be accurate, reliable, and controlled. A quality forensic program consists of properly trained personnel and appropriate equipment, software, and procedures to collectively ensure these attributes [6].

5.2 Monitoring Social Media Propaganda for Law Enforcement

The Internet has become a primary platform for communication and it has also become a tool for spreading extremist propaganda, and for terrorist recruiting, training, and planning. It is a means of social networking for like-minded extremists including those who are not yet radicalized, but who may become so through the anonymity of cyberspace. In other words, the Internet has become a facilitator and an accelerant for *domestic antisocial groups* and *domestic fanatics* as well as criminal activity [7].

To stay ahead of domestic and international extremists, it has become necessary to monitor the social media propaganda disseminated by known extremist groups as well as propaganda that may be targeting a particular community or jurisdiction. While national attention is focused on the substantial threat posed by international terrorists to the homeland, local law enforcement officials must often contend with an ongoing threat posed by domestic terrorists based and operating strictly within the U.S. Domestic terrorists motivated by a number of political or social agendas— including white supremacists, black separatists, animal rights/environmental terrorists, anarchists, anti-abortion extremists, and self-styled militia—continue to employ violence and criminal activity in furtherance of these agendas. There are several known groups that have posed a threat.

Animal rights and environmental extremists, operating under the umbrella of the Animal Liberation Front (ALF) and Earth Liberation Front (ELF), utilize a variety of tactics against their targets, including arson, sabotage/vandalism, theft of research animals, and the occasional use of explosive devices. Serious incidents caused by animal rights supporters and *eco-terrorists* decreased in 2004, a fact attributed to a series of law enforcement successes that are likely deterring large-scale arsons and property destruction. Following a rash of serious incidents of animal rights/eco-terrorism, including a $50 million arson in San Diego and two bombing incidents in the San Francisco area, law enforcement authorities achieved several significant successes that have likely deterred additional terrorist activity. Despite these successes, it is anticipated that animal rights extremism and eco-terrorism will continue to threaten certain segments of government and private industry, specifically in the areas of animal research and residential/commercial development.

The potential for violence by anarchists and other emerging revolutionary groups, such as the Anarchist Black Cross Federation (ABCF), will continue to be an issue for law enforcement. The stated goals of the ABCF are the abolishment of prisons, the system of laws, and the Capitalist state. The ABCF believes in armed resistance to achieve a stateless and classless society. ABCF has continued to organize, recruit, and train anarchists in the tactical use of firearms. U.S.-based black separatist groups follow radical variants of Islam, and in some cases express solidarity with Al Qaeda and other international terrorist groups.

Incidents of organized white supremacist group violence decreased in 2004. This was due to several high profile law enforcement arrests over the last several years, as well as the continued fragmentation of white supremacist groups because of the deaths or the arrests of leaders. However, the violence on the part of white supremacists remains an ongoing threat to government targets, Jewish individuals and establishments, and non-white ethnic groups. White supremacists' social media propaganda and activities increased during and after the 2016 U.S. elections.

The right-wing Patriot movement consisting of militias, common law courts, tax protesters, and other anti-government extremists remains a continuing threat. Sporadic incidents resulting in direct clashes with law enforcement are possible and will most likely involve state and local law enforcement personnel, such as highway patrol officers and sheriff's deputies.

Potential violent anti-abortion extremists linked to terrorism ideologies or groups pose a current threat. The admiration of violent high-profile offenders by extremists highlight continued concerns relating to potential or similar anti-abortion threat activity including gun violence at abortion clinics and harassment of people visiting the clinics [8].

There are a variety of evolving tools to help monitor extremist social media propaganda. The Homeland Security Systems Engineering and Development Institute (HS SEDI™) published research in 2014 that reviewed social media

Table 5.2   Social Media Monitoring Tools

Babel street™	Marketwired Sysomos™
Crimson hexagon™	Meltwater Buzz™
DataSift™	NetVibes™
Geofeedia™	SAS™
Graphika™	Salesforce Radian6™
Hashtagify.me™	SocialMention™
HootSuite™	SocialOomph™
HumanGeo™	Spiral16™
Nuvi™	SproutSocial™
Recorded future™	TweetDeck™
InTENSITY™	Twitter Gnip App™

monitoring tools. Many of these tools may be beyond the budgets of local law enforcement agencies but the report can help local agencies better understand tool capability [9]. Social media monitoring tools covered in the report are shown in Table 5.2. Tools are constantly evolving and interested agencies should research their current capabilities and pricing structure.

Smaller law enforcement agencies with very slim budgets can still monitor social media propaganda through applications like Google Alerts and the use of hashtag searches on Twitter or other simple searches on various social media platforms. Once it is determined what should be monitored and searches are developed, it is a rather easy process. If, for example, there is a known hate group in the geographical area and their user names are known, they can be followed in social media services. Another approach is to monitor mentions by community or jurisdiction name on various social media platforms.

5.3 Joint Terrorism Task Forces

The FBI's Joint Terrorism Task Forces, or JTTFs, are small cells of highly trained, locally based, investigators, analysts, linguists, SWAT experts, and other specialists from dozens of U.S. law enforcement and intelligence agencies. Extremist social media propaganda is of great interest to them and the JTTFs can provide a valuable resource to local law enforcement agencies. These units investigate terrorism, chase down leads, gather evidence, make arrests, provide security for special events, conduct training, collect and share intelligence, and respond to threats and incidents at a moment's notice. The task forces are based in 104 cities nationwide, including at least one in each of the 56 FBI field offices. A total of 71 of these JTTFs have been created since 9/11; the first was established in New York City in 1980.

The JTTFs currently include approximately 4,000 members nationwide hailing from over 500 state and local agencies and 55 federal agencies (DHS, the U.S. military, Immigration and Customs Enforcement, and the Transportation Security Administration, to name a few). The JTTFs provide one-stop shopping for information regarding terrorist activities. They enable a shared intelligence base across many agencies. They create familiarity among investigators and managers before a crisis. Perhaps most importantly, they pool talents, skills, and knowledge from across the law enforcement and intelligence communities into a single team that responds together.

The task forces coordinate their efforts largely through the interagency National Joint Terrorism Task Force, working out of FBI Headquarters, which makes sure that information and intelligence flows freely among the local JTTFs and beyond [10].

5.4 Law Enforcement and Justice System Personnel Can Be Extremists

The Internet has had a profound impact on radicalization. It has become a key platform for spreading extremist propaganda and has been used as a tool for terrorist recruiting, training, and planning. It also serves as a means of communication for like-minded extremists [11]. The Internet is available to much of the U.S. population including law enforcement and Justice System personnel, some of whom have been found to be extremists. There have been several cases in the last decade when a police or court officer has revealed their racism and bigotry in social media posts.

Incident like the shooting death of Michael Brown in Ferguson, Missouri, and Eric Garner in New York have inflamed both sides of the conflict for equal justice. The Black Lives Matter movement emerged out of such incidents but has met extreme resistance from the pro-police movement, which considers any questioning of police conduct to be an affront to the profession. This conflict has played out in years of social media propaganda laden with racist content and often condoning violence.

For almost 40 years, the U.S. Commission on Civil Rights has been at the forefront of the police practices debate. Through its report *Who Is Guarding the Guardians?* as well numerous subsequent reports, the Commission has made important recommendations to improve the quality of police protection while ensuring the protection of civil rights for all Americans. The Commission has consistently endeavored to underscore these connected goals.

Law enforcement work is undeniably difficult. Officers must constantly be aware of the pressures to reduce crime and make arrests, while balancing concerns about officer safety and the constant stress of making split-second decisions that could mean the difference between life and death. The Commission applauds the efforts of many law enforcement agencies to improve themselves by increasing diversity among the ranks of officers, developing new training methods on the use of force, and bolstering their internal affairs divisions. Many police departments have also worked to strengthen their relationships with communities of color and have updated their policies in order to adequately respond to the needs of an ever-changing constituency. Some police departments have drastically reduced crime and fundamentally changed the communities in which they serve. Indeed, the Commission found that cities like New York City and Los Angeles, for example, have made great strides in lowering crime rates.

Regrettably, their crime reduction achievements often have come at a significant cost to the vulnerable communities in greatest need of police protection. Reports, many brought to light by *citizen journalists*, of alleged police brutality, harassment, and misconduct continue to spread throughout the country. People of color, women, and the poor are groups of Americans that seem to bear the brunt of the abuse, which compounds the other injustices that they may suffer as a result of discrimination against their racial, ethnic, gender, or economic status. In their eagerness to achieve important goals such as lowering crime, some police officers become extremist and overstep their authority, trample on individuals' civil rights, and may cause entire communities to fear the same people they hired and trusted to protect them.

Based on the Commission's research, the problem of police misconduct has affected every facet of police culture and policies. Perpetrators can come from any race, ethnicity, or gender, but all police officers are essentially trained by the same law enforcement methods that fail to adequately address cultural diversity and civil rights. Moreover, although law enforcement agencies may significantly reduce crime and the number of police shootings, these improvements come at a terrible price. Incidents of police officers committing crimes, engaging in racial profiling, and harassing individuals continue to make the headlines.

The Commission has a long history of examining the police in their administration of justice and has made numerous recommendations to improve law enforcement as a whole. Many of the Commission's recommendations have been implemented and have positively affected those communities. Despite this fact, reports of abuse and misconduct seem to be incessant, and they typically prompt a complex series of responses: community leaders cry out for change; law enforcement agencies assert that they are doing their job; federal investigators evaluate rogue police officers and entire departments; politicians debate about policies that purport to be tough on crime, yet strong on civil rights. What emerges from these opposing accounts is the need for a reasoned, systematic approach to honestly and sufficiently address police misconduct, once and for all.

Some of the Commission's key findings and recommendations have been previously made in other reports. For example, the Commission reiterates the need to increase diversity in all law enforcement agencies from the officer patrolling the street to the precinct captain. There is also a continuing need to implement successful models of *community engagement* and to improve police officer training so that it will encompass cultural sensitivity issues and the proper use of force.

In addition, the Commission makes findings and recommendations on the issue of racial profiling that need to be given the highest priority in order to confront this pressing contemporary problem. It has been established that racial profiling exists in many areas of law enforcement. However, profound differences exist between the perceptions of the police and the public, particularly with regard to people of color. People of color and other civilians often conclude that law enforcement officers disproportionately target their communities because of misperceptions about their racial and ethnic backgrounds, rather than crime patterns or citizen complaints. In contrast, many law enforcement officers view race and ethnicity as appropriate elements of proper police investigations. Despite efforts to monitor racial profiling, some police officers and officials resist collecting statistics on alleged suspects' race or ethnicity. It is clear that modified policing techniques, based on facts rather than myths about communities of color, would begin to remedy many of the current problems surrounding this issue. The collection of racial profiling data is needed to examine the extent of its use, to enact legislation to prosecute those who utilize it, and to realize the total elimination of this practice in law enforcement.

Law enforcement personnel generally do not reflect the communities they serve. There continues to be a serious underutilization of people of color and women, as well as bilingual officers. Although police forces have tried to implement affirmative action policies, they have been unable to accomplish or sustain diversity. Several reasons account for this problem. Recruitment efforts do not specifically target women and people of color. Despite attempts to attract members of these groups, many people of color and women continue to have negative perceptions of law enforcement.

Within law enforcement agencies, claims of sexual and racial harassment, disparity in pay, and low job satisfaction make police careers unattractive. Additionally, the selection process for police officers often contains biases that, in effect, eliminate candidates of color and noncitizen permanent residents. The Commission recommended, among other things, that law enforcement agencies:

- Develop creative strategies to increase diversity at all levels.
- Improve public perception of the police to attract more applicants.
- Encourage recruits to have college degrees.
- Eliminate biases in the selection system.
- Revise recruitment and selection methods.

The Commission finds that the promotion and reward systems of many law enforcement agencies are seriously flawed. The emphasis on certain questionable crime reduction strategies may negatively affect civil rights by encouraging officers to engage in unlawful practices in the hopes of gaining a promotion. Indeed, racial profiling may be encouraged by this reward system because communities of color are frequently targeted as high-crime areas. To remedy this situation, law enforcement agencies should re-evaluate their retention and promotion processes, recognizing that a system of rewards that promotes crime prevention over the protection of civil rights should be replaced with one that incorporates and reinforces the two concerns. They should also seek ways to improve the promotion rate for officers of color.

Good basic training on diversity issues, especially at the earliest stages of law enforcement careers, would significantly improve the overall effectiveness of officers. In contrast, inadequate training usually reveals itself during the most precarious circumstances: when officers are responding to a volatile crime scene or in the process of making an arrest, and are called upon to make instantaneous, life-altering decisions.

Law enforcement agencies should police themselves primarily because they possess the tools to internally change policies and practices. The Commission finds problems, however, with the internal regulation of the use of deadly force, racial profiling, as well as misconduct investigations and dispositions of radicalized officers. Different jurisdictions have varying interpretations of the legitimate use of deadly force and the legal standards of reasonable behavior. Civilian deaths caused by police error continue to mount, and it is increasingly evident that officers need clear guidance from their chiefs of police and immediate supervisors on the use of excessive force, as well as internal misconduct policies and disciplinary procedures related to that behavior.

Internal affairs divisions, charged with investigating allegations of police misconduct and resolving complaints, increasingly lose credibility and effectiveness when they are accused of unequally disciplining the same types of offenses, taking too long to investigate complaints, being unable to break through the code of silence among police officers, failing to keep the public apprised of complaint dispositions, and lacking computerized data systems to track needed information on misconduct incidents. City officials continue to hold the most influence over how external review procedures are conducted. They guide the overall attitude of their officers regarding police misconduct issues. Officials at every level of city government should make a concerted effort to eliminate all forms of police misconduct.

State prosecution of police misconduct cases is not effective primarily because district or county attorneys rely heavily upon the support and cooperation of police departments. The appointment of an independent or special prosecutor assigned solely to police misconduct cases would increase the frequency and quality of those investigations and prosecutions.

Civilian oversight boards continue to play an important role in the external oversight of police misconduct; however, most boards have little or no investigative or disciplinary powers. Civilian review boards should be endowed with disciplinary authority over investigations of police abuse incidents. In addition, criminal remedies should be pursued in every police misconduct case when there is sufficient evidence to support the charges. Through vigorous criminal prosecution of accused police officers, the federal government can work to remedy the problem of police misconduct and enhance *constitutional and effective policing* and reduce *discriminatory policing practices* [12].

5.5 Anti-Cop versus Pro-Cop Propaganda in Social Media

It is a rather commonly held opinion that there is an anti-police culture in the U.S. This is fueled by several high profile incidents were police officer were gunned down in the line of duty. The shooting deaths of police officers in Dallas, Texas, in 2016 are considered the worst attacks on U.S. law enforcement in decades. The assassin was intent on killing as many police officers as possible. FBI statistics show that 66 law enforcement officers were feloniously killed in the line of duty in 2016 in the U.S. This was an increase of 61% when compared with the 41 officers killed in 2015. At the time the 66 law enforcement officers were fatally wounded:

- 17 were ambushed (entrapment/premeditation).
- 13 were answering disturbance calls (seven were domestic disturbance calls).
- Nine were investigating suspicious persons/circumstances.
- Six were engaged in tactical situations.
- Five were performing investigative activities.
- Four were conducting traffic pursuits/stops.
- Three were investigating drug-related matters.
- Three were victims of unprovoked attacks.
- One was answering a robbery in progress call or pursuing a robbery suspect(s).
- One was answering a burglary in progress call or pursuing a burglary suspect(s).
- Four were attempting other arrests.

Offenders used firearms in 62 of the 66 felonious deaths. These included 37 incidents with handguns, 24 incidents with rifles, and one incident with a shotgun. Four victim officers were killed with vehicles used as weapons. Of the 66 officers killed, 50 were confirmed to be wearing body armor at the times of the incidents. Fourteen of the 66 slain officers fired their service weapons, and 10 officers attempted to fire their weapons. Three victim officers had their weapons stolen; one officer was killed with his own weapon.

In 2016, an additional 52 officers were killed in line-of-duty accidents, which are officer deaths that were found not to be willful and intentional. This is an increase of 16% when compared with the 45 officers who were accidentally killed in 2015. Twenty-six of the officers died as a result of automobile accidents, 12 were struck by vehicles, and seven were fatally injured in motorcycle accidents. Three officers died in accidental shootings, two victim officers drowned, one died in an aircraft accident, and one victim officer was fatally injured when thrown from a horse. Of the 26 officers who died due to automobile accidents, eight were wearing seatbelts. Eleven officers were not wearing seatbelts (five of whom were partially or totally ejected from the vehicles), and seatbelt use was not reported for seven of the officers who were killed in automobile accidents [13].

There has also been a steady stream of people being killed by police officers and that has drawn considerable public concern and sparked hatred of police by targeted minorities, especially when the victim was unarmed. Many cases quickly become *consumer-generated content* somewhere on the Internet. The U.S. government does not collect or publish data on how many people are killed by law enforcement officers every year. However, several independent trackers, primarily journalists and academics who study criminal justice, contend that the accurate number of people shot and killed by police officers is consistently upwards of 1,000 each year.

Between June 1, 2015, and March 31, 2016, media reviews identified 1,348 potential arrest-related deaths. During this period, the number of deaths consistently ranged from 87 to 156 arrest-related deaths per month, with an average of 135 deaths per month. To confirm and collect more information about the 379 deaths identified through open sources from June to August 2015, the Bureau of Justice Statistics (BJS) conducted a survey of law enforcement agencies and medical examiners' and coroners' offices. The survey findings identified 425 arrest-related deaths during this three-month period, which is 12% more than the number of deaths identified through the open source review. Extrapolated to a full calendar year, an estimated 1,900 arrest-related deaths occurred in 2015. Nearly two-thirds (64%) of the deaths that occurred from June to August 2015 were homicides, about a fifth (18%) were suicides, and a tenth (11%) were accidents [14].

These circumstances in general, as well as high profile incidents involving deaths caused by law enforcement officers, spark propaganda wild fires on social media. There have also been instances of *cyberbullying* and *cyber-stalking* of people that have expressed their views on police violence and *policing style*. There are a few Twitter accounts that focus on posting about law enforcement officers. Copwatch, WeCopwatch, and Arizona Copwatch post that their mission is to hold cops accountable. Police Support USA, Working For You, and BlueLivesMatter are very pro-police oriented. A search of social media shows a variety of perspectives in thousands of posts samples, some of which are shown in Table 5.3.

Table 5.3 Sample Anti-Cop Pro-Cop Social Media Posts

Indicative of the current anti police agenda in the media
Kill these cops, F*** that cop
Anti-police brutality is the opposite of being anti-police
More cops, more arrests, more policing, more prisoners, more lives ruined
We are not anti-police, we are anti-police brutality
Dotard Donald is now anti-police
Hate cops in Washington, Obama=cop hater
Cop hater HUSSEIN OBAMA murdered another officer!
If you're a Democrat you must be a cop hater
He's a lying race-baiting cop hater
Cops investigate themselves, clear themselves, reward each other
My business will be a cop-free zone
LEOs received awards for their anti-black terror

5.6 Summary

Extremist propaganda in social media has perpetuated the turmoil for the profession of law enforcement as a whole. Extremist propaganda that promotes violence is also a challenge for law enforcement because they are often the target of the violence or the communities they police are targets. This chapter examines training for law enforcement on dealing with extremist propaganda, monitoring social media, the radicalization of law enforcement officers, and anti-cop versus pro-cop propaganda in social media. Key points covered in this chapter include:

- Jihadist recruitment has reached into small and mid-sized cities in every state of the U.S. and attracted followers from some 40 different ethnicities and every race in America.
- Given the diversity of American homegrown terrorism offenders, there is no common denominator, no common grievances, or even common motivations, that can predict who may opt to join groups espousing violent jihad.
- Digital evidence is information stored or transmitted in binary form that may be relied on in court. It can be found on a computer hard drive, a mobile phone, a personal digital assistant (PDA), a CD, and a flash card in a digital

camera, among other places. Digital evidence is commonly associated with electronic crime, or e-crime, such as child pornography or credit card fraud, and digital evidence is now used to prosecute all types of crimes, not just e-crime.

- NICE, led by NIST in the U.S. Department of Commerce, is a partnership between government, academia, and the private sector focused on cybersecurity education, training, and workforce development.
- All activity relating to the seizure, storage, examination, or transfer of digital evidence must be recorded in writing and be available for review and testimony.
- The Internet has become a primary platform for communication. It has also become a tool for spreading extremist propaganda and for terrorist recruiting, training, and planning.
- Smaller law enforcement agencies with very slim budgets can monitor social media propaganda through applications like Google Alerts and the use of hashtag searches on Twitter or other simple searches on various social media platforms.
- The FBI's Joint Terrorism Task Forces, or JTTFs, are small cells of highly trained, locally based, investigators, analysts, linguists, SWAT experts, and other specialists from dozens of U.S. law enforcement and intelligence agencies.
- The Internet has had a profound impact on radicalization. It has become a key platform for spreading extremist propaganda and has been used as a tool for terrorist recruiting, training, and planning. It also serves as a means of communication for like-minded extremists.
- It is a rather commonly held opinion that there is an anti-police culture in the U.S. This is fueled by several high profile incidents where police officers were gunned down in the line of duty.
- High profile incidents involving deaths caused by law enforcement officers spark propaganda wild fires on social media.

5.7 Course Activities

Course project number one: Design a questionnaire of five to ten questions to interview law enforcement personnel about the impact of social media extremist propaganda on their work and their lives. Compare the developed questionnaires with those of other class members. Then formulate a questionnaire that all class members can use to interview law enforcement professionals about extremist propaganda on their work and their lives.

Course project number two: Interview three to five law enforcement professionals about the impact of social media extremist propaganda on their work and their lives.

Course project number three: Compare the results of the interviews of the impact of social media extremist propaganda on the work and lives of law enforcement professionals that were interviewed.

Course project number four: Read, review, and discuss one of the suggested readings listed in the introduction.

References

1. National Institute of Justice. *The Role of Social Media in the Evolution of Al Qaeda-Inspired Violent Extremism*, September 6, 2017. Accessed December 2, 2017 https://nij.gov/topics/crime/terrorism/Pages/role-of-social-media-in-evolution-of-al-qaeda-inspired-terrorism.aspx.
2. National Institute of Justice. *Digital Evidence and Forensics*. Accessed December 3, 2017 https://www.nij.gov/topics/forensics/evidence/digital/Pages/welcome.aspx.
3. NIST National Institute of Standards and Technology. *Digital & Multimedia Evidence*. Accessed December 2, 2017 https://www.nist.gov/topics/digital-multimedia-evidence.
4. NIST. National Initiative for Cybersecurity Education (NICE). Accessed December 2, 2017 https://www.nist.gov/itl/applied-cybersecurity/nice/about.
5. Federal Law Enforcement Training Centers. *Internet Investigations Training Program*. Accessed December 2, 2017 https://www.fletc.gov/training-program/internet-investigations-training-program.
6. U.S. FBI. *Digital Evidence: Standards and Principles*. Forensic Science Communication, April 2000—Volume 2—Number 2. Accessed December 3, 2017 https://archives.fbi.gov/archives/about-us/lab/forensic-science-communications/fsc/april2000/swgde.htm.
7. R. S. Mueller, III. FBI. *Statements to the Preparedness Group Conference*, Washington, DC, October 6, 2010. Accessed December 3, 2017 https://archives.fbi.gov/archives/news/speeches/countering-the-terrorism-threat.
8. R. S. Mueller, III. FBI. *Statements to the Senate Committee on Intelligence of the United States Senate*, Washington, DC, February 16, 2005. Accessed December 3, 2017 https://archives.fbi.gov/archives/news/testimony/global-threats-to-the-u.s.-and-the-fbis-response-1.
9. Homeland Security Systems Engineering and Development Institute. *First Responder Big Data Analytics Roadmap Recommendations*, February 5, 2014. Accessed December 3, 2017 https://www.dhs.gov/sites/default/files/publications/First-Responder-Big-Data-Analytics-Roadmap-Recommendation-508.pdf.
10. FBI. *Joint Terrorism Task Forces*. Accessed December 3, 2017 https://www.fbi.gov/investigate/terrorism/joint-terrorism-task-forces.
11. R. S. Mueller, III. FBI. *Statement Before the Senate Appropriations Committee, Subcommittee on Commerce, Justice, Science, and Related Agencies*, Washington, DC, May 16, 2013. Accessed December 3, 2017 https://archives.fbi.gov/archives/news/testimony/fbi-budget-request-for-fiscal-year-2014.
12. U.S. Commission on Civil Rights. *Revisiting Who is Guarding the Guardians?* Executive Summary, November 2000. Accessed December 3, 2017 http://www.usccr.gov/pubs/guard/exsum.htm.

13. FBI. *FBI Releases 2016 Preliminary Statistics for Law Enforcement Officers Killed in the Line of Duty*, May 15, 2017. Accessed December 4, 2017 https://www.fbi.gov/news/pressrel/press-releases/fbi-releases-2016-preliminary-statistics-for-law-enforcement-officers-killed-in-the-line-of-duty.
14. U.S. Bureau of Justice Statistics. *Arrest-Related Deaths Program Redesign Study, 2015–2016: Preliminary Findings*, December 15, 2016. Accessed December 4, 2017 https://www.bjs.gov/content/pub/pdf/ardprs1516pf_sum.pdf.

Chapter 6

The Corporate Extremist Propaganda Machine

6.1 The Corporate Extremist Propaganda Culture

The focus on extremist propaganda generated by hate groups and terrorist organizations has overshadowed the fact that corporations also generate and disseminate vast amounts of extremist propaganda. Corporations do not necessarily motivate or inspire people to go kill other people, but their extremist propaganda has resulted in the deaths of millions of people and has had a societal cost in the hundreds of billions of dollars.

The primary propaganda technique used by corporations is misinformation, which is delivered through their lobbying efforts, the creation of research reports to conceal their guilt, and their ability to take their *deceptive marketing* efforts into the halls of legislators through campaign contributions and buying votes necessary to protect their profit-oriented enterprises. Corporations go far beyond deceptive and false advertising. They have become experts in executing the process of disseminating extremist propaganda. They do this all in the name of capitalism and profits. The major culprits that come to mind are the tobacco and pharmaceutical industries.

When consumers see or hear an advertisement—whether it's on the Internet, radio or television, or anywhere else—U.S. federal law says that ad must be truthful, not misleading, and, when appropriate, backed by scientific evidence. The Federal Trade Commission (FTC) enforces these truth-in-advertising laws, and it applies the same standards no matter where an ad appears, be it in newspapers and magazines, online, in the mail, or on billboards or buses. The FTC looks especially closely at advertising claims that can affect consumers' health or their pocketbooks, including claims about food, over-the-counter drugs, dietary supplements, alcohol, and tobacco and on conduct related to high-tech products and the Internet. The FTC also monitors and writes reports about ad industry practices regarding the marketing of alcohol and tobacco. When the FTC finds a case of fraud perpetrated on consumers, the agency files actions in federal district court for immediate and permanent orders to stop scams, prevent fraudsters from perpetrating scams in the future, freeze their assets, and get compensation for victims [1]. The FTC has a broad mandate to protect consumers from fraud and deception in the marketplace. To fulfill this goal, the FTC takes law enforcement actions; provides consumer and business education; issues reports and policy guidance; leads workshops; and participates in other forums. Actions taken by the FTC include:

■ Dallas Auto Dealer Settles Charges It Deceptively Advertised Sale and Lease Terms (December 1, 2017)
■ Online Lingerie Marketer Prohibited from Deceiving Shoppers about Negative-Option Programs (November 21, 2017)
■ FTC Charges Office Supply Scheme with Bilking Millions of Dollars from Small Businesses for Free Samples of Cleaning Products (November 8, 2017)
■ Administrative Law Judge Upholds FTC's Complaint that 1-800 Contacts Unlawfully Harmed Competition in Online Search Advertising Auctions, Restricting the Availability of Truthful Advertising to Consumers (October 30, 2017)
■ FTC Releases Reports on 2015 Cigarette and Smokeless Tobacco Sales and Marketing Expenditures (October 25, 2017)
■ Victory Media Settles FTC Charges Concerning Its Promotion of Post-Secondary Schools to Military Consumers (October 19, 2017)
■ FTC Sending Refund Checks Totaling More than $9.8 Million to People Who Were Charged for Free Trials for Health Products (October 10, 2017)
■ Illinois Firm Barred from Making Misleading Baby Mattress Claims (September 28, 2017)
■ FTC Revises Fuel Economy Guide (September 15, 2017)
■ CSGO Lotto Owners Settle FTC's First-Ever Complaint against Individual Social Media Influencers (September 7, 2017)
■ FTC Obtains Temporary Restraining Order Halting Work-at-Home Scheme (August 17, 2017)
■ FTC Stops False Advertising, Phony Reviews by Online Trampoline Sellers (May 31, 2017)
■ FTC Obtains Court Order Against Envelope-Stuffing Scheme (April 24, 2017)
■ FTC Staff Reminds Influencers and Brands to Clearly Disclose Relationship (April 19, 2017)
■ FTC Approves Final Consents Settling Charges that Two Companies Made Misleading Made-in-the-USA Claims (April 18, 2017)
■ FTC Settlement Bars Spam Email Marketing, Baseless Weight-Loss Claims by Diet-Pill Operation (March 17, 2017)

- Business Opportunity Scheme Operators Banned from Telemarketing and Selling Investment Opportunities; Will Return Millions to Consumers (March 13, 2017)
- Federal Trade Commission, Class Action Settlements Require Volkswagen to Repair or Buy Back 3.0 Liter TDI Diesel Vehicles (February 1, 2017)
- Breathometer Marketers Settle FTC Charges of Misrepresenting Ability to Accurately Measure Users' Blood Alcohol Content (January 23, 2017)
- Uber Agrees to Pay $20 Million to Settle FTC Charges That It Recruited Prospective Drivers with Exaggerated Earnings Claims (January 19, 2017)
- FTC, New York State Charge the Marketers of Prevagen with Making Deceptive Memory, Cognitive Improvement Claims (January 9, 2017)
- CarMax and Two Other Dealers Settle FTC Charges That They Touted Inspections While Failing to Disclose Some of the Cars Were Subject to Unrepaired Safety Recalls (December 16, 2016)
- DeVry University Agrees to $100 Million Settlement with FTC (December 15, 2016)
- FTC Approves Final Order Settling Charges that Mars Petcare Made False Health Claims for Its Eukanuba Brand Dog Food (December 13, 2016)
- FTC Rules California Naturel, Inc. Misled Consumers, Violated the FTC Act (December 12, 2016) [2]

6.2 The Case of Big Tobacco

Tobacco use is the leading cause of preventable disease and death in the U.S. and cigarettes are the most commonly used tobacco product among U.S. adults. Since the 1950s, the tobacco industry has used extremist propaganda techniques to distort the science and research about the health dangers of smoking. The tobacco industry implemented a strategy, new in the history of U.S. industry, to erode, confuse, and condemn the science that was beginning to threaten its highly profitable business. It was the beginning of extremist propaganda use by U.S. businesses and it was very successful for a very long time.

In the U.S., the total number of cigarettes reported sold by the major manufacturers was 244.2 billion in 2015 which was a decrease of 9.6 billion units (3.8%) from 2014. Advertising and promotional expenditures increased during that same period, from $8.031 billion to $8.240 billion. The largest single category of these expenditures in 2015 was *price discounts paid to cigarette retailers* in order to reduce the price of cigarettes to consumers, which accounted for $5.447 billion (66.1% of total advertising and promotional expenditures) [3]. Clearly tobacco sales in the U.S. are a big business.

On January 11, 1964, Luther L. Terry, M.D., Surgeon General of the U.S. Public Health Service, released the first report of the Surgeon General's Advisory Committee on Smoking and Health. On the basis of more than 7,000 articles relating to smoking and disease already available at that time in the biomedical literature, the Advisory Committee concluded that cigarette smoking is a cause of lung cancer and laryngeal cancer in men and is a probable cause of lung cancer in women and the most important cause of chronic bronchitis. The release of the report was the first in a series of steps, still being taken more than 40 years later, to diminish the impact of tobacco use on the health of the American people. For several days, the report furnished newspaper headlines across the country and lead stories on television newscasts. Later, it was ranked among the top news stories of 1964.

During the 50-plus years that have elapsed since that report, individual citizens, private organizations, public agencies, and elected officials have pursued the Advisory Committee's call for appropriate remedial action. Early on, the U.S. Congress adopted the Federal Cigarette Labeling and Advertising Act of 1965 and the Public Health Cigarette Smoking Act of 1969. These laws required a health warning on cigarette packages, banned cigarette advertising in the broadcasting media, and called for an annual report on the health consequences of smoking.

In September 1965, the Public Health Service established a small unit called the National Clearinghouse for Smoking and Health. Through the years, the Clearinghouse and its successor organization, the Centers for Disease Control and Prevention's Office on Smoking and Health, have been responsible for over two dozen reports on the health consequences of smoking [4].

In the twentieth century, extremist media helped create new generations of tobacco users even as evidence mounted about tobacco's terrible toll on health. Despite a roughly 50% decline in adult smoking prevalence over the past 40 years, about one in five Americans continues to smoke, and more than 4,000 young people smoke their first cigarette each day. A fundamental theme in research is the dynamic interplay between the forces that work to promote tobacco use and those that work to control or prevent it. For example, whereas tobacco control media campaigns warn about the dangers of smoking, smoking proponents send out the message that smoking confers social status, athleticism, and glamour. Key research findings include:

- Much tobacco advertising targets the needs of adolescents, who can be influenced by even brief exposure to tobacco advertising.
- There is a causal relationship between tobacco advertising and promotion and increased tobacco use. Substantial evidence from the U.S. and other countries shows that partial bans on tobacco advertising do not work because the industry modifies its use of the media, for example by expanding point-of-sale advertising and promotions on the Internet. Therefore, comprehensive bans on tobacco advertising and promotion need to be considered.
- Canadian and European restrictions on tobacco marketing are stronger than those in the United States.
- Smoking has often been pervasive in the movies, occurring in three-quarters or more of contemporary box-office hits. Smoking is more common in adult-rated movies.

- There is evidence of a causal relationship between exposure to tobacco use in movies and youth smoking initiation.
- Media campaigns to prevent and control tobacco use can reduce smoking. Anti-tobacco advertising with strong negative messages works better in reaching audiences; messages that use humor or other tactics are less successful. In contrast, anti-tobacco youth campaigns sponsored by the tobacco industry are not effective and may even increase smoking among adolescents.
- Organized media advocacy efforts on behalf of the tobacco control community generally lack sufficient resources. Very little is known about how the content and volume of news coverage related to tobacco affects attitudes and behavior [5].

Other research has shown that:

- Cigarette smoking is a major cause of disease and death and differences in the magnitude of disease risk are directly related to differences in patterns of smoking. African-Americans bear the greatest health burden.
- Tobacco use varies within and among racial/ethnic minority groups; among adults, American Indians and Alaska Natives have the highest prevalence of tobacco use, and African-American and Southeast Asian men also have a high prevalence of smoking. Asian American and Hispanic women have the lowest prevalence.
- Among adolescents, cigarette smoking prevalence increased in the 1990s among African-Americans and Hispanics after several years of substantial decline among adolescents.
- No single factor determines patterns of tobacco use among racial/ethnic minority groups; these patterns are the result of complex interactions of multiple factors, such as socioeconomic status, cultural characteristics, acculturation, stress, biological elements, targeted advertising, price of tobacco products, and varying capacities of communities to mount effective tobacco control initiatives [6].

Surgeon General C. Everett Koop's first official act after his confirmation was to issue the 1982 Surgeon General's Report on Smoking and Health, the most authoritative statement to date on the connection between smoking and cancer of the lung, oral cavity, larynx, esophagus, stomach, bladder, pancreas, and kidneys. Reports issued by Koop in 1983, 1984, 1985, and 1988, respectively, showed that smoking caused even more deaths from heart disease than from cancer.

Koop was prepared to stand up to the powerful tobacco industry and its allies in Congress and in the administration of President Ronald Reagan. Koop castigated the tobacco industry for spending $4,000 on advertising for every dollar the U.S. Public Health Service spent on broadcasting anti-smoking messages. In 1982, he testified before Congress in favor of a series of rotating labels warning against the specific dangers of smoking (heart disease, cancer, emphysema, the risk to unborn children of pregnant women who smoke) in place of the current single generic label, "Warning: The Surgeon General Has Determined That Cigarette Smoking Is Dangerous to Your Health." He continued to advocate rotating warning labels even after the Reagan White House withdrew its support under pressure from the tobacco industry. In 1986, he succeeded in having the Surgeon General's health warning placed on packages of smokeless tobacco such as chewing and snuff tobacco, a product the tobacco industry suggested was a less harmful alternative to cigarettes [7].

On June 17, 1998, the U.S. Senate refused to vote on a bill to reduce teen smoking. President Clinton supported legislation introduced by Senator John McCain (Republican-Arizona) that contained the strongest anti-youth smoking provisions in U.S. history. It was legislation designed to cut youth smoking in half over the next five years. The tobacco industry reportedly spent $40 million to defeat the legislation [8].

In 1998, the Attorneys General of 46 states and the District of Columbia signed the Master Settlement Agreement (MSA) with the four largest tobacco companies in the U.S. (The other four states had already reached separate agreements with the tobacco companies). Since the agreement was signed, about 40 other tobacco companies have signed on and are also bound by its terms. The agreement was designed to halt much of the aggressive propaganda generated by the tobacco industry [9]. Table 6.1 summarizes what the Master Settlement Agreement required of tobacco companies.

Finally, in 2009, the Family Smoking Prevention and Tobacco Control Act (Tobacco Control Act), was signed into law, giving the U.S. Food and Drug

Table 6.1 Master Settlement Agreement Requirements

Pay the states billions of dollars annually to compensate for tobacco-related health care costs
Limitations on advertising, marketing, and promotion of cigarettes
Prohibition on tobacco advertising that targets people younger than 18, including the use of cartoons
Limitations on outdoor, billboard, and public transit advertising
Prohibition on the use of cigarette brand names on other products
Provide tobacco company internal documents to the public

Source: U.S. Department of Health & Human Services, About tobacco marketing laws and policies, https://betobaccofree.hhs.gov/index.html, Accessed December 8, 2017.

Administration (FDA) authority to regulate the manufacture, distribution, and marketing of tobacco products. The Tobacco Control Act gave the FDA immediate authority to regulate cigarettes, cigarette tobacco, roll-your-own tobacco and smokeless tobacco. For other kinds of tobacco products, the statute authorizes the FDA to issue regulations deeming them to be subject to such authorities. Consistent with the statute, once a tobacco product is deemed, the FDA may put in place restrictions on the sale and distribution of a tobacco product, including age-related access restrictions as well as advertising and promotion restrictions, if the FDA determines the restrictions are appropriate for the protection of the public health.

The deeming rule issued on May 5, 2016, extended the FDA's tobacco product authorities to additional categories of products that meet the statutory definition of a tobacco product, including Electronic Nicotine Delivery Systems or ENDS (e.g., e-cigarettes, vape pens), cigars, pipe tobacco, gels, hookah (waterpipe) tobacco, and future tobacco products, but not including accessories of newly deemed products. The final deeming rule triggers automatic provisions and contains additional restrictions. Newly deemed tobacco products automatically are required to comply with all provisions regarding tobacco products found in the Federal Food, Drug, and Cosmetic (FD&C) Act. These automatic provisions require industry, which includes manufacturers and retailers, to take certain actions, such as:

- Ensure that tobacco products are not adulterated or misbranded. For example, a tobacco product is adulterated if the product is marketed with an unauthorized modified risk claim on its label, labeling, or advertisements. An example of a misbranded tobacco product is one where the manufacturer of the product fails to include a required warning on the label of the product package.
- Provide the FDA with ingredient listings for all tobacco products.
- Register manufacturing establishments and provide FDA with product listings for all tobacco products.
- Obtain premarket authorization for newly deemed products that meet the definition of new tobacco product via one of the pathways specified in the FD&C Act (e.g., Substantial Equivalence or SE, Premarket Tobacco Application or PMTA, Exemption from Substantial Equivalence).
- Requirement for a minimum age of purchase and verification of age via photographic identification. Retailers may not sell newly deemed tobacco products to individuals under 18 years of age; retailers must verify the age of any person who is 26 years of age or younger. States may require a higher minimum age for purchase of tobacco products.
- Prohibition of vending machine sales, unless the vending machine is located in a facility where the retailer ensures that individuals under 18 years of age are prohibited from entering at any time.
- Health warnings for product packages and advertisements [10].

Meanwhile, it is important recognize that tobacco companies have worked for several decades to develop global businesses and leverage their brand and marketing expertise worldwide. This strategy has generated controversy similar to the controversy created by the extremist propaganda the tobacco companies disseminated in the U.S. for over 50 years. One case that illustrates continued corruption in the industry occurred in August 2010, when the U.S. Securities and Exchange Commission (SEC) charged two major tobacco companies, Universal Corporation, Inc. and Alliance One International, Inc., with violating, among other things, the anti-bribery provisions of the Foreign Corrupt Practices Act of 1977 (FCPA) for their involvement in a multi-million dollar bribery scheme with government officials in Thailand to obtain nearly $30 million in sales contracts to supply tobacco. The SEC also charged Alliance One with paying bribes in Kyrgyzstan and making improper payments in China, Greece, and Indonesia and Universal with making improper payments in Malawi and Mozambique. Moreover, the SEC's complaints alleged Universal and Alliance One engaged in books and records and internal control violations.

According to the SEC's complaint, between 2000 and 2004, Universal, in coordination with two of its competitors, Dimon, Inc. (Dimon) and Standard Commercial Corporation (Standard), paid approximately $800,000 to bribe officials of the government-owned Thailand Tobacco Monopoly (TTM) in exchange for securing approximately $11.5 million in sales contracts for its subsidiaries in Brazil and Europe. From 2004 through 2007, Universal also made a series of payments in excess of $165,000 to government officials in Mozambique through corporate subsidiaries in Belgium and Africa. Universal made these payments, among other things, to secure an exclusive right to purchase tobacco from regional growers and to procure legislation beneficial to the company's business. Between 2002 and 2003, Universal subsidiaries paid a total of $850,000 to high-ranking Malawian government officials. Universal did not accurately record these payments in its books and records.

From 2000 to 2004, in a coordinated bribery scheme with Universal, Dimon and Standard paid bribes of more than $1.2 million to government officials of the TTM in order to obtain more than $18.3 million in sales contracts. (In May 2005, Dimon and Standard merged to form Alliance One). Dimon characterized the payment of bribes to TTM officials as commissions paid to Dimon's agent in Thailand. Similarly, Standard personnel authorized improper payments to TTM officials and failed to record those payments accurately in Standard's books and records.

The SEC's complaint also alleges that, from 1996 through 2004, Dimon International Kyrgyzstan (DIK), a wholly-owned subsidiary of Dimon, paid more than $3 million in bribes to Kyrgyzstan government officials to purchase Kyrgyz tobacco for resale to Dimon's customers. Most of these payments were delivered in bags filled with $100 bills to a high-ranking government official. DIK also made improper payments to Kyrgyzstan tax officials.

Additionally, Dimon made improper payments to tax officials in Greece and Indonesia. Standard also made an improper payment to a political candidate and provided gifts, travel, and entertainment expenses to foreign government officials in the Asian Region, including China and Thailand. Dimon and Standard failed to record these payments accurately in the companies' books and records.

Without admitting or denying the SEC's allegations, defendants Universal and Alliance One consented to the entry of final judgments permanently enjoining each of them from violating the anti-bribery, books and records, and internal control provisions of the FCPA, codified as Sections 30A, 13(b)(2)(A), and 13(b)(2)(B) of the Securities Exchange Act of 1934. Universal and Alliance One are ordered to pay disgorgement of $4,581,276.51 and $10,000,000, respectively, and each is ordered to retain an independent monitor for three years.

In related criminal proceedings, the U.S. Department of Justice (DOJ) filed criminal actions against a Universal subsidiary and two Alliance One subsidiaries, charging each of them with one count of conspiring to violate the FCPA and one count of violating the anti-bribery provisions of the FCPA. Universal and Alliance One have entered into non-prosecution agreements with the DOJ and agreed to pay criminal penalties of $4,400,000 and $9,450,000, respectively, and retain independent monitors for a period of three years [11].

6.3 Corporations Are Seen as Terrorist Organizations

Ethnocentrism is basically a belief in the intrinsic superiority of a nation, culture, or group to which individuals, groups, or classes of people belong. This is usually accompanied by feelings of disdain, dislike, or hate for other groups. These perspectives far too often are used to justify the exploitation, oppression, or death of people of a different race, color, sex, or religion. Capitalistic and imperialistic nations are rather ethnocentric by nature and that is reflected in how corporations view their rights to exploit *indigenous groups* in countries where they have operations as well as to commit environmental atrocities where and whenever they operate.

A typical environmental crime such as knowingly discharging raw sewage to one of the U.S. waterways or killing a bald eagle is investigated by Special Agents of the Environmental Protection Agency's Criminal Investigation Division, by Special Agents of the Fish and Wildlife Service, or by other investigative organizations as necessary. Generally speaking, an environmental crime is a negligent, knowing or willful violation of a federal environmental law. Knowing violations are those that are deliberate and not the product of an accident or mistake. Typical violations that result in investigations may involve, but are not limited to

■ Illegal disposal of hazardous waste.
■ Export of hazardous waste without the permission of the receiving country.
■ Illegal discharge of pollutants to a water of the United States.

- The removal and disposal of regulated asbestos containing materials in a manner inconsistent with the law and regulations.
- Illegal importation of certain restricted or regulated chemicals into the United States.
- Tampering with a drinking water supply.
- Mail fraud/wire fraud.
- Conspiracy.
- Money laundering relating to environmental criminal activities.

The Environment and Natural Resources Division (ENRD) Environmental Crimes Section (ECS) DOJ prosecutors often get involved early in an investigation, such as when the investigator swears out a search warrant or when a grand jury's investigative power is needed. Once the necessary evidence is collected, the prosecutor presents the case to the grand jury for indictment. After indictment, the prosecutor guides the case through complex white collar and environmental law issues and prepares it for trial. Although many cases settle through plea agreements, some do not. ECS has an excellent track record in federal court. From October 1, 1998, through September 30, 2014, ECS concluded criminal cases against more than 1,083 individuals and 404 corporate defendants, leading to 774 years of incarceration and $825 million in criminal fines and restitution (903 years with incarceration, halfway house and home detentions) [12]. Specific cases include:

- Volkswagen Senior Manager Sentenced to 84 Months in Prison for Role in Conspiracy to Cheat U.S. Emissions Tests (2017).
- Saltwater Disposal Well Operators Sentenced on Multiple Felony Charges in Connection with Operation of Well (2017).
- Terminix Companies Sentenced for Applying Restricted-Use Pesticide to Residences in the U.S. Virgin Islands (2017).
- Owner and Employee of Metal Plating Government Contractor Pled Guilty to Hazardous Waste Crimes (2017).
- Tyson Poultry Pleads Guilty to Clean Water Act Violations in Connection with Discharge of Acidic Feed Supplement (2017).
- Black Elk Energy Offshore Operations LLC. Convicted of Worker Safety and Clean Water Act Violations in Connection to Offshore Explosion (2017).

Corporations do everything they can to hide their illegal and unethical actions. Many corporations also have propaganda campaigns boasting of their socially responsible activities and the causes or charities they support. Prosecutors and investigators seldom refer to the activities of corporations as terrorist acts. However, there are many people making social media posts and using hashtags like #CorporateTerrorism that specifically express views on corporate terrorism. A sampling of such social media posts is shown in Table 6.2.

Table 6.2   Sample Corporate Terrorism Social Media Posts

#CorporateTerrorism hides behind the guise of a free market society
People will suffer, some will eventually die from exposure to toxins
#DAPL hired TigerSwan mercenaries to terrorize Native water protectors and nobody is talking about 700 people charged on bogus charges
Pollution is ending 9 million lives early, every year. Imagine if terrorists were doing that
Shocking how passive #Americans & #Canadians are to #CorporateTerrorism
No @DonaldTrump is not running the country Big Pharma bankers & corporations are running the country #CorporateTerrorism
I'm sick to death of the wealthy using their resources for #CorporateTerrorism

6.4 Corporate Propaganda in the Classroom

Over the last several decades, propaganda materials with extreme ideological bias or solely for product promotion purposes from industries, corporations, lobbying groups and trade associations have made it into public school classrooms. In April 2017, Ranking Members Raúl M. Grijalva (Democrat-Arizona) of the Committee on Natural Resources, Eddie Bernice Johnson (Democrat-Texas) of the Committee on Science, Space and Technology, and Bobby Scott (Democrat-Virginia) of the Committee on Education and the Workforce condemned the Heartland Institute's distribution of politically motivated and scientifically inaccurate materials on climate change to science teachers at the nation's public schools.

They also stated that the campaign they were referring to was uncovered by the PBS program Frontline, which reported that Heartland was seeking to send a book and DVD distorting the scientific consensus on climate change to every public-school science teacher in the nation—approximately 200,000 teachers across the U.S. The materials were accompanied by a cover letter from a Heartland official urging teachers to consider the possibility that climate science is still being debated and students would be better served by letting them know a vibrant debate is taking place among scientists.

Right-wing funders, including the Koch and Scaife financial networks, have contributed millions of dollars to Heartland Institute projects. The organization previously worked with and accepted money from the tobacco giant Philip Morris to question the validity of research on smoking and cancer, among other activities. A Texas district court judge rebuked its president, Joseph Bast, in a 2014 ruling for declaring that public schools are socialism and that his organization was dedicated to using school vouchers to destroy American public education. Grijalva, Johnson and Scott called on Heartland to end its campaign immediately and for education officials across the country to dismiss the materials out of hand. The scientific consensus that man-made emissions are worsening the process of climate change has been widely accepted, including by the DoD, for many years.

Representative Johnson indicated that he was not really surprised to see a right-wing organization sending scientifically inaccurate materials on climate change to public school teachers across the country and that this isn't the first time Heartland has targeted teachers. As early as 1998, a group of fossil fuel officials, lobbyists and conservative think tanks planned to distribute climate-change skeptical curricula for classrooms nationwide. In 2012, an internal Heartland document outlined plans to do the same [13].

The issue of commercial activity in schools has been on the agenda of many school districts and states since the late 1980s. In September 2000, pursuant to a congressional request, the GAO provided information on commercial activities in public schools, focusing on: (1) laws, regulations, and policies that regulate commercial activities in schools; and (2) the nature and extent of such activities. The GAO noted that:

1. State laws and regulations governing commercial activities in public schools are not comprehensive.
2. Nationwide, only general laws and regulations that apply to all businesses or that govern school finance usually cover school-based commercial activities.
3. However, 19 states have statutes or regulations that address school-related commercial activities, but in 14 of these states, statutes and regulations are not comprehensive and permit or restrict only specific types of activities.
4. In most states, local school officials are responsible for making decisions about commercial activities.
5. No single source of information about local school board policies exists, and policies varied greatly in the districts GAO visited.
6. GAO found no policies that specifically addressed market research activities.
7. The visibility, profitability, and type of commercial activities varied widely, and the high schools GAO visited had more commercial activities than middle or elementary schools.
8. Product sales, primarily the sale of soft drinks by schools or districts under exclusive contracts and short-term fundraising sales, were the most common and lucrative type of commercial activity at the schools GAO visited, although they represented a very small percentage of the districts' budgets.
9. The most visible examples of direct advertising appeared on soft drink vending machines and high school scoreboards.
10. Although some high school sports facilities displayed banners and signs with the names of businesses that had contributed to sports programs, several placed these signs to acknowledge donations rather than in exchange for them.

11. Advertisements were delivered through the media in some schools.
12. GAO observed indirect advertising in all the schools, yet its presence was usually limited and subtle.
13. None of the schools GAO visited reported engaging students in market research, although one principal said he has been approached about doing research.
14. Often the values of school board members, district officials, and parents determine whether an activity is controversial or not, rather than the nature of the activity.
15. Because most of the decisions are made at the local level, varying preferences of local officials result in different levels of commercial activities across districts and across schools in the same districts [14].

In 2004, the GAO reported that 13 states had established laws addressing commercial activities in public schools, and at least 25 states are considering such legislation. Of the states establishing new laws, six established laws affecting market research by addressing the use of student data for commercial activities. Almost all of the proposed bills target the sale of food and beverages. Prior to 2000, 28 states established laws addressing commercial activities, particularly product sales and advertising. At that time, only one state passed a provision affecting market research [15].

6.5 Summary

The focus on extremist propaganda generated by hate groups and terrorist organizations has overshadowed the fact that corporations generate and disseminate vast amounts of extremist propaganda. This chapter examines the extremist propaganda being disseminated by corporations, with the tobacco industry as the primary case study. Key points covered include:

■ Corporations go far beyond deceptive and false advertising. They have become experts in executing the process of disseminating extremist propaganda. They do this all in the name of capitalism and profits.
■ Since the 1950s, the tobacco industry has used extremist propaganda techniques to distort the science and research about the health dangers of smoking. The tobacco industry implemented a strategy, new in the history of U.S. industry, to erode, confuse, and condemn the science that was beginning to threaten its highly profitable business.
■ In the twentieth century, extremist media helped create new generations of tobacco users even as evidence mounted about tobacco's terrible toll on health.
■ Media campaigns to prevent and control tobacco use can reduce smoking. Anti-tobacco advertising with strong negative messages works better in reaching audiences; messages that use humor or other tactics are less successful.

- Anti-tobacco youth campaigns sponsored by the tobacco industry are not effective and may even increase smoking among adolescents.
- Corporations do everything they can to hide their illegal and unethical actions. Many corporations also have propaganda campaigns boasting of their socially responsible activities and the causes or charities they support.
- Over the last several decades, propaganda materials with extreme ideological bias or solely for product promotion purposes from industries, corporations, lobbying groups and trade associations have made it into public school classrooms.

6.6 Course Activities

Course project number one: Find three social media posts made on behalf of a corporation that you determine are extremist propaganda. Compare your findings with others in the class.

Course project number two: Find three social media posts made about a corporation that you determine are extremist propaganda. Compare your findings with others in the class.

Course project number three: Once the findings in projects number one and two are compared, analyze the posts to determine if there is any pattern to the content.

References

1. FTC. *Truth in Advertising*. Accessed December 7, 2017 https://www.ftc.gov/news-events/media-resources/truth-advertising.
2. FTC. *Protecting Consumers from Fraud and Deception*. Accessed December 7, 2017 https://www.ftc.gov/news-events/media-resources/truth-advertising/protecting-consumers.
3. FTC. Cigarette Report for 2015 released in 2017. Accessed December 7, 2017 https://www.ftc.gov/system/files/documents/reports/federal-trade-commission-cigarette-report-2015-federal-trade-commission-smokeless-tobacco-report/2015_cigarette_report.pdf?utm_source=govdelivery%20.
4. U.S. Centers for Disease Control and Prevention. *History of the Surgeon General's Reports on Smoking and Health*. Accessed December 7, 2017 https://www.cdc.gov/tobacco/data_statistics/sgr/history/index.htm.
5. U.S. National Cancer Institute. *The Role of the Media in Promoting and Reducing Tobacco Use*. Accessed December 7, 2017 https://cancercontrol.cancer.gov/brp/tcrb/monographs/19/docs/M19MediaFactSheet.pdf.
6. U.S. Surgeon General. *Tobacco Use Among U.S. Racial/Ethnic Minority Groups*, 1998. Accessed December 8, 2017 https://www.cdc.gov/tobacco/data_statistics/sgr/1998/complete_report/index.htm.

7. U.S. National Library of Medicine. The C. Everett Koop papers. *Tobacco, Second-Hand Smoke, and the Campaign for a Smoke-Free America.* Accessed December 8, 2017 https://profiles.nlm.nih.gov/ps/retrieve/Narrative/QQ/p-nid/85.
8. *U.S. President Clinton: Fighting For Legislation to Reduce Teen Smoking,* June 19, 1998. Accessed December 8, 2017 https://clintonwhitehouse4.archives.gov/textonly/WH/Work/061998.html.
9. U.S. Department of Health & Human Services. *About Tobacco Marketing Laws and Policies.* Accessed December 8, 2017 https://betobaccofree.hhs.gov/index.html.
10. Division of Program Coordination, Planning, and Strategic Initiatives. *National Institutes of Health, About the FSPTCA,* January 5, 2017. Accessed December 9, 2017 https://prevention.nih.gov/tobacco-regulatory-science-program/about-the-FSPTCA.
11. U.S. SEC. *SEC Files Anti-Bribery Charges Against Two Global Tobacco Companies,* August 6, 2010. Accessed December 9 2017 https://www.sec.gov/litigation/litreleases/2010/lr21618.htm.
12. U.S. DOJ. *Environmental Crimes Section,* May 13, 2015. Accessed December 10, 2017 https://www.justice.gov/enrd/environmental-crimes-section.
13. U.S. House Committee on Natural Resources. *Ranking Members of Natural Resources, Science and Ed & Workforce Committees Condemn Group Misleading Students on Climate Science,* April 3, 2017. Accessed December 7, 2017 https://democrats-naturalresources. house.gov/media/press-releases/ranking-members-of-nat-resources-science-and-ed-and-workforce-committees-condemn-group-misleading-students-on-climate-science.
14. GAO. *Public Education: Commercial Activities in Schools.* HEHS-00-156: September 14, 2000. Accessed December 16, 2017 http://www.gao.gov/products/HEHS-00-156.
15. GAO. *Commercial Activities in Schools Use of Student Data is Limited and Additional Dissemination of Guidance Could Help Districts Develop Policies,* August 2004. GAO-04-810. Accessed December 16, 2017 http://www.gao.gov/new.items/d04810.pdf.

Chapter 7

Extremist Propaganda and Recruitment Targeting Youth

7.1 Students as Recruitment Targets

Youth are embracing many forms of extremism, including those perpetrated by terrorist organizations or domestic extremist movements and those maintaining biases towards others due to their race, religion, or sexual orientation. As this threat evolves and more youth embrace extremist ideologies, it places a growing burden on the educational system to provide appropriate services to students who view hatred or targeted violence as acceptable outlets for their grievances. To complicate matters, youth possess inherent risk factors making them susceptible to extremist ideologies or possible recruitment. Schools are being encouraged to remain vigilant in educating their students about catalysts that drive violent extremism and the potential consequences of embracing extremist beliefs.

Many people believe that educators are in a unique position to affect change, impart affirmative messaging, or facilitate intervention activities due to their daily interactions with students. These interactions allow for observing and assessing concerning behaviors and communications of students embracing extremist ideologies and progressing on a trajectory toward violence. There are many hurdles to schools accomplishing positive messaging and intervention, including knowledge, training, time and financial resources. Nevertheless, societies have placed a considerable burden on educators and schools to address social problems and psychological problems that students face.

Researchers contend that youth can be easily tempted by the false allure of quick and easy social connections amidst an individualistic society from which they feel alienated. Physical contact with extremist organizations has diminished over time. The Internet now affords extremists a veritable playground for spotting and assessing individuals who are receptive to a specific grievance or ideology and for sharing radical thoughts and beliefs. A growing body of research suggests the Internet acts as a catalyst to sustain radicalized beliefs more so than acting as a primary catalyst towards radicalization.

Regardless of the mechanism, once a violent extremist makes contact with youth, they begin assessing his or her responsiveness for supporting a violent extremist belief or acting on behalf of its underlying grievance. While online recruitment is one potential vulnerability, social media also provides youth a platform for identifying violent extremists or becoming curious about the subject matter to conduct research and gaining an appreciation or understanding of its principles. Youth may find the content appealing or attractive, especially when they meet others (peers or young adults) online, who are violent extremists but are viewed as rational people. These online contacts can offer meaning and understanding to the ideological underpinnings that drive acceptance of radical beliefs or support for future actions. These interactions often result in bringing new supporters into the fold.

As with any age group, no single element is responsible for making a student vulnerable to violent extremists seeking to impart radical views on them. Extremist recruiters often encourage their followers to transition their means of communication from open social media platforms to encrypted chat rooms, transitioning from overt lines of communication to covert, encrypted chats, facilitating extremism discussions, and allowing for various forms of *electronic aggression*. This is a way to hinder law enforcement's ability to obtain electronic communications or evidence pursuant to a court order or warrant. Law enforcement defines these phenomena as *Going Dark*, thus limiting an understanding of extremist communications or future intentions.

The Internet provides access to endless streams of violent propaganda inspiring others to action, glorifying extremist lifestyles, or perpetuating the spread of hatred and intolerance. The difference between protected speech and illegal incitement can be a very fine line. Espousing anti-U.S. sentiment or extremist rhetoric is not a crime and is protected First Amendment activity. As individuals consume violent propaganda, it might resonate with them or reinforce their perceived grievance. Consumption of violent propaganda is a primary catalyst in self radicalization.

A threat landscape, once dominated by terrorist organizations and their hierarchical command and control structures, is now characterized by decentralized and distributed nodes of influence. While the volume of violent extremist propaganda may vary depending on the type of network structure, the ease of access to extremist propaganda on social media platforms frequented by youths remains a concern. Even limited exposure to extremist propaganda may result in a path towards radicalization to violent extremism. Vast social networks promote agility in recruitment, radicalization, planning, and mobilizing to violence.

Several extremist organizations have disseminated online magazines intended for their supporters. The magazines are professionally designed and of high quality and are disseminated on a massive scale, ensuring penetration of their radical messages, and disseminated in multiple languages, allowing them to target a particular population for manipulation or radicalization. Posting these magazines in online forums in English specifically targets western and European audiences. Further, these organizations either have access to individuals from the regions they are targeting with their messaging or are very adept at synthesizing the region's local concerns and manipulating those issues to advocate their position. They also contain flashy graphics, mimicking those in present-day video games. The primary motivators behind these online magazines are drawing attention to their cause and enticing more supporters into the fold.

Law enforcement attention to these publications is important but it is also important to pay attention to local activities and various streams of hate propaganda including racism, religious discrimination and gender preference bias. People of all ages are exposed to hate messages and news of hate crimes in their own communities. Television and online news feeds in the U.S. are well populated with news of hate and discrimination. In addition, hate and prejudice is present in communities across the country. The rhetoric of politicians and religious leaders serves to further fuel the hate message and provide some validation to those who hate that their hate is legitimate.

Online gaming adds yet another level of vulnerability for our youth because it is sometimes used to communicate, train, or plan terrorist activities. Many youths are very proficient in gaming techniques, online communications, and user forums, leading to interactions with online gaming enthusiasts, who are assessing vulnerable youth for possible recruitment opportunities. These online contacts might be supporters of an extremist organization and actively recruiting for their cause.

A 2002 Guide to Managing Threatening Situations and Creating Safe School Climates, drafted jointly by the U.S. Secret Service and the U.S. Department of Education, suggested acts of targeted violence are rarely impulsive and some may be preventable through the detection of planning behavior. This concept also applies within the violent extremism context, as students on the pathway to becoming radicalized or mobilizing often exhibit behaviors, indicating support for extremist ideologies or highlighting future intentions.

The FBI contends that countering violent extremism is a shared responsibility between law enforcement, civic leaders, and their communities. Schools share in this responsibility within their local communities, which builds resiliency against the catalysts driving violent extremist activities. Schools should remain a healthy environment for learning, personal growth, physical and cognitive development, and not be infused with extremist or hateful rhetoric. Communities can grow stronger against outside influences targeting youth by informing them about the perils of violent extremism [1].

Much of the counter messaging and intervention strategies in the U.S. contend that engaged families and active schools are the first defense to monitor Internet usage, content, or violent propaganda alerting to possible extremist beliefs, contacts, or future intentions. This is true only to the extent that the hate and extremism that youth are exposed to do not originate in their homes, families, schools, or social groups.

7.2 Hate and Violence Are Parts of Life for Youth in the U.S.

Crimes of hatred and prejudice, from lynchings to cross burnings to vandalism of synagogues, are a sad fact of American history, but the term *hate crime* did not enter the nation's vocabulary until the 1980s, when emerging hate groups like the Skinheads launched a wave of bias-related crime [2]. Of the 6,121 hate crime incidents reported for 2016, 6,063 were single-bias incidents (there were also 58 multiple-bias incidents). Of the single-bias incidents:

- 57.5% were motivated by a race, ethnicity or ancestry bias.
- 21.0% were motivated by a religious bias.
- 17.7% were motivated by a sexual orientation bias.
- The remaining incidents were motivated by a gender identity, disability, or gender bias.

The two largest percentages of hate crime incidents took place in or near residences (27.3%) and on or near some type of roadway (18.4%). The remaining incidents were perpetrated at a variety of other locations, including schools and houses of worship, commercial and government buildings, restaurants and nightclubs, parking lots and garages, playgrounds and parks, and even medical facilities. During 2016, there were 664 hate crime offenders under 18 while 3,436 over 18 years old [3]. Preliminary analysis of hate crimes in 2017 shows an almost 20% increase in major U.S. cities after increasing nationally by 5% from 2015 to 2016. The motivations behind hate crimes generally fall into four major categories:

- Thrill-seeking or the desire for excitement (66%)
- Defensive to protect a neighborhood from perceived outsiders (25%)
- Retaliatory in response to a hate crime either real or perceived (8%)
- Mission of those so strongly committed to bigotry that they make hate a career (1%) [3]

Although not all violence is considered a hate crime, violence is a national crisis that affects approximately two out of every three children and millions of children can expect to have their lives touched by violence, crime, abuse, and psychological trauma every year. In 1979, U.S. Surgeon General Julius B. Richmond declared *violence exposure* a public health crisis of the highest priority, and yet over 35 years later that crisis remains. Whether the violence occurs in children's homes, neighborhoods, schools, playgrounds or playing fields, locker rooms, places of worship, shelters, streets, or in juvenile detention centers, *children exposed to violence* is a uniquely traumatic experience that has the potential to profoundly derail the child's security, health, happiness, and ability to grow and learn with effects lasting well into adulthood.

This exposure to violence is not limited to one community or one group of children. It occurs among all ethnic and racial groups; in urban, suburban, and rural areas; in gated communities and on tribal lands. Advances in neuroscience and child development have taught us that the trauma children experience when they are exposed to physical, sexual, and emotional violence harms their ability to mature cognitively and emotionally and it scars them physically and emotionally. Exposure to violence in any form harms children, and different forms of violence have different negative impacts.

Sexual abuse places children at high risk for serious and chronic health problems, including post-traumatic stress disorder (PTSD), depression, suicidality, eating disorders, sleep disorders, substance abuse, and deviant sexual behavior. Sexually abused children often become hyper vigilant about the possibility of future sexual violation and experience feelings of betrayal by the adults who failed to care for and protect them.

Physical abuse puts children at high risk for lifelong problems with medical illness, PTSD, suicidality, eating disorders, substance abuse, and deviant sexual behavior. Physically abused children are also at a heightened risk for cognitive and developmental impairments, which can lead to violent behavior as a form of self-protection and control. These children often feel powerless when faced with physical intimidation, threats, or conflict and may compensate by becoming isolated (through truancy or hiding) or aggressive (by bullying or joining gangs for protection). Physically abused children are at risk for significant impairment in memory processing and problem solving and for developing defensive behaviors that lead to consistent avoidance of intimacy.

Intimate partner violence within families puts children at high risk for severe and potentially lifelong problems with physical health, mental health, and school and peer relationships as well as for disruptive behavior. Witnessing or living with domestic or intimate partner violence often burdens children with a sense of loss or profound guilt and shame because of their mistaken assumption that they should have intervened or prevented the violence or, tragically, that they caused the violence. They frequently castigate themselves for having failed in what they assume to be their duty to protect a parent or sibling(s) from being harmed, for not having taken the place of their horribly injured or killed family member, or for having caused the offender to be violent. Children exposed to intimate partner violence often experience a sense of terror and dread that they will lose an essential caregiver through permanent injury or death. They also fear losing their relationship with the offending parent, who may be removed from the home, incarcerated, or even executed. Children will mistakenly blame themselves for having caused the batterer to be violent. If no one identifies these children and helps them heal and recover, they may bring this uncertainty, fear, grief, anger, shame, and sense of betrayal into all of their important relationships for the rest of their lives.

Community violence in neighborhoods can result in children witnessing assaults and even killings of family members, peers, trusted adults, innocent bystanders, and perpetrators of violence. Violence in the community can prevent children from feeling safe in their own schools and neighborhoods. Violence and ensuing psychological trauma can lead children to adopt an attitude of hyper vigilance, to become experts at detecting threat or perceived threat and never able to let down their guard in order to be ready for the next outbreak of violence. They may come to believe that violence is normal, that violence is here to stay, and that relationships are too fragile to trust because one never knows when violence will take the life of a friend or loved one. They may turn to gangs or criminal activities to prevent others from viewing them as weak and to counteract feelings of despair and powerlessness, perpetuating the cycle of violence and increasing their risk of incarceration.

They are also at risk for becoming victims of intimate partner violence in adolescence, and in adulthood the picture becomes even more complex when children are polyvictims (exposed to multiple types of violence). As many as one in ten children in the U.S. are polyvictims, according to the DOJ and Centers for Disease Control and Prevention's (CDCP) groundbreaking National Survey of Children's Exposure to Violence (NatSCEV). The toxic combination of exposure to intimate partner violence, physical abuse, sexual abuse, and/or exposure to community violence increases the risk and severity of posttraumatic injuries and mental health disorders by at least twofold and up to as much as tenfold. Polyvictimized children are at very high risk for losing the fundamental capacities necessary for normal development, successful learning, and a productive adulthood.

The financial costs of children's exposure to violence are astronomical. The financial burden on public systems, including child welfare, social services, law enforcement, juvenile justice, and, in particular, education is staggering when combined with the loss of productivity over children's lifetime [4].

There are not many safe places for children. During the academic year 2013/2014 there were 48 school-associated violent deaths. In 2015, among students ages 12–18, there were about 840,000 nonfatal victimizations at school and 545,000 nonfatal victimizations away from school. In 2015, about 21% of students ages 12–18 reported being bullied at school during the school year. Of the 804 total hate crimes reported on college campuses in 2014, the most common type of hate crime was intimidation, followed by destruction, damage, and vandalism and simple assault [5].

Situations surrounding crime at school locations vary based on the offender's motive and the intended victim. For example, incidents involving student offenders and student victims constitute the stereotypical definition of crime at schools, colleges, and universities where the offender and victim are present to participate in the activities occurring at the institution. However, there are situations involving adult and/or juvenile offenders and victims where the school serves only as an offense location because neither the offender nor the victim is present to participate in school functions. Criminal acts due to political motivation, hate crimes, and crimes perpetrated by offenders against victims who are not instructors or students and have no other relation to the school are examples of such situations.

By far, the relationship type most often reported for crime in schools was Acquaintance, with 107,533 instances occurring during the 5-year study period from 2000 and 2004. When Acquaintance was combined with the Otherwise Known category (50,486 instances), these two categories were 3.3 times more likely to occur as the relationship than were all other victim-to-offender relationships in which the relationship was known. The relationship Victim was Offender was reported for 15,539 occurrences, or 7.5% of known relationships. This type of relationship is one in which all participants in the incidents were victims and offenders of the same offense, such as assaults being reported as a result of a brawl or fight. Stranger was reported for 7.5% (15,511 instances) of the relationships. The remaining percentages were widely dispersed among all other relationship categories [6].

In 2014, there were 27,000 criminal incidents against persons and property on campus at public and private 2-year and 4-year postsecondary institutions that were reported to police and security agencies, representing a 2% decrease from 2013, when 27,400 criminal incidents were reported. The number of on-campus crimes per 10,000 full-time equivalent (FTE) students also decreased, from 18.4 in 2013 to 17.9 in 2014.

Among the various types of on-campus crimes reported in 2014, there were 13,500 burglaries, constituting 50% of all criminal incidents. Other commonly reported crimes included forcible sex offenses (6,700 incidents, or 25% of crimes) and motor vehicle theft (2,900 incidents, or 11% of crimes). In addition, 2,100 aggravated assaults and 1,100 robberies were reported. These estimates translate to 9.0 burglaries, 4.5 forcible sex offenses, 1.9 motor vehicle thefts, 1.4 aggravated assaults, and 0.7 robberies per 10,000 FTE students [7].

In addition to being traumatic, the exposure to violence can normalize the existence of violence and children grow up being accustomed to violence and some even comfortable being around violence or being violent themselves. This creates a circumstance where extremist recruiters do not have to get their target recruit accustomed to violence, they just need to convince the recruit that the extremists ideology is a worthy cause for which to perform violent acts.

7.3 Don't Be a Puppet: Pull Back the Curtain on Violent Extremism Website

The FBI is reaching out to teenagers and those who care for them, to provide awareness about the risks associated with violent extremists. The FBI has created a website to counter extremist propaganda (https://cve.fbi.gov/home.html)

that is designed to provide counter and alternative messaging to those people who would like to learn how extremists recruit youth and people of all ages, in order to resist the negative messaging in the propaganda. The Don't Be a Puppet interactive website teaches teens how to recognize violent extremists and the tactics they use to radicalize people. The goal is to help people better understand the destructive nature of violent extremism and learn to recognize the deceptive recruiting strategies of violent extremists who seek to turn people into puppets to carry out their orders.

The section that describes what violent extremism is has several subparts. The subsection on groupthink states that groups can be a powerful way to bring people together to achieve common goals. Groupthink happens, however, when those in the group stop stating their opinions or using critical thinking because they wish to avoid conflict. This can result in extremely poor decision making. Violent extremist organizations are highly vulnerable to groupthink. They are often headed or motivated by a strong leader who is rarely challenged. Different beliefs or ideas are not accepted. Violent extremist groups often work in secret, not only because their activities and plans are illegal, but also because they want to keep out other opinions.

The subsection on symbols explains that a symbol is something that stands for something else. For example, common American symbols such as the U.S. flag, Statue of Liberty, White House, and bald eagle represent the U.S. and its freedoms. A symbol can build pride or create a positive emotional connection. Symbols can also be used to create fear and to control people. Violent extremists have used various symbols over the years to fuel feelings of revenge and hatred. They have also attacked many symbols of America and other countries to make their actions seem more important.

The subsection on propaganda explains that violent extremists often use propaganda with misleading or biased information that supports a particular point of view, to trick people into believing their ideologies. It's the primary extremist recruiting tool, and you could be a target. The goal of propaganda is to create a compelling story that people will buy into by twisting the facts.

The subsection on extremist groups and individuals explains that they often appear in communities struggling with social or political issues. Rather than improving these situations or their own lives through constructive actions, violent extremists often place the blame on another person or group. They argue that the only solution to these problems or injustices is to violently oppose and even destroy those they claim are responsible. Placing blame is an effective way to recruit people with feelings of frustration and turn them into a group united by a sense of purpose. It enables extremists to invent an enemy that must be destroyed. This makes violence seem like the best solution and even a moral duty.

The subsection on distorted principles explains that violent extremists are driven by twisted beliefs and values or ideologies that are tied to political, religious, economic, or social goals. For example:

- Many violent extremist ideologies are based on the hatred of another race, religion, ethnicity, gender, or country/government.
- Violent extremists often think that their beliefs or ways of life are under attack and that extreme violence is the only solution to their frustrations and problems.
- Despite what they sometimes say, violent extremists often do not believe in fundamental American values like democracy, human rights, tolerance, and inclusion.
- Violent extremists sometimes twist religious teachings and other beliefs to support their own goals.

The section on why people become violent extremists declares that no single reason explains why people become violent extremists, but it often happens when someone is trying to fill a deep personal need. For example, a person may feel alone or lack meaning and purpose in life. Those who are emotionally upset after a stressful event also may be vulnerable to recruitment. Some people also become violent extremists because they disagree with government policy, hate certain types of people, do not feel valued or appreciated by society, or think they have limited chances to succeed.

The section on known violent extremist groups explains that groups that commit acts of violent extremism can have very different beliefs and goals. They are located in many countries around the world. Most have websites or use social media, so they can now reach and recruit people just about anywhere. Keep in mind that some of those who carry out extremist attacks and hate crimes are only loosely motivated by these groups and may not be actual members. More than 50 violent extremist groups around the world have been named terrorist organizations by the U.S. government. The website also gives background on several violent extremist groups.

The subsection on Al Qaeda defines the term as *The Base* in Arabic. It is a global extremist network started in 1988 by the now deceased Osama bin Laden. It seeks to free Muslim countries from the influence of Western countries and attacks Muslim nations that don't agree with its version of the Islamic religion. Al Qaeda attacks those it believes are enemies of Islam. In 1988, Al Qaeda said that it is the duty of its followers to kill Americans and citizens of other countries that support the U.S. Al Qaeda has carried out many bombings and other acts of violence, including the attacks of September 11, 2001.

Al Shabaab is described as a violent extremist organization based in Somalia that seeks to replace the current government through violence. Al Shabaab has recruited dozens of U.S. citizens to train and fight with them. Al Shabaab has carried out many bombings and murders in Somalia and in nearby countries like Kenya. It not only targets government officials and military troops but also Somali peace activists, international aid workers, police officers, and others. Al Shabaab has a history of kidnapping and hurting women and girls.

Hizballah, or Party of God, is described as an extremist group based in Lebanon. Hizballah supports the global rise of Shia Islam, and it is inspired by the Iranian revolution. Hizballah also supports certain Palestinian groups in their struggle against Israel. Hizballah targets Israel and its supporters and is responsible for some of the deadliest extremist attacks against the U.S. in history, including the bombing of a Marine base in Lebanon in 1983 that killed more than 250 Americans. Hizballah has supporters worldwide, including in the U.S.

ISIL (DAESH) is described as a highly violent extremist group that has killed thousands of men, women, and children, mostly Muslims. The group calls itself the Islamic State, but its members follow an extreme, fringe interpretation of Islamic law. They do not represent mainstream Islam, and the vast majority of Muslims are horrified by their actions. ISIL members work to enslave or kill anyone who disagrees with them and have taken over parts of Iraq and Syria. ISIL continues to actively recruit U.S. citizens, especially young people. ISIL has attacked the people of Iraq, Syria, and other nations including government and military officials as well as journalists and school children. ISIL also has targeted Americans and has killed U.S. troops and civilian hostages.

Kahane Chai (Kahane Lives) is described as a group that was started by the son of a radical Israeli-American rabbi named Meir Kahane, who was killed in 1990. The group seeks to expand the borders of Israel. Kahane Chai has targeted Arabs, Palestinians, and Israeli government officials. Its last major attack was in 1994, when a Kahane Chai supporter opened fire at a mosque in the southern West Bank, killing 29 people.

Fuerzas Armadas Revolucionarias de Colombia (Revolutionary Armed Forces of Colombia), or FARC, is described as a violent rebel group. Since it was created in 1964, FARC has tried to overthrow the Republic of Colombia, South America's oldest democracy. It also sends a lot of illegal drugs into the U.S. and other countries. FARC mostly targets the people and government of Colombia through bombings, murder, and other attacks. FARC sees U.S. citizens as military targets and has kidnapped and murdered several Americans in Colombia.

The section on Domestic Extremist Ideologies states that violent extremists based in the U.S. have different beliefs that lead them to commit crimes and acts of violence. It is important to note that it is legal to have hateful or extremist beliefs as long as you don't commit crimes or violence based on those beliefs. The right to assemble (or gather) in groups is also protected by the U.S. Constitution.

The subsection on Sovereign Citizen Extremists states that sovereign citizens believe they are separate or sovereign from the U.S. even though they live in the country. They think they don't have to answer to any government authority. Sovereign citizens use their beliefs to justify fraud and other non-violent crimes. Some sovereign citizen extremists turn to violence and commit murder, threaten public officials, and destroy property as part of their anti-government, anti-tax beliefs. Sovereign citizen violent extremists usually target members of the government including judges, police officers, and tax officials. In 2010, for example, a sovereign citizen extremist killed two Arkansas police officers during a routine traffic stop.

The subsection on Abortion Extremists states that some abortion extremists believe that violence and bloodshed are justified to support their different beliefs on abortion. These violent extremists have turned to murder, bombings, assault, vandalism, kidnapping, and arson. They have also made death threats and sent hate mail and suspicious packages. Violent anti-abortion extremists have targeted women's reproductive clinics and the health care professionals and staff who work in these facilities, including doctors, nurses, receptionists, and even security guards. In one case in 2009, for example, a Kansas doctor who performed abortion services was shot and killed in his local church by an anti-abortion extremist. Those who use violence to defend abortion rights have murdered, threatened, and attacked those who oppose abortion.

The subsection on Animal Rights Extremists and Environmental Extremists states that some animal rights and environmental extremists believe violence is needed to stop those they think are hurting animals or the environment. These violent extremists usually don't seek to kill or injure people, but their crimes including property damage, vandalism, threats, cyber attacks, arson, and bombings have caused millions of dollars in damages and disrupted many lives. Violent animal rights extremists attack those they believe are linked to the abuse of animals. Typical targets include the fur industry, companies and individuals involved in animal research, and businesses that ship animals. Violent environmental extremists target those they believe are destroying the environment, such as businesses and individuals involved in construction or automobile sales.

The subsection on Militia Extremists states that a militia is a group of citizens who come together to protect the country, usually during an emergency. Some militia extremists, however, seek to violently attack or overthrow the U.S. government. Often calling themselves patriots, they believe the government has become corrupt, has overstepped its constitutional limits, or has not been able to protect the country against global dangers. Violent militia extremists mainly target those they believe could violate their constitutional rights, such as police officers and judges. In one 2010 case, a Michigan militia group planned to kill a police officer and later attack the parade of cars in the funeral, hoping to start a large battle. The FBI and its partners stopped them from carrying out their plan.

The subsection on Anarchist Extremists states that anarchist extremists believe that society should have no government, laws, or police, and they are loosely organized, with no central leadership. Violent anarchist extremists believe that such a society can only be created through force. Violent anarchist extremists usually target symbols of capitalism they believe to be the cause of all problems in society such as large corporations, government organizations, and police agencies. They damage property, cause riots, and set off firebombs. In some cases, they have injured police officers.

The subsection on White Supremacy Extremists states that white supremacy extremists are motivated by a hatred of other races and religions. Some try to achieve their political and social goals through violence. These violent extremists often wrongly believe that the U.S. government is hurting the country or secretly planning to destroy it. White supremacy violent extremists target the federal government and racial, ethnic, and religious minorities. Their methods have included murder, threats, and bombings. As just one example, white supremacists attacked a pair of Middle Eastern men on New Year's Eve in 2011, punching one victim in the face and head.

The section on How Do Violent Extremists Make Contact has three subsections that cover contact methods used on the Internet, cell phone, and flyers. The subsection on the Internet explains online forums and chat rooms are places where violent extremists and hate groups find many new recruits. In these sites, young people often talk about things that interest them, sometimes in secret areas only for members. Violent extremists look for those who might be open to their beliefs. The subsection on social networking explains how violent extremists have joined the many popular social networking sites, created fake profiles and are looking for people who are vulnerable to recruitment. Violent extremists also spread propaganda on these sites through videos, pictures, and messages that glorify their causes. There is also a subsection on Internet gaming sites and mobile applications.

There is also a section that provides videos of interviews with people who have survived terrorist attacks and a section that shows various places teenagers can get help and learn more about extremists. Once a website visitor reviews each of the sections and subsections, a puppet on the site is set free from the ropes that have had it tied up during the tour [8].

7.4 Gangs as Extremist Groups

The proliferation of gang problems in large and small cities, suburbs, and even rural areas led to the development of a comprehensive, coordinated response to America's gang problem by the Office of Juvenile Justice and Delinquency Prevention (OJJDP). These gangs, like other extremist groups, are using social media for recruitment, indoctrination, communications, and mobilization.

OJJDP has long supported a combination of activities, including research, evaluation, training and technical assistance, and demonstration programs, aimed at combating youth gangs. Since the 1980s, OJJDP has developed, funded, and evaluated community-based anti-gang programs that coordinate prevention, intervention, enforcement, and reentry strategies.

Recognizing that street gang activities transcend ages of members, in October 2009, the Office of Justice Programs (OJP) merged its existing resources to create a new National Gang Center (NGC), developing a comprehensive approach to reduce gang involvement and gang crime. The reinvigorated NGC is a single, more efficient entity, responsive to the needs of researchers, practitioners, and the public. The NGC website (https://www.nationalgangcenter.gov/) features the latest research about gangs; descriptions of evidence-based, anti-gang programs; and links to tools, databases, and other resources to assist in developing and implementing effective community-based gang prevention, intervention, and suppression strategies. There is also data analysis of the findings from nearly 20 years of data collected by the annual National Youth Gang Survey (NYGS) of 2,500 U.S. law enforcement agencies. Users can read and download publications related to street gangs, request training and technical assistance as they plan and implement anti-gang strategies, and register for a variety of anti-gang training courses.

Based on law enforcement responses to the NYGS, nearly one-third of all responding law enforcement agencies reported gang activity in 2012. It is estimated that there were 30,700 gangs and 850,000 gang members throughout 3,100 jurisdictions with gang problems in the U.S. in 2012. The number of reported gang-related homicides increased 20% from 2011 to 2012.

A national assessment of gang problems and programs provided the foundation for OJJDP's Comprehensive Gang Model, a project developed in the mid-1980s. Its key components reflect the best features of existing and evaluated programs across the country. The model outlines five strategies: community mobilization, social intervention, opportunities for educational and vocational advancements, suppression, and organizational change and development. As most gang members join between the ages of 12 and 15, prevention is a critical strategy within a comprehensive response to gangs that includes intervention, suppression and reentry.

OJJDP collaborates with the Bureau of Justice Assistance to ensure that OJP has an array of information and resources available on gangs. OJJDP's strategy is to reduce gang activity in targeted neighborhoods by incorporating a broad spectrum of research-based interventions to address the range of personal, family, and community factors that contribute to juvenile delinquency and gang activity. This approach attempts to integrate federal, state, and local resources to incorporate state-of-the-art practices in prevention, intervention, and suppression.

At the direction of President Obama, the Departments of Justice and Education launched the National Forum on Youth Violence Prevention (Forum) in order to begin a national conversation concerning youth and gang violence, raising awareness and elevating the issue to one of national significance. In addition, the Forum was created to build the capacity of localities across the country to more effectively address the youth violence through multi-disciplinary partnerships, balanced approaches, data-driven strategies, comprehensive planning and the sharing of common challenges and promising strategies. The Forum was created as a model for federal and local collaboration, encouraging Forum members to change the way they do business through increased communication and coordinated action.

The Forum has convened a diverse array of stakeholders at the federal, state and local levels. Along with Justice and Education, participating federal agencies include the Departments of Health and Human Services, Housing and Urban Development, Labor and the White House Office of National Drug Control Policy. Communities that participated in the Forum include Boston, Camden, Chicago, Detroit, Memphis, Minneapolis, New Orleans, Philadelphia, Salinas, San Jose,

Long Beach, Cleveland, Louisville, Seattle, and Baltimore. Other participants included local faith and community-based groups, youth and family representatives, as well as businesses and philanthropies.

The Community-Based Violence Prevention Initiative was adapted from the best violence reduction work in several cities and the public health research of several decades. Evaluation research has identified programs that have demonstrated effectiveness in reducing the impact of risk factors. These efforts identified that responses must be comprehensive, long-term strategic approaches that contain the spread of gang activity, protect those youth who are most suscep-tible, and mitigate risk factors that foster gang activity. The four-pronged approach of effective anti-gang strategies included targeted suppression of youth who com-mit the most serious and chronic offenses; intervention with youthful gang mem-bers; prevention efforts for youth identified as being at high risk of entering a gang; and implementation of programs that addressed risk and protective fac-tors and targeted the entire population in high-crime, high-risk areas. Additional public health research conducted over decades showed success in those programs, which focused on managing not only incidents of serious youth violence and gang violence, but also those that included proactive interventions to prevent further retaliatory acts of youth or gang violence.

For example, in FY2011, OJJDP supported the national Boys & Girls Clubs of America (BGCA) organization of Atlanta, GA, to help local affiliate clubs prevent youth from joining gangs, intervene with gang members in the early stages of gang involvement, and divert youth from gangs into more constructive activities. That program reflects a long-term collaboration between OJJDP and BGCA to reduce problems of juvenile gangs, delinquency, and violence. The national organization provides training and technical assistance to local gang prevention and interven-tion sites and to other clubs and organizations through regional training sessions and national conferences. Each year, dozens of new gang prevention sites, gang intervention sites, and targeted reintegration sites are added to the many existing programs implementing these strategies across the country.

The Gang Resistance Education and Training (G.R.E.A.T.) Program is a school-based, law enforcement officer-instructed, classroom curriculum administered by OJJDP (https://www.great-online.org/GREAT-Home). Using a communitywide approach to combat risk factors, the goal of the G.R.E.A.T. Program is to help youth develop positive life skills that will help them avoid gang involvement and violent behavior. The G.R.E.A.T. Program consists of four interrelated components, each designed to target different audiences: Elementary School Component, Middle School Component, Summer Component, and Families Component. The components can stand alone to teach the necessary skills and attitudes that will help youth resist the pressures to become involved in gang behavior and avoid situations that could lead to violence.

The Urban Institute and Temple University received grant funding to look at norms and networks of Latino gang youth. That study, *Norms and Networks of Latino*

Gang Youth, employed a social network framework to understand the patterns of relations by examining two levels of social processes for the unit of analysis (individual and group relationships) through both egocentric and sociocentric network analysis, and extending network analysis to include different types of relationships (e.g., friend, relative, neighbor). This study examined multiple research questions that have not yet been addressed in delinquency and gang literature.

The National Gang Center website (https://www.nationalgangcenter.gov/) has featured research about gangs; descriptions of evidence-based, anti-gang programs; and links to tools, databases, and other resources to assist in developing and implementing effective community-based gang prevention, intervention, and suppression strategies.

youth.gov has been the U.S. government website that helps create, maintain, and strengthen effective youth programs. Included are youth facts, funding information, and tools to help you assess community assets, generate maps of local and federal resources, search for evidence-based youth programs, and keep up-to-date on the latest, youth-related news [9].

Over the last two decades the term *cyberbanging* has been used to describe a variety of social media activities that gangs have participated in, including intimidation, recruitment and indoctrination. The use of social media for law enforcement gang investigations is an emerging discipline and there is a great deal of work to be done in order to maximize the approach. Many people are aware of the use of social media by terrorist groups or Internet predators; however, gangs use similar tactics. There are hundreds of thousands of gang-related photos and videos circulating on the Internet. MS-13 and other gangs promote propaganda and glorification of gang lifestyle as a recruitment tool. The gangs also use these platforms to intimidate and threaten their rivals, which can lead to violent retaliation. Law enforcement can use these photos and videos as powerful evidence and parents are advised to monitor their children's computers to look for signs of gang involvement and protect them from recruitment [10].

Gangs are also becoming more sophisticated in the use of technology to bolster their efforts. Social networking sites on the web are replacing graffiti on walls as places for gangs to boast of their exploits and recruit members. Perhaps most chilling are reports from Mexico where gangs have adopted the media techniques of Middle Eastern terrorists and show scenes of torture and murder on these sites to scare off competitors and boast of their prowess. National gangs such as The Latin Kings, Bloods, and Crips have had websites on the Internet. They are savvy at protecting the contents of the sites from nonmembers by creating viruses that attack a nonmember's computer if they get onto the sites. This allows people from all over the country to communicate with each other. The site Myspace.com was highly popular with gangs, promoting gang culture to other teens and posting photos of young members holding weapons and other criminal proceeds. Most drug gangs have begun using anonymous, throwaway phones and switching out chips in phones to avoid wire taps [11].

7.5 Summary

The constant exposure of youth to violence in the U.S. contributes to their viewpoint that violence is a normal and acceptable response to many social situations. This makes them ideal targets for recruitment by extremist groups ranging from neo Nazis to anti-abortion organizations to ISIL. This chapter examines teenagers as a recruitment target and the methods that extremist groups use to recruit them. Key points covered include:

- Youth are embracing many forms of extremism including those perpetrated by terrorist organizations or domestic extremist movements and they possess inherent risk factors making them susceptible to extremist ideologies or possible recruitment.
- Researchers contend that youth can be easily tempted by the false allure of quick and easy social connections amidst an individualistic society from which they feel alienated.
- The Internet provides access to endless streams of violent propaganda inspiring others to action, glorifying extremist lifestyles, or perpetuating the spread of hatred and intolerance.
- The FBI contends that countering violent extremism is a shared responsibility between law enforcement, civic leaders, and their communities. Schools share in this responsibility within their local communities.
- Although not all violence is considered a hate crime, violence is a national crisis that affects approximately two out of every three children and millions of children can expect to have their lives touched by violence, crime, abuse, and psychological trauma every year.
- Exposure to violence is not limited to one community or one group of children. It occurs among all ethnic and racial groups; in urban, suburban, and rural areas; in gated communities and on tribal lands.
- The FBI has created a website to counter extremist propaganda (https://cve.fbi.gov/home.html) that is designed to provide counter and alternative messaging to those people that would like to learn how extremists recruit youth and people of all ages, so that they can resist the negative messaging in the propaganda.
- Many people are aware of the use of social media by terrorist groups or Internet predators; however, gangs use similar tactics. There are hundreds of thousands of gang-related photos and videos circulating on the Internet.

7.6 Course Activities

Course project number one: Design a questionnaire with 10–12 questions to use in interviews with high school principals, teachers, or administrators on the impact of social media propaganda on students. Compare your questionnaire with those of other people in the course. Then create a final version of the questionnaire to use as an interview tool.

Course project number two: Using the questionnaire, conduct interviews with five high school principals, teachers, or administrators on the impact of social media propaganda on students. Compare your interview results with those of other people in the course.

Course project number three: In a panel discussion setting, openly discuss the results of the interviews.

Course project number four: Read and discuss A Clockwork Orange (1995) by Anthony Burgess.

References

1. FBI Office of Partner Engagement. *Preventing Violent Extremism in Schools*, January 2016. Accessed December 16, 2017 http://cdpsdocs.state.co.us/safeschools/Resources/FBI/PreventingViolentExtremismInSchools_Jan2016.pdf.
2. FBI. *Hate Crimes*. Accessed December 18, 2017 https://www.ncjrs.gov/spotlight/hate_crimes/summary.html.
3. FBI. *2016 Hate Crime Statistics Released*, November 13, 2017. Accessed December 18, 2017 https://www.fbi.gov/news/stories/2016-hate-crime-statistics.
4. DOJ. *Report of the Attorney General's National Task Force on Children Exposed to Violence*, December 12, 2012. Accessed December 18, 2017 https://www.justice.gov/defendingchildhood/cev-rpt-full.pdf.
5. BJS. *Indicators of School Crime and Safety: 2016*, May 16, 2017. Accessed December 18, 2017 https://www.bjs.gov/index.cfm?ty=pbdetail&iid=5926.
6. FBI. UCR. *Crime in Schools and Colleges*. Accessed December 18, 2017 https://ucr.fbi.gov/nibrs/crime-in-schools-and-colleges.
7. U.S. Department of Education, National Center for Education Statistics 2017/College Crime. Accessed December 18, 2017 https://nces.ed.gov/fastfacts/display.asp?id=804.
8. FBI. Don't be a puppet. Accessed December 19, 2017 https://cve.fbi.gov/home.html.
9. Office of Juvenile Justice and Delinquency Prevention. Comprehensive anti-gang initiative. Accessed December 20, 2017 https://www.ojjdp.gov/programs/antigang/.
10. United States House of Representatives Committee on Homeland Security testimony by Detective Sergeant Michael Marino, Commanding Officer, Gang Investigations Squad, Nassau County Police Department regarding MS-13 testimony, June 20, 2017. Accessed December 21, 2017 http://docs.house.gov/meetings/HM/HM05/20170620/106122/HHRG-115-HM05-Wstate-MarinoM-20170620.pdf.
11. Prepared testimony of Paul Logli Chairman of the National District Attorneys Association Winnebago County, Illinois. Before the House Judiciary Subcommittee on Crime, Terrorism, and Homeland Security. Making communities safer: Youth violence and gang interventions that work, February 15, 2007. Accessed December 21, 2017 https://judiciary.house.gov/_files/hearings/February2007/021507logli.pdf?ID=740.

Chapter 8

Electronic Aggression or Free Speech

8.1 The Rise of Electronic Aggression

Electronic Aggression is any type of intimidation, harassment or bullying that occurs through any e-mail, chat room, instant messaging, website (including blogs), text messaging, or social media posts the content of which is often associated with some expression of anger and negativity. This includes teasing, telling lies, making fun of someone, making rude or mean comments, spreading rumors, making threatening or aggressive comments, or disseminating propaganda that is harmful to individuals or segments of society [1]. Table 8.1 shows various examples of electronic aggression.

Extremist propaganda usually contains several forms of electronic aggression. Perpetrators of electronic aggression can act as lone wolves, small groups, or a large network of affiliated people and they can come from a variety of social positions, anywhere from a fast food worker to the White House staff, the halls of the U.S. Congress, and the highest elected offices and board rooms of the country. Extremist propaganda and electronic aggression are often intertwined to provide the perpetrator with some form of extrinsic benefits.

The U.S. military has published that some forms of speech are deemed unprotected in both the civilian and military community, which means the speech can be freely regulated and punished. For instance, fighting words, obscenity and dangerous speech are all types of speech that have not been afforded constitutional protections. In the military, dangerous speech includes speech that interferes with the military mission or affects morale and discipline [2].

Table 8.1 Examples of Electronic Aggression

Disclosing someone else's personal information in a public area in order to cause embarrassment or harm a reputation
Posting rumors or lies about someone in a public area
Distributing embarrassing pictures of someone
Assuming another person's electronic identity to post or send messages about others with the intent of causing the other person harm
Sending mean, embarrassing, or threatening text messages
Sexting is commonly used to describe the creation and transmission of sexual images

Social networking websites Twitter, Facebook, and Google, among others are under pressure from advocacy groups as well as the U.S. government to address how their services can be used as an electronic aggression tool or to disseminate extremist propaganda. On the other side of that argument, free-speech activists are concerned that the efforts of a social media company could lead to some ideas and speech being censored. This debate came to the forefront in 2017 when it was determined that Russia had attempted to meddle in the 2016 U.S. election.

Elected officials in the U.S. are complicating issues further by claiming that any news they do not like is fake news. The Federal Communications Commission (FCC) receives numerous complaints that television and/or radio networks, stations or their employees or guests have broadcast extreme, incorrect or somehow improper political, economic or social statements—complaints that then spill into social media feeds. In some cases, the complaints allege that certain broadcast statements may endanger the U.S. or its people, or threaten the form of government, the economic system or established institutions like family or marriage. They say these statements are un-American and an abuse of freedom of speech. The FCC also receives complaints that some broadcast statements criticize, ridicule, stereotype or demean individuals or groups because of the religion, race, nationality, gender or other characteristics of the group or individual.

The FCC is barred by law from trying to prevent the broadcast of any point of view. The Communications Act prohibits the FCC from censoring broadcast material, in most cases, and from making any regulation that would interfere with freedom of speech. Expressions of views that do not involve a clear and present danger of serious, substantive evil come under the protection of the Constitution, which guarantees freedom of speech and freedom of the press and prevents suppression of these expressions by the FCC. According to an FCC opinion on this subject, the public interest is best served by permitting free expression of views. This principle ensures that the most diverse and opposing opinions will be expressed, even though some may be highly offensive. The FCC, however, does have enforcement responsibilities in certain limited instances. For example, the Courts have said that indecent material is protected by the First Amendment to the Constitution and cannot be banned entirely. It may be restricted, however, in order to avoid its broadcast when there is a *reasonable risk* that children may be in the audience. Between 6 a.m. and 10 p.m. (when there is the greatest likelihood that children may be watching) airing indecent material is prohibited by FCC rules. The courts have ruled that obscene material is not protected by the First Amendment and cannot be broadcast at any time [3].

In his remarks to the Hungarian Association of Journalists on October 17, 2017, Chargé d'Affaires David Kostelancik said that "A democratic society with a free press is a messy place, especially with the proliferation of blogs, social media, online news, and the nonstop news cycle. I don't claim to have all the answers about how to navigate this new media environment, though it's clear to me that as government representatives—as servants of our citizens—we must work harder to illuminate, to present the evidence, to show and not just tell, and to adhere to logic and reason when we engage in debate. We should consider other points of view, and urge our colleagues and citizens to do the same. And we must urge responsibility and professionalism and integrity on the part of the press, and should not be afraid to speak up when we see shortcomings. We must also be responsible, discerning consumers and refrain from spreading incomplete, inaccurate, or deliberately misleading information. Above all, there is one temptation to which we must not succumb: democratic governments must not attempt to silence their critics" [4].

It is sufficiently clear that the proponents of freedom of speech and those who practice electronic aggression and those who advocate for civility will have a lot to argue about in the future. Expect continued debate but also evolving legislation.

8.2 Electronic Aggression Models

There are endless configurations of ways by which electronic aggression can be perpetrated. For several years, the major concern among care givers and educators was one individual, most often a minor, being aggressive against another minor, but clearly this also happens among adults. Since the 2016 election in the U.S., electronic aggression has become more of a norm. Several cases have occurred where an individual would receive thousands of e-mails or text messages over a long period of time. Very often, such cases involve personal animosities and sexual harassment.

There have also been instances when an extremist group was electronically aggressive toward an individual. Such cases have most often been based on traditional hate crime models of intimidation and harassment because of race, ethnicity, or religion. They have also been rooted in dislike of an individual's political perspectives or social beliefs. Jennifer Longdon, a gun safety advocate, has suffered considerable electronic abuse but has also been abused physically and emotionally in public for her personal position on guns, according to numerous sources. There were also fake news stories about her in right-wing publications. She is not the only person who has suffered at the hands of gun rights advocates for their activism. The gun rights advocates in these cases were motivated by tribalism; they did not know each other, they just identify with their cause and joined together to abuse their victims electronically and in person.

Another form of electronic aggression is similar to shooting a gun into the air—not aiming at anything in particular and not hitting anything as well. These rants are usually perpetrated by individuals as a way of expressing their dislike or hatred of something or somebody. For years people would make aggressive and often obscene posts in social media about Barack Obama. These posts were usually poorly written and tended to blame Obama for everything the creator thought was wrong with the world. Of course, Barack Obama would probably never see the posts.

One element of aggressive electronic posts that grew popular over time is the inclusion of *visual content* including photographs, drawings, charts, or graphs. The visual element was usually designed to mock or disparage the target subject, person, or organization the aggressors had issues about. Some of the visual content was rather amusing but much of it was racist, rude, and despicable.

8.3 Electronic Aggression at the Tribal Level

Many politicians in the U.S. have become extremist propagandists and some political parties thrive on white nationalism, regionalism, and tribalism as a divide-and-conquer tactic to canvass for votes as part of their campaign strategy. Tribes are most active and easily mobilized as political, social, and economic entities at the village level, but social media can help mobilize tribal members across the U.S. when Election Day comes. Tribe members relate to their virtual leaders and other tribe members through extremist social media propaganda and thus do not need to have physical contact with each other to feel tribe membership.

Tribe members also seem to respond positively to electronic aggression that targets the perceived enemy or nontribal individuals or groups. Watching electronic aggression unfold on social media motivates and binds the tribe members. Many observers feel that Donald Trump has mastered electronic aggression and his tribal members thrive on seeing it happen. There have been an endless stream of social media posts, articles and news broadcasts highlighting his aggressive electronic messaging.

On Christmas Eve, 2017, for example, President Donald Trump retweeted an altered image of himself that showed a splatter covering the CNN logo on the bottom of his shoe; the photo was captioned: Winning. As with most of Donald

Trump's social media posts, this one received thousands of likes and retweets from his 45 million followers. The tribe members are loyal social media followers and support Trump's posts regardless of how aggressive they are or how blatantly inaccurate the posts may have been.

In addition, the Trump tribe members help to aggressively attack any social media posts that criticize, doubt, expose, or otherwise disparage Trump, regardless of the validity of the content of the posts. The same type of propaganda, misinformation, and social media aggression has contributed to the fanatical anti-American and anti-Semitic incitement that has permeated much of the Arab world. It also constitutes a real threat to long-term U.S. interests and security [5]. The long-term effects this electronic aggression can have on U.S. politics, culture, and global standing could end up being seriously damaging.

Electronic aggression by tribe members does not require continuous prompting or direction from a tribal leader. Once a person or organization has been repeatedly victimized by the electronic aggression of a tribal leader, members will carry on that aggression at any opportunity. The case studies here are Barack Obama and Hillary Clinton. Although Trump did sometimes signal attacks by using his social media posts to aggressively attack Obama and Clinton, they were also attacked by the tribe on a constant basis across social media platforms. At the end of December 2017, Twitter was afire with the posts about Barack Obama being named most admired man, beating out Donald Trump, and of course this set the tribe off on an aggressive social media tangent.

Extremists can use social media to customize their *personal propaganda feed* to coincide with their individual beliefs or those of their tribe. One dangerous result of this is that, even if a specific extremist article, post, or discussion thread is proven to be fake news or just a blatant lie, the extremist may never be exposed to that revelation. If their ideas are never challenged or they never encounter an alternative narrative, the extremist will get so locked into their belief system it may be impossible to ever break the belief pattern or set.

The governments of the world collaborate to counter extremist propaganda on a regional and global basis, but within the U.S. there is little formal structure or process to counter home-grown extremist propaganda. There are some liberal organizations that work to do so, and several media organizations perform fact checking duties and provide weekly reports that expose the lies and misleading information that politicians and other would-be influencers spread, but those that close off their social media feeds may never encounter that information.

8.4 The Electronic Aggression of White Nationalism

There is a growing consensus that white nationalists, Nazis and Nazi sympathizers are increasing their use of social media. During the 2016 election in the U.S., social media became the grandstand for white nationalism and remains so at this writing. Since the August 2017 white nationalist rally in Charlottesville when hundreds of torch-bearing white nationalists, white supremacists, Klansmen, and neo-Nazis chanted racist, anti-Semitic, and anti-immigrant slogans and violently engaged with counter-demonstrators on and around the grounds of the University of Virginia in Charlottesville, that use has been accelerated. In addition, groups such as these have been recruiting college students and spreading leaflets and flyers on college campuses.

There has also been increased social media activity by those who oppose white nationalism. Dozens if not hundreds of elected officials across the U.S. have denounced totalitarian impulses, violent terrorism, xenophobic biases, and bigoted ideologies that are promoted by white nationalists and neo-Nazis. One such effort was a joint resolution passed by the U.S. Congress condemning the violence and domestic terrorist attack that took place during events between August 11 and August 12, 2017, in Charlottesville, Virginia, recognizing the first responders who lost their lives while monitoring the events, offering deepest condolences to the families and friends of those individuals who were killed and deepest sympathies and support to those individuals who were injured by the violence, expressing support for the Charlottesville community, rejecting white nationalists, white supremacists, the Ku Klux Klan, neo-Nazis, and other hate groups, and urging the President and the President's cabinet to use all available resources to address the threats posed by those groups [6].

Many of those opposing white nationalism and racism consider President Trump to be largely responsible for its rise, including his appointments of white nationalists to government positions. Congressman Al Green's Articles of Impeachment against President Trump claim that under the inane pretext of dispensing with *political correctness*, he produced a demonstrable record of inciting white supremacy, sexism, bigotry, hatred, xenophobia, race-baiting, and racism by demeaning, defaming, disrespecting, and disparaging women and certain minorities. In doing so, he has fueled and is fueling an alt-right hate machine and its worldwide covert sympathizers engendering racial antipathy, LGBTQ enmity, religious anxiety, stealthy sexism, and dreadful xenophobia, perfidiously causing immediate injury to American society. Further, on September 23, 2017, Donald Trump incited race-baiting and racism, engendering stealthy sexism and racial antipathy when he disrespected, disparaged, and demeaned mothers of professional football players by calling them dogs as he made the widely published statement: "Wouldn't you love to see one of these NFL owners, when somebody disrespects our flag, to say, 'Get that son of a bitch off the field right now, out, he's fired! He's fired!'" [7].

In October 2017, J. Richard Cohen, President of the Southern Poverty Law Center, testified before the Committee on Health, Education, Labor and Pensions of the U.S. Senate Exploring Free Speech on College Campuses. He made several major points on the subject:

- The debate over free speech on college campuses is taking place against the backdrop of increased activity by a white nationalist movement that has been emboldened by President Trump's rhetoric and that is targeting colleges and universities.
- Although university officials and students may find white nationalism abhorrent, they must respect the First Amendment rights of white nationalist speakers and of the students who want to listen to them.
- University administrators and public officials, particularly the President, must speak out forcefully against white nationalism and in support of the First Amendment. The President also should heed Congress's call to use his administration's resources to fight the growing prevalence of hate groups in our country [8].

The white power symbol and the discussion of that symbol have become more prevalent in social media posts. Not all people even understand the symbols when they see them. There are several hate-oriented hand signals, and the Anti-Defamation League (ADL) hosts a Hate on Display™ Hate Symbols Database. This database provides an overview of many of the symbols most frequently used by a variety of white supremacist groups and movements, as well as some other types of hate groups (https://www.adl.org/education/references/hate-symbols).

8.5 Extremist Religious Propaganda in the U.S.

The debate on freedom of religion in the U.S. has evolved into a yelling contest about the concept of religious liberty. However, protecting religious freedom does not include creating a right to harm or discriminate against others. U.S. House of Representatives Democrats feel that the Trump Administration has chosen to use the protection of religious liberty as a justification to take away women's access to contraceptive care and to undermine the civil rights of lesbian, gay, bisexual, and transgender Americans. The Administration's executive actions could allow corporations, whether publicly-traded or closely-held, to deny essential health coverage for women and allow entities receiving federal funds to engage in invidious discrimination against people based on their gender, sexual orientation, or gender identity, among other bases [9].

What it has all boiled down to it that the religious Christian right in the U.S. wants to be able to discriminate against LGBTQ citizens as well as anyone else that does not adhere to Christian beliefs or does not act in accordance to the right-wing Christian interpretation of the Bible. That is clear enough and can be worked out in Federal court over time. However, this yelling contest has resulted in a large volume of extremist propaganda in social media.

Conservative Christian leaders, especially those of the mega churches and the television evangelists, have long condemned LGBTQ citizens by making statements like LGBTQ people poison children's minds and are pedophiles, LGBTQ must be banned from our military, and why has this evil ever been allowed to exist?

In August 2017, The Council on Biblical Manhood and Womanhood (CBMW), during the annual conference of the Ethics and Religious Liberty Commission of the Southern Baptist Convention in Nashville, Tennessee, published the Nashville Statement. The statement, which strongly condemned homosexuality and same-sex marriage, was signed by more than 150 Evangelical Christian leaders, some of whom have either worked closely with President Donald Trump or served on his Evangelical Advisory Board. Those leaders wanted to push their agenda with the hope that under the Trump Administration they would garner support to combat the LGTBQ population, which they consider to be evil. Social media went wild with extremist propaganda from numerous directions.

The CBMW was going into full throttle extremist propaganda mode with the Nashville Statement. However, it crashed and burned rather swiftly and the backlash to the statement was encouraging for the LGBTQ and other civilized communities. Nashville Mayor Megan Barry tweeted that the document is poorly named and does not represent the inclusive values of the city and people of Nashville. The hashtag #NashvilleStatement is still steeped in controversy on Twitter.

8.6 Extremist Propaganda through Censorship

Donald Trump has been well known for rejecting inclusion and political correctness. One of his campaign complaints was that the U.S. has become too politically correct and that keeps people from using the phrase Merry Christmas. Numerous social media posts made it clear that people never stopped saying Merry Christmas and questioned Trump's grip on reality.

In a twist on that saga, in December 2017, print, broadcast, and social media were again in flames over the reported censorship of the Centers for Disease Control and Prevention, which had reportedly been warned not to use seven hot-button words in future budget proposals. The banned words were diversity, fetus, transgender, vulnerable, entitlement, science-based and evidence-based. We will see how that unfolds in the future.

In a similar move, the term *climate change* has reportedly been removed from U.S. government websites. In typical fashion, when exposed, Trump Administration loyalists denied such censorship. However, at the time of this writing the National Oceanographic and Atmospheric Administration (NOAA) Climate.gov website was still operational. Its mission is to provide science and information for a climate-smart nation. NOAA Climate.gov is a source of timely and authoritative scientific data and information about climate. Our goals are to promote public understanding of climate science and climate-related events, to make data products and services easy to access and use, to provide climate-related support to the private sector and the nation's economy, and to serve people making climate-related decisions with tools and resources that help them answer specific questions.

8.7 Summary

Extremist electronic aggression is permeating social media. Even though much of that aggressive expression is protected by the First Amendment, it is no less antagonistic or harmful to society. The extremists are setting a tone for more hate and intolerance to spread. This chapter examined electronic aggression and how it is driven by nationalism, tribalism, clan conflict, and bigotry. Key points covered include:

- Electronic aggression is any type of intimidation, harassment or bullying that occurs through any e-mail, chat room, instant messaging, website (including blogs), text messaging, or social media posts, the content of which is often associated with some expression of anger and negativity.
- Extremist propaganda and electronic aggression are often intertwined to provide the perpetrator with some form of extrinsic benefits.
- It is sufficiently clear that the proponents of freedom of speech and those who practice electronic aggression and those who advocate for civility will have a lot to argue about in the future.
- There are endless configurations of ways by which electronic aggression can be perpetrated. For several years, the major concern among care givers and educators was one individual, most often a minor, being aggressive against another minor, but clearly this also happens among adults.
- Many politicians in the U.S. have become extremist propagandists and some political parties thrive on white nationalism, regionalism, and tribalism as a divide-and-conquer tactic to canvass for votes as part of their campaign strategy.
- Extremists can use social media to customize their propaganda feed to coincide with their individual beliefs or those of their tribe. One dangerous result of this is that even if a specific extremist article, post, or discussion thread is

proven to be fake news or just a blatant lie, the extremist may never be exposed to that revelation.

■ There is a growing consensus that white nationalists, Nazis and Nazi sympathizers are increasing their use of social media.

■ The debate on freedom of religion in the U.S. has evolved into a yelling contest about the concept of religious liberty. However, protecting religious freedom does not include creating a right to harm or discriminate against others.

8.8 Course Activities

Course project number one: Read and discuss *It Can't Happen Here* (2014) by Sinclair Lewis.

Course project number two: Research two articles on any of the subtopics in this chapter that take opposite perspectives on the topic. Write a 500-word summary of the opposing viewpoints.

Course project number three: In a panel setting, discuss the articles and opposing viewpoints from course assignment number two.

References

1. Centers for Disease Control and Prevention. *Technology and Youth: Protecting Your Child from Electronic Aggression.* Accessed December 24, 2017 https://www.cdc.gov/violenceprevention/pdf/ea-tipsheet-a.pdf.
2. Staff Sgt. Jenifer Piovesan, U.S. Air Force Warfare Center Judges Advocate. *Military Members: Freedom of Speech, Social Media,* August 28, 2013. Accessed December 24, 2017 http://www.nellis.af.mil/News/Commentaries/Display/Article/665415/military-members-freedom-of-speech-social-media/.
3. FCC Consumer Guides. *The FCC and Freedom of Speech.* Accessed December 24, 2017 https://www.fcc.gov/consumers/guides/fcc-and-freedom-speech.
4. Chargé d'Affaires David Kostelancik remarks to the Hungarian Association of Journalists, October 17, 2017. Accessed December 30, 2017 https://hu.usembassy.gov/freedom-press-enduring-values-dynamic-media-environment/.
5. Words have consequences: The impact of incitement and Anti-American and Anti-Semitic propaganda on American interests in the Middle East. Hearing before the Subcommittee on the Middle East and South Asia of the Committee on International Relations House of Representatives. *One Hundred Seventh Congress Second Session,* April 18, 2002. Accessed December 28, 2017 http://commdocs.house.gov/committees/intlrel/hfa78802.000/hfa78802_0f.htm.
6. S.J.Res.49—A joint resolution condemning the violence and domestic terrorist attack that took place during events between August 11 and August 12, 2017, Charlottesville, VA, September 14, 2017 Became Public Law No: 115-58. Accessed December 29, 2017 https://www.congress.gov/bill/115th-congress/senate-joint-resolution/49/text.

7. Congressman Al Green's articles of impeachment against Donald J. Trump President of the United States, October 16, 2017. Accessed December 29, 2017 https://algreen.house. gov/press-release/articles-impeachment-against-donald-j-trump-president-united-states.
8. Testimony of J. Richard Cohen, President, Southern Poverty Law Center, before the Committee on Health, Education, Labor and Pensions United States Senate. *Exploring Free Speech on College Campuses*, October 26, 2017. Accessed December 29, 2017 https://www.help.senate.gov/imo/media/doc/Cohen5.pdf.
9. Conyers and Cohen: Trump administration conflates religious liberty with the right to discriminate in latest troubling actions. *House Judiciary Committee Ranking Member John Conyers, Jr. (D-MI) and Subcommittee on the Constitution and Civil Justice Ranking Member Steve Cohen (D-TN)*, October 6, 2017. Accessed December 30, 2017 https://democrats-judiciary.house.gov/news/press-releases/ conyers-and-cohen-trump-administration-conflates-religious-liberty-right.

Chapter 9

Countering Extremist Anti-Science Propaganda

9.1 The Anti-Science Movement Gained Momentum over Many Years

It has been difficult to determine on what day and in what year the current anti-science movement actually started. What happened along the way is that many people that are anti-science found a tool to express their views, cheaply, quickly, and free from validation. That tool is extremist anti-science propaganda in social media. Through social media propaganda the religious right, fiscal conservatives and corporate interests converged to deny, attack, and defund science in the U.S., which was once considered to be the nation that led the growth of science, medical research, and technological innovation for the world.

One of the oldest standing anti-science protests has been over the teaching of evolution in schools and universities and favoring that over the teaching of creationism, which is a sacred conservative religious belief. Although the question of the origins of humankind is not new and was a debated topic even before Charles Darwin published Origin of Species in 1859, it was the Scopes Monkey Trial in 1925 that brought the controversy into the mainstream in the U.S. Many people consider the Dayton, Tennessee case to be one of the landmark legal decisions of the twentieth century. Table 9.1 provides directions to find more information on the Scopes Trial. The trial would have been great drama if social media as we now know it would have been in existence at the time.

Fast forward to April 2017 when there was a worldwide protest against the anti-science Trump Administration. The March for Science movement saw rallies in hundreds of communities across the U.S. and around the world to voice

Table 9.1   Scopes Monkey Trial Information

The Tennessee State Library and Archives (TSLA) host and exhibit, "A Monkey on Tennessee's Back: The Scopes Trial in Dayton." The exhibit presents the history behind the famous Scopes Trial, a court case that received national attention as attorney Clarence Darrow battled William Jennings Bryan on behalf of a John Scopes, a Tennessee teacher who decided to teach evolution in a public school.

Source: http://sharetngov.tnsosfiles.com/tsla/exhibits/scopes/index.htm

concerns about proposed budget cuts for the National Institutes of Health and the Department of Energy's Office of Science as well as the growing climate change denial that was spewing from the White House.

March for Science's @ScienceMarchDC is a very active Twitter account with over 350,000 followers. The Twitter profile states that the March for Science champions robustly funded and publicly communicated science as a pillar of human freedom and prosperity. Numerous Congressional Representatives have supported the March for Science, as have communities, organizations, and corporations around the world.

Among the Congressional supporters is U.S. Senator Tom Udall of New Mexico, a member of the Senate Commerce, Science and Transportation Committee. Udall, along with a group of other Senators, urged President Trump to appoint well-qualified experts for critical science posts at the White House Office of Science and Technology Policy (OSTP) and throughout the federal government. That urging was done in conjunction with the March for Science in April, 2017. At the heart of the issue at that time was the fact that nearly 100 days into his presidency, President Trump still had not appointed a science advisor, director for the White House OSTP, or chief technology officer. Many Senators consider the White House Office of Science and Technology Policy to be a critical office responsible for advising the president on scientific and technical matters related to national security, the economy, and innovation. The office has been severely short-staffed as scores of scientists and technology experts resigned since Trump was elected [2].

9.2 Educational Attainment in the U.S.

The anti-science movement is also changing the perceptions of people in making career choices and how to pursue higher education if they pursue it at all. Few U.S. students pursue expertise in science, technology, engineering, and mathematics (STEM) fields and there is an inadequate pipeline of teachers skilled in those subjects. Many young people find STEM fields too difficult to study for and choose easier curriculums.

Now, many youths do not even have access to quality STEM learning opportunities and too few students see these disciplines as springboards for their careers. For example, only 81% of Asian-American high school students and 71% of white high school students attend high schools where the full range of math and science courses are offered (algebra I, geometry, algebra II, calculus, biology, chemistry, and physics). The access to these courses for American Indian, Native-Alaskan, black, and Hispanic high school students is significantly worse. Children's race, zip code, and socioeconomic status largely determine their STEM fluency. In addition, only 16% of U.S. high school seniors are proficient in math and interested in a STEM career. Even among those who do go on to pursue a college major in the STEM fields, only about half choose to work in a related career field. The U.S. is also falling behind internationally, ranking 29th in math and 22nd in science among industrialized nations [3].

STEM careers generally require a higher level of education than most U.S. residents have, with only about 30% of the population having attained a Bachelor's degree or above. Over 99% of STEM employment is in occupations that typically require some type of postsecondary education for entry, compared with 36% of overall employment. Table 9.2 shows educational attainment in the U.S.

There were nearly 8.6 million STEM jobs in May 2015, representing 6.2% of U.S. employment. Computer occupations made up nearly 45% of STEM employment, and engineers made up an additional 19%. Mathematical science occupations and

Table 9.2 Educational Attainment in the U.S.

Educational Attainment 2016 (people over 18 years old)	*Percent of population*
High School Graduate	28.9
Some College (no degree)	19.1
Associate's degree, occupational	4.0
Associate's degree, academic	5.5
Bachelor's degree	19.5
Master's degree	8.3
Professional degree	1.3
Doctoral degree	1.6
Less than High School	11.8

Source: U.S. Census Bureau, Educational attainment in the United States: 2016, https://www.census.gov/data/tables/2016/demo/education-attainment/cps-detailed-tables.html, Accessed January 3, 2018.

architects, surveyors, and cartographers combined made up less than 4% of STEM employment. Employment in STEM occupations grew by 10.5%, or 817,260 jobs, between May 2009 and May 2015, compared with 5.2% net growth in non-STEM occupations.

Ninety-three out of 100 STEM occupations had wages above the national average. Wages for STEM occupations varied vastly. The national average wage for all STEM occupations was $87,570, nearly double the national average wage for non-STEM occupations ($45,700). Ninety-three out of 100 STEM occupations had wages significantly above the national average wage for all occupations of $48,320. Petroleum engineers were the highest paid STEM occupation, with an annual mean wage of $149,590, over $100,000 higher than the national average across all occupations. Physicists ($118,500) were also among the highest paid STEM occupations. The STEM group that is projected to grow fastest from 2014 to 2024 is the mathematical science occupations group at 28.2%, compared with the average projected growth for all occupations of 6.5% [5].

Learning about and understanding science can be rewarding for those who are motivated to pursue science. But science is also a complex and difficult set of academic disciplines that most people do not want to put the time into in order to expand their understanding. Thus, there is a void in knowledge about science. That void is far too often filled with pop-science or junk science, which is fundamentally extremist propaganda just as fake news is a propaganda instrument. Then, when real science is on the agenda, it is struggling against a world full of false unproven information that is disseminated by various interest groups trying to discredit real science and replace it with self-serving propaganda, just as the tobacco industry did for decades. When confronted with science that does not support a capitalist agenda, as in the case of the big tobacco companies, industries and their supporters will quickly label it junk science, just as politicians label news they do not like as fake news. Science supporters face a complex set of issues in the face of the anti-science movement, including:

■ Countering wide-spread anti-science sentiment and propaganda
■ Attracting young people to science occupations
■ Protecting the U.S. science infrastructure from being decimated by an anti-science Congress
■ Countering junk science with real research and real science

These are all major challenges, especially because so many people have become not only anti-science but anti-intellectual across society. This is driven in part because of the higher than average salaries that STEM occupations pay, which creates jealousy from non-STEM workers and breeds deep-rooted resentment. STEM workers and educated people in general can afford a better quality of life than the average U.S. citizen and that just widens the gap between two subparts of the population.

9.3 Countering Extremist Anti-Vaccine Social Media Propaganda

Beyond the high-level debates about the origin of the species and the present-day budget battles on science funding, social media has become a battleground of a wide selection of perspectives and one of the hottest areas is the topic of vaccines. In the past there has been an incredible viciousness in many social media posts targeting vaccine havers and pushers on one side and vaccine deniers and protesters on the other side. The intensity of the social media posts rises and falls with various news stories about vaccines.

There are also numerous posts making claims about the impact of vaccines or spreading unverified stories about what has happened because of vaccines. There are several repeat posters and trolls that keep posting the same misinformation and attack social media users that disagree with them. It is an area where extremist social media propaganda can flourish while causing panic and jeopardizing public health. Some of the social media topics include:

■ I was pro vaccine until it happened to my child.
■ Fear of vaccines is an imaginary first world problem.
■ Alcohol with vaccination may raise effectiveness.
■ For #flatearthers, #antivaxxers, advocates, there's no amount of fact or reason that matters.
■ Study claims vaccines-autism link using fake data.
■ This is a vaccine-related autism epidemic.
■ Ingredients in vaccines may cause autism, but not the vaccines themselves.
■ Immunizations are not effective vaccines can kill.
■ Scientists told to destroy evidence linking vaccines to autism.
■ Our child was brain damaged by his vaccines and then came autism.
■ Mandatory vaccines are secret genocide.
■ Half of all Americans suspect vaccines cause autism.
■ Vaccines are being used as a tool to control people.
■ People who are anti-vaccines are not learning both sides.
■ Pro Vaccine lovers don't like listening to the truth.

The CDC frequently reiterates that vaccines protect the health of children in the U.S. so well that most parents today have never seen first-hand the devastating consequences of diseases now stopped by vaccines. This could very well explain why so many people got sucked into the anti-vaccine propaganda resulting in the 2014 measles count being the highest number since measles was declared eliminated in 2000 [6]. This is representative of the post *Sabin* and *Salk* mentality. Polio was very common in the U.S. and caused severe illness in thousands of people each year before polio vaccine was introduced. Once polio was largely conquered the panic about such diseases diminished because they were not such a large part of everyday life.

Before vaccines, many children died from diseases such as whooping cough and polio, which are diseases that vaccines are now able to prevent. However, according to reports from the Centers for Disease Control and Prevention (CDCP), there has been a resurgence of certain vaccine-preventable diseases in the U.S. in recent years. For example, since 2010, there have been between 10,000 and 50,000 cases of whooping cough each year in the U.S., with cases reported in every state [7].

Extremist propaganda pours disinformation into social media. In this case, it can impact homeland security in the U.S. by negatively impacting the health of the nation. This, combined with other forms of extremist propaganda in social media, starts shredding the social fiber of the country. Reasonable debate builds societies but alarmism, information that leads to poor decision making or propaganda that spreads confusion is not only counterproductive but can be very destructive. The CDCP provides a wide range of information about vaccines including:

- Vaccines and Immunizations www.cdc.gov/vaccines/index.html
- Vaccine—Official Site www.vaccines.gov/
- Immunization Schedules www.cdc.gov/vaccines/schedules/index.html
- Vaccines—Food and Drug Administration (FDA) www.fda.gov/BiologicsBloodVaccines/Vaccines/default.htm
- Vaccine Basics www.vaccines.gov/basics/index.html
- Parents Vaccines for Your Children www.cdc.gov/vaccines/parents/index.html
- Vaccine Safety www.vaccines.gov/basics/safety/index.html
- Who & When www.vaccines.gov/who_and_when/index.html
- Recommended Vaccinations by Age www.cdc.gov/vaccines/vpd/vaccines-diseases.html
- Vaccines Work www.vaccines.gov/basics/work/index.html
- Vaccine Types www.vaccines.gov/basics/types/index.html
- Influenza (Flu) www.vaccines.gov/diseases/flu/index.html

The shortcoming of the CDCP outreach approach is that it requires people to go the website and seek the information and data. This is an observation, not a criticism of the outreach approach. Even though there are articles and positive news stories about vaccines, the world of extremist propaganda on social media can better be countered with a more direct approach in dealing with those who post junk science, fake news, and false personal stories. The obstacle is of course the First Amendment and the rules of engagement that federal agencies must follow when dealing with the public.

9.4 Extremist Anti-Climate Change Science Propaganda

Anti-climate change science propaganda is about as widespread as television commercials for junk food brands. Politicians decry climate change programs and supporting legislation as a threat to the U.S. economy and the American way of life.

The Trump Administration has taken climate change off the list of national security issues and announced intent to withdraw from the Paris Climate Agreement. These actions were taken under the influence of an ever-growing body of extremist propaganda about what climate change is and why it is occurring so rapidly at this time. This is basically a subtopic of the anti-science movement but has resulted in the appointment of cabinet-level executives in the U.S. government that do not know science but reject science and in turn are willing to risk the future of homeland security based on the lobbying of corporate interests and the knee-jerk reactions of an uneducated populace. Remember that candidate Trump said during the 2016 presidential race that he loves poorly educated people, the core population that propaganda is the most effective in influencing and swaying.

In April 2016, Congressman Ted W. Lieu (Democrat-Los Angeles County) reported that the board of the 62,000-member American Geophysical Union (AGU) had decided to sell its scientific integrity for $35,000 in ExxonMobil Money. Evidence showed that the oil giant was still funding climate science denial nearly a decade after it said it would stop. It was also learned that ExxonMobil continued funding groups that spread disinformation on climate science in 2015. The science-denying groups American Legislative Exchange Council (ALEC), American Enterprise Institute, National Black Chamber of Commerce (NBCC), and Manhattan Institute of Policy Research received more than $860,000 in 2015 alone. That does not include the $5,000,000 Exxon gave the anti-science U.S. Chamber of Commerce from 2014 to 2018. In November 2016, the NBCC president described global warming as a farce and a ghost.

Since 1997, ExxonMobil has spent more than $30 million funding dozens of groups that spread disinformation about climate science and climate solutions. They never stopped funding such groups even though they appeared to promise otherwise in their 2007 Corporate Citizenship Report [8]. Former ExxonMobil chairman and chief executive officer (2006–2016) Rex W. Tillerson was sworn in as the 69th U.S. Secretary of State on February 1, 2017.

When Barack Obama was president, he vigorously pursued action to address climate change issues. A search of his archived records, speeches, and press briefings shows a high proportion of climate change topics consistent with the global perspective that climate change must be addressed. There have also been a considerable number of social media posts supporting efforts to address climate change through positive actions.

When Donald Trump became president, he was determined to dismantle all things Obama said so in speech after speech to voters during the 2016 election. This played well with his supporters in part because of their leaning toward white nationalism, which fostered hate for Barack Obama. President Trump then declared that the U.S. would withdraw from the Paris Climate Agreement based on the unsubstantiated claim that the Agreement is detrimental to U.S. interests.

President Trump has since proceeded to gut climate change research and reduce funding for renewable energy projects. In May 2017, U.S. Senator

Catherine Cortez Masto (Democrat-Nevada) among many other Senators and Representatives condemned President Trump's budget proposal for its unprecedented cuts targeting federal environmental protection programs, efforts to address the threat of climate change, and investments for renewable energy production. She contended that the irreversible effects of climate change are preventable if we remain committed to science-based solutions, and yet President Trump's budget demonstrates his continued support for Big Oil companies over the protection of our planet [9].

Previously, Congresswoman Elizabeth Esty (Connecticut) spoke against H.R. 1430, the Honest and Open New EPA Science Treatment (HONEST) Act during debate of the bill on the House floor in March 2017. She contended that although the HONEST Act is framed as requiring additional transparency by the EPA about the research it relies on, the requirements it sets would preclude the EPA from using studies related to one-time events and longitudinal studies, which are essential for developing sound public health policy [10]. These events and others during 2017 demonstrated that the conflict between anti-science and real science was unfolding at a rapid pace.

One of the major hurdles to overcoming extremist anti-climate change propaganda is that in 2017/2018 the sources of that propaganda, including corporate interests that want to pollute and profit at the same time, had a strong hold in the U.S. government. As nations around the world work to deal with climate change, the U.S. government is not taking an active leadership role. In fact, the U.S. Congress is awash with climate change deniers and leading scientists are seeking positions outside the government research complex so they can effectively continue their work.

U.S. Secretary of Energy Rick Perry announced in September 2017 the availability of approximately $36 million in federally-funded financial assistance to advance carbon capture technologies. Under the Department of Energy's (DOE's) Office of Fossil Energy (FE), the Design and Testing of Advanced Carbon Capture Technologies funding opportunity announcement (FOA) will support cost-shared research and development projects that will continue the development of carbon capture technologies to either the engineering scale or to a commercial design [11].

However, in June 2017, Secretary of Energy Rick Perry denied in a television interview that CO_2 emissions are primarily responsible for climate change, contending that the primary control knob to climate change is the ocean waters and this environment that we live in. In response, Congressman Earl Blumenauer (Oregon-Republican) sent a letter to Perry with educational materials outlining the basic established science behind climate change. Blumenauer and 32 of his colleagues sent the same materials to Environmental Protection Agency Administrator Scott Pruitt in March following Pruitt's similar comments on CO_2 emissions [12]. A visit to the EPA website page on climate change on January 4, 2018, yielded the note in Table 9.3 [13].

Table 9.3   Note on EPA Climate Change Page

> This page is being updated. Thank you for your interest in this topic. We are currently updating our website to reflect EPA's priorities under the leadership of President Trump and Administrator Pruitt. If you're looking for an archived version of this page, you can find it on the January 19 snapshot.

Subsequently, the EPA released a report in October 2017 about promoting energy independence and economic growth that was said to review actions that may burden the development or use of domestically produced energy resources and recommend changes to any regulations. In other words, the Trump Administration was trying to protect the domestic coal industry, so went the anti-climate science extremist propaganda campaign. This part of the story has a long way to go before it is finished.

A note of optimism: In the struggle to counter extremist anti-climate science propaganda, nations around the world and cities and states across the U.S., along with governors, mayors, scientists, and concerned citizens, have expressed their support for the Paris Agreement and other efforts to address climate change. They have also used social media to make their perspectives and feelings clear on the matter and have worked to counter the anti-science propaganda.

9.5   Anti-Fetal Tissue Research Extremist Propaganda

Fetal tissue research has been a controversial topic since the Roe v. Wade decision in 1973, which legalized abortion nationwide in the U.S. Research by means of human fetal tissue obtained from abortions benefits countless people worldwide and also has great promise for the development of lifesaving vaccines and therapies. Since abortion became legal nationwide, fetal tissue research has, time and again, become entangled in the abortion controversy. One element of the controversy has grown out of abortion opponents' long-standing campaign to vilify abortion and abortion providers and put fetal tissue research in jeopardy [14]. Fetal tissue research remains uniquely and critically important and has resulted in significant improvements in maternal and infant health. It also remains critical to understanding and advancing treatments and cures for a broad range of conditions that impact millions [15].

Congress passed the NIH Revitalization Act in 1993 with overwhelming bipartisan support. This law prohibits the receipt of any valuable consideration for fetal tissue while expressly permitting reasonable payments for costs, including transportation, implantation, processing, preservation, quality control, or storage of human fetal tissue [16].

In 2015, David Daleiden produced videos that he claimed proved that Planned Parenthood was illegally selling fetus material obtained through abortions. The videos were edited into extremist propaganda and the U.S. House of Representatives male Republicans got sucked in by that propaganda. There were several House hearings that attempted to torpedo Planned Parenthood, and they were as dramatic as the *Salem Witch trials* were portrayed. As the House hearings continued they became extremist propaganda machines. The House Judiciary Committee held a hearing entitled Planned Parenthood Exposed: Examining the Horrific Abortion Practices at the Nation's Largest Abortion Provider. The title and the content were full-blown extremist propaganda.

Dozens of claims were made about Planned Parenthood, including that the undercover videos showed Planned Parenthood trafficking in fetal tissue for profit in violation of federal law, even though the videos included no credible evidence that Planned Parenthood profits from its fetal tissue donation program. Planned Parenthood was accused of being paid for fetal tissue donations in violation of federal law and it was eventually determined that Planned Parenthood was receiving reasonable reimbursement for its tissue donation services, as expressly permitted by law.

Other claims included that Planned Parenthood doctors change the method, timing, and procedure for abortions to obtain fetal tissue in violation of federal law. However, no credible evidence to support the claim was ever presented. In the end, there was not credible evidence that Planned Parenthood had violated any laws, but it had become clear that the videos had been heavily edited and deceptively manipulated. The first video released intentionally omitted ten instances in which Planned Parenthood's Director of Medical Services stated that Planned Parenthood does not profit from tissue donations.

Even though most of the services Planned Parenthood provides are not abortion related, the propaganda portrayed Planned Parenthood as an abortion-focused business. Daleiden's Center for Medical Progress eventually became engaged in a full-fledged lobbying effort to pass legislation to withhold federal funds from Planned Parenthood [17]. The debate continues in social media with posts like:

- Attorney General Turns Blind Eye to Violations in Fetal Tissue Investigation
- Researcher selling fetal parts to a private company
- Current vaccines contain aborted fetal tissue
- Aborted fetal tissue injected into your body through VAX
- University launches investigation into fetal tissue transfer
- Quit murdering babies and selling of fetal tissue for profit
- Republicans say abortion is murder and call fetal tissue body parts

Countering extremist propaganda being disseminated by the U.S. Congress is a challenge but their atrocity did not go unanswered. Women became very vocal and in social media there were tidal waves of testimonies about how Planned Parenthood had contributed to their health and their lives. The declaration of "I stand by Planned Parenthood" was made tens of thousands of times. Women also took to the streets by the thousands to protest men trying to make decisions about women's health and those protests will continue. One symbol of the movement was the hand-knitted pink pussy hat, which is now heavily mocked on social media by right-wing misogynists. One other response to the misbehavior by the white Republican males in Congress is that more women are pursuing elected office and doing so successfully, meaning more change may yet come.

9.6 Ethics and Codes of Conduct Violations in the U.S. Government

The U.S. Congress has been behaving badly. Violations of ethical norms and principles of ethical behavior by a Member of Congress are enforced, principally, at the ballot box by the Member's constituents who choose their representatives in Congress but are also enforced internally in each House of Congress by other Members of the House or the Senate. Members of Congress have no general immunity from criminal prosecutions and are subject to prosecution for violations of federal criminal laws by the U.S. Attorneys of the DOJ. Unlike criminal laws or other federal statutory provisions, however, there exist broad ethical standards, codes of conduct or behavior, and general principles of morality, written or unwritten, by which a Member of Congress may also be judged.

As part of the assurance of an independent legislature, one not fettered or intimidated by a powerful law-enforcing executive, the Constitution expressly grants a limited immunity to Members of Congress from prosecution when the conduct involves official legislative activities. The so-called "speech or debate" clause immunity provides that a Member shall not be questioned in any other place concerning official legislative conduct. Since a Member may not be questioned in any other place regarding certain conduct in the legislative process, this speech or debate immunity provides a cogent and practical reason for the countervailing authority and responsibility within the Constitution for congressional self-discipline and the necessity for internal enforcement of legislative standards of conduct [18].

The rules of the House of Representatives 114th congress established by and for the House a Code of Official Conduct, which requires that "[a] Member, Delegate, Resident Commissioner, officer, or employee of the House shall behave at all times in a manner that shall reflect creditably on the House." In addition, "[a] Member, Delegate, Resident Commissioner, officer, or employee of the House shall adhere to the spirit and the letter of the Rules of the House and to the rules of duly constituted committees thereof" [19].

Given the earlier terms regarding conduct of Members of Congress, and the process of self-discipline, the behavior of Members can only be governed by Congress. The conclusion is that the behavior of Members during hearings where witnesses are abused, berated, disparaged, intimidated, or otherwise threatened is allowable as long as the majority feels those behaviors are allowable.

The requirement that "[a] Member, Delegate, Resident Commissioner, officer, or employee of the House shall behave at all times in a manner that shall reflect creditably on the House" is largely ignored, especially during political campaigns. This was obvious during the 2016 U.S. elections, during which numerous Members were seeking the Presidency or just reelection to their then-current positions. The campaigns of 2016 descended into yelling contests laden with name calling, accusations, and threats accompanied by misleading statements and lie after lie. On the home front, it was disgusting—in the international arena, it was an embarrassment and a disgrace.

There are also Principles of Ethical Conduct for all government officers and employees. The following Principles are an excerpt from Executive Order 12674 of April 12, 1989, as modified by Executive Order 12731. These Principles apply to all employees of the federal government.

Section 101. Principles of Ethical Conduct. To ensure that every citizen can have complete confidence in the integrity of the Federal Government, each Federal employee shall respect and adhere to the fundamental principles of ethical service as implemented in regulations promulgated under sections 201 and 301 of this order:

- Public service is a public trust, requiring employees to place loyalty to the Constitution, the laws, and ethical principles above private gain.
- Employees shall not hold financial interests that conflict with the conscientious performance of duty.
- Employees shall not engage in financial transactions using nonpublic Government information or allow the improper use of such information to further any private interest.
- An employee shall not, except pursuant to such reasonable exceptions as are provided by regulation, solicit or accept any gift or other item of monetary value from any person or entity seeking official action from, doing business with, or conducting activities regulated by the employee's agency, or whose interests may be substantially affected by the performance or nonperformance of the employee's duties.
- Employees shall put forth honest effort in the performance of their duties.
- Employees shall make no unauthorized commitments or promises of any kind purporting to bind the Government.
- Employees shall not use public office for private gain.
- Employees shall act impartially and not give preferential treatment to any private organization or individual.
- Employees shall protect and conserve Federal property and shall not use it for other than authorized activities.
- Employees shall not engage in outside employment or activities, including seeking or negotiating for employment, that conflict with official Government duties and responsibilities.
- Employees shall disclose waste, fraud, abuse, and corruption to appropriate authorities.

- Employees shall satisfy in good faith their obligations as citizens, including all just financial obligations, especially those such as Federal, State, or local taxes that are imposed by law.
- Employees shall adhere to all laws and regulations that provide equal opportunity for all Americans regardless of race, color, religion, sex, national origin, age, or handicap.
- Employees shall endeavor to avoid any actions creating the appearance that they are violating the law or the ethical standards promulgated pursuant to this order [20].

The ethics of the Trump Administration will be scrutinized and studied for decades to come. The concerns in this chapter are specifically directed at extremist propaganda, which many Trump appointees may be guilty of disseminating and perpetuating. Questions arose during the early days of the Administration as to ethical behavior on many fronts. However, when it comes to elected officials, appointed advisors or cabinet members, or civil service members the importance of maintaining a proper etiquette when tweeting or speaking cannot be overstated.

Federal employees must cooperate and provide testimony, information, and documents during investigations by the Office of Special Counsel (OSC). The same rule requires federal agencies to make employees available to testify, on official time, and to provide pertinent records. It is unlawful for agency management to retaliate against a person for providing information to OSC. If necessary, OSC may issue subpoenas for documents or the attendance and testimony of employees. During an investigation, OSC may require employees and others to testify under oath, sign written statements, or respond formally to written questions.

Generally, the information provided to OSC will remain confidential. Information in OSC investigative files is protected from disclosure under the Freedom of Information Act. Neither the complainant nor the agency will ordinarily have access to information provided to OSC. In a limited number of cases where OSC determines that a violation has occurred, OSC may include the information gathered in an investigation in a report to an agency, the MSPB, or the Office of Personnel Management.

The U.S. Office of Special Counsel (OSC) routinely receives questions from federal employees and others about when the use of social media and e-mail could violate the Hatch Act. Social media and e-mail and the ease of accessing those accounts at work, either on computers or smartphones, have made it easier for federal employees to violate the Hatch Act. Yet there are many activities employees can do on social media and e-mail that do not violate the law. OSC has created a Frequently Asked Questions (FAQs) page to help employees understand what the Hatch Act does and does not allow when using social media and e-mail (https://osc.gov/Pages/The-Hatch-Act-Frequently-Asked-Questions-on-Federal-Employees-and-the-Use-of-Social-Media-and-Email.aspx). In general, all federal employees may use social media and e-mail and comply with the Hatch Act if they remember the following guidelines:

■ Do not engage in political activity while on duty or in the workplace. Federal employees are on duty when they are in a pay status, other than paid leave, or are representing the government in an official capacity. Federal employees are considered on duty during telecommuting hours.
■ Do not engage in political activity in an official capacity at any time.
■ Do not solicit or receive political contributions at any time. Political activity refers to any activity directed at the success or failure of a political party or partisan political group (collectively referred to as partisan groups), or candidate in a partisan race. In addition, some federal employees are considered further restricted, which means they are prohibited from taking an active part in partisan political management or partisan political campaigns. Thus, they may not engage, via social media and e-mail, in any political activity on behalf of a partisan group or candidate in a partisan race.

Federal employees may express their opinions about a partisan group or candidate in a partisan race (e.g., post, like, share, tweet, retweet), but there are a few limitations. Specifically, the Hatch Act prohibits employees from:

■ Engaging in any political activity via Facebook or Twitter while on duty or in the workplace.
■ Referring to their official titles or positions while engaged in political activity at any time (note that inclusion of an employee's official title or position on one's social media profile, without more, is not an improper use of official authority).
■ Suggesting or asking anyone to make political contributions at any time. Thus, they should neither provide links to the political contribution page of any partisan group or candidate in a partisan race nor like, share, or retweet a solicitation from one of those entities, including an invitation to a political fundraising event. An employee, however, may accept an invitation to a political fundraising event from such entities via Facebook or Twitter.

Further Restricted Employees also may express their opinions about a partisan group or candidate in a partisan race (e.g., post, like, share, tweet, retweet), but there are a few limitations. In addition to the earlier limitations, the Hatch Act prohibits further restricted employees from:

■ Posting or linking to campaign or other partisan material of a partisan group or candidate in a partisan race
■ Sharing these entities' Facebook pages or their content
■ Retweeting posts from these entities' Twitter accounts

A federal employee may engage in political activity on Facebook or Twitter if she is friends with or has followers who are subordinate employees, but she remains subject to the limitations described in other related questions and the following guidelines. If a supervisor's statements about a partisan group or candidate in a partisan race are directed at all of his Facebook friends or Twitter followers, for example, posted on his Facebook page, then there is no Hatch Act violation. Such statements would be improper if the supervisor specifically directed them toward her subordinate employees, or to a subset of friends that includes subordinate employees. For example, a supervisor should not send to a subordinate employee a Facebook message or tweet that shows her support for a partisan group or candidate in a partisan race.

Any social media account created in a federal employee's official capacity should be limited to official business matters and remain politically neutral. Any political activity must be confined to the employee's personal Facebook or Twitter account, subject to the limitations described in other related questions. A federal employee may become a friend, like, or follow the social media page of a partisan group or candidate in a partisan race but not while on duty or in the workplace.

A federal employee may continue to friend, like, or follow an official social media page of a government official after he has become a candidate for reelection; for example, a federal employee may continue to friend, like, or follow the official government Facebook or Twitter account of the President or Member of Congress, even after the President or Member begins his reelection campaign.

If a federal employee has listed his official title or position on Facebook, he may also complete the political views field, simply identifying one's political party affiliation on a social media profile, which also contains one's official title or position, without more, is not an improper use of official authority.

A federal employee may display a political party or campaign logo or candidate photograph as her cover or header photo on Facebook or Twitter and display a political party or campaign logo or a candidate photograph as his profile picture on Facebook or Twitter, but because a profile picture accompanies most actions on social media, a federal employee would not be permitted, while on duty or in the workplace, to post, share, tweet, or retweet any items on Facebook or Twitter, because each such action would show their support for a partisan group or candidate in a partisan race, even if the content of the action is not about those entities.

If a federal employee receives a partisan political e-mail in her government e-mail account, she may send that e-mail to her personal e-mail account while at work. Simply forwarding such an e-mail to one's personal e-mail account, without more, does not violate the Hatch Act. A federal employee cannot send or forward a partisan political e-mail from either his government e-mail account or his personal e-mail account (even using a personal device) while at work.

The Hatch Act does not prohibit federal employees from engaging in non-partisan political activities. Accordingly, employees may express their opinions about current events and matters of public interest at work so long as their actions are not considered political activity. For example, employees are free to express their views and take action as individual citizens on such questions as referendum matters, changes in municipal ordinances, constitutional amendments, pending legislation or other matters of public interest, like issues involving highways, schools, housing, and taxes. Of course, employees should be mindful of their agencies' computer use policies prior to sending or forwarding any non-work-related e-mails. It is an improper use of official authority for a supervisor to send or forward a partisan political e-mail to subordinates, at any time. The Hatch Act prohibits federal employees from soliciting or receiving political contributions, which includes inviting individuals to political fundraising events, at any time [21].

9.7 Survey of Public Attitudes toward and Understanding of Science and Technology

The National Science Foundation (NSF) regularly collects nationally representative data about public attitudes toward and understanding of science and technology (S&T). NSF has changed its means of collecting these data over time. Since 2006, National Center for Science and Engineering Statistics (NCSES), a division of NSF, has funded an S&T module on the biennial General Social Survey (GSS) (http://gss.norc.org/). The GSS is a nationally representative, face-to-face survey covering a broad range of behavior and attitudes. The Survey of Public Attitudes Toward and Understanding of Science and Technology monitored public attitudes towards science and technology, including the public's level of scientific understanding and policy preferences on selected issues. The survey was closely coordinated with surveys in several other countries in order to facilitate international comparisons. Key findings from the 2016 report include:

- About 4 out of 10 Americans say they are very interested in new scientific discoveries, and 6 out of 10 say they are very interested in new medical discoveries.
- Interest in environmental pollution has declined slowly since 1990, when more than 6 in 10 Americans said they were very interested in the topic. Only about 4 in 10 Americans gave this response in 2014.
- Nearly half of Americans cited the Internet as their primary source of science and technology (S&T) information in 2014, compared with about one-tenth of Americans in 2001. Television and newspapers continue to be used less often as sources of science news and information.
- Americans correctly answered an average of 5.8 out of 9 factual knowledge questions in 2014, a score similar to those in recent years but high in terms

of the overall historical trend. Americans with more formal education tend to provide a greater number of correct answers on science knowledge questions.

■ Levels of factual scientific knowledge in the United States are comparable with those in Europe and are generally higher than levels in countries in other parts of the world.

■ Americans perceive far more benefits than harms from science and want governments to fund research. About 7 in 10 Americans say that they believe the benefits from science are greater than the harms, and almost 9 in 10 agree that S&T will create more opportunities for future generations.

■ Americans increasingly worry that science is making life change too fast. About half of Americans expressed this view in 2014, up from about one-third in 2004.

■ About 4 in 10 Americans say we are spending too little to support scientific research. This number has stayed relatively steady for many years, although relatively few Americans (1 in 10) now say we spend too much.

■ Although the medical community remains one of the most respected groups in America, the percentage of Americans who express a great deal of confidence in the medical community has decreased since the 1970s and has tied with its previous low in 2002, with slightly fewer than 4 in 10 expressing high confidence.

■ In 2015, about half of Americans said the environment should be made a priority over economic growth, up from about 3 in 10 in 2011. This level is still, however, below the nearly 6 in 10 who gave this response in 2001.

■ Americans are, on average, less likely to choose the environment over the economy than residents of many other countries. About 3 in 10 Americans say they worry a great deal about the quality of the environment, similar to the historic low in 2014.

■ Slightly more than half of Americans say they worry about climate change, a percentage that is relatively low compared with surveys conducted since 1989. Fewer than 4 in 10 think it will pose a serious threat to their own way of life. Only about 6 in 10 Americans believe there is scientific consensus on the fact that climate change is occurring.

■ About 6 in 10 consumers say they would choose to prioritize conservation over fossil fuel development; the same proportion would focus on alternative energy over fossil fuel development. The vast majority of Americans (about 8 in 10) say they would like to see more emphasis on both fuel efficiency standards for vehicles and renewable energy development.

■ Three in 10 Americans see GE foods as safe to eat, and a similar proportion believes that scientists understand the risks of these foods.

■ Most Americans view using stem cells from human embryos in medical research as morally acceptable.

■ Most Americans think other countries are doing a better job on science, technology, engineering, and mathematics (STEM) education [22].

9.8 Summary

The growing anti-science movement is entangled with an anti-intellectual sentiment among conservatives, which is fueling an anti-education attitude. Many major party candidates for political office during the 2016 election took anti-science positions. This chapter examines how the extremist propaganda in media and social media is being countered. Key points covered include:

■ Through social media propaganda the religious right, fiscal conservatives and corporate interests converged to deny, attack, and defund science in the U.S., which was once considered to be the nation that led the growth of science, medical research, and technological innovation for the world.

■ The anti-science movement is changing the perceptions of people in making career choices and how to pursue higher education if they pursue it at all. Few U.S. students pursue expertise in science, technology, engineering, and mathematics (STEM) fields and there is an inadequate pipeline of teachers skilled in those subjects.

■ STEM careers generally require a higher level of education than most U.S. residents have, with only about 30% of the population having attained a Bachelor's degree or above.

■ Social media has become a battleground of a wide selection of perspectives and one of the hottest areas is the topic of vaccines. There has been an incredible viciousness in many social media posts targeting vaccine havers and pushers on one side and vaccine deniers and protesters on the other side.

■ The CDC frequently reiterates that vaccines protect the health of children in the U.S. so well that most parents today have never seen first-hand the devastating consequences of diseases now stopped by vaccines.

■ Extremist propaganda pours disinformation into social media. In the case of vaccines, it can impact homeland security in the U.S. by negatively impacting the health of the nation.

■ Politicians decry climate change programs and supporting legislation as a threat to the U.S. economy and the American way of life.

■ In the struggle to counter extremist anti-climate science propaganda, nations around the world and cities across the U.S. along with governors, mayors, scientists, and concerned citizens have expressed their support for the Paris Agreement and other efforts to address climate change.

■ Research by means of human fetal tissue obtained from abortions benefits countless people worldwide and also has great promise for the development of lifesaving vaccines and therapies. Since abortion became legal nationwide, fetal tissue research has, time and again, become entangled in the abortion controversy.

■ Even though most of the services Planned Parenthood provides are not abortion-related, propaganda has portrayed Planned Parenthood as an abortion-focused business selling fetus tissue for profit.

- The behavior of Members of Congress during hearings where witnesses are abused, berated, disparaged, intimidated, or otherwise threatened seems to be allowable as long as the majority feels those behaviors are allowable.
- Members of the U.S. Congress have been responsible for a great volume of anti-science, anti-climate change, and anti-fetal tissues research extremist propaganda.

9.9 Course Activities

Course project number one: Schedule a class viewing of *Inherit the Wind*, which is a movie about the Scopes Monkey Trial (1960) (http://www.imdb.com/title/tt0053946/). Before viewing the movie, each student should establish a Twitter account and during the viewing have access to that account so they can post a step-by-step account of the trial as if it were happening in real time. Also, before the viewing, decide upon a hashtag like #scopesmonkeytrial.

Course project number two: Publicize the scheduled viewing through social media and to friends, family, school mates, and so on. Recruit as many people as possible to logon to their Twitter feed and follow the postings about the trial and the responses those postings may generate. Also, encourage followers to retweet the postings.

Course project number three: Launch the experiment by viewing the movie and making postings to Twitter. Get dramatic in the postings.

Course project number four: Follow-up on the postings and retweets to determine how much interest was generated.

References

1. Tennessee State Library and Archives. A Monkey on Tennessee's Back: The Scopes Trial in Dayton. Accessed January 2, 2018 http://sharetngov.tnsosfiles.com/tsla/exhibits/scopes/index.htm.
2. Ahead of March for Science, Udall Urges President Trump to Fill Key Science Posts Throughout Administration, April 21, 2017. Accessed January 2, 2018 https://www.tomudall.senate.gov/news/press-releases/ahead-of-march-for-science-udall-urges-president-trump-to-fill-key-science-posts-throughout-administration.
3. U.S. Department of Education. *Science, Technology, Engineering and Math: Education for Global Leadership*, March 2015. Accessed January 3, 2018 https://www.ed.gov/Stem.
4. U.S. Census Bureau. *Educational Attainment in the United States: 2016.* Accessed January 3, 2018 https://www.census.gov/data/tables/2016/demo/education-attainment/cps-detailed-tables.html.
5. S. Fayer, A. Lacey, and A. Watson. *STEM Occupations: Past, Present, and Future.* U.S. Bureau of Labor Statistics, Division of Information and Marketing Services, January 2017.

Accessed January 3, 2018 https://www.bls.gov/spotlight/2017/science-technology-engineering-and-mathematics-stem-occupations-past-present-and-future/home.htm.

6. CDC statement regarding 2004 pediatrics article, age at first measles-mumps-rubella vaccination in children with autism and school-matched control subjects: A population-based study in metropolitan Atlanta, December 7, 2015. Accessed January 1, 2018 https://www.cdc.gov/vaccinesafety/concerns/autism/cdc2004pediatrics.html.

7. National Center for Complementary and Integrative Health. *Vaccinations/Immunizations for Children.* Accessed January 1, 2018 https://nccih.nih.gov/health/vaccinations.

8. Congressman Ted W. Lieu (Democrat-Los Angeles County). Climate scientist group has one more chance to cut ties to anti-science ExxonMobil, July 13, 2016. Accessed January 1, 2018 https://lieu.house.gov/media-center/in-the-news/climate-scientist-group-has-one-more-chance-cut-ties-anti-science.

9. Cortez Masto denounces Trump's anti-science budget proposal, May 30, 2017. Accessed January 4, 2018 https://www.cortezmasto.senate.gov/news/press-releases/cortez-masto-denounces-trumps-anti-science-budget-proposal.

10. Esty opposes GOP anti-science bill on House floor, March 29, 2017. Accessed January 4, 2018 https://esty.house.gov/media-center/press-releases/esty-opposes-gop-anti-science-bill-house-floor.

11. U.S. DOE. Secretary of Energy Rick Perry announces $36 million for projects to advance carbon capture technologies, September 22, 2017. Accessed January 4, 2018 https://www.energy.gov/articles/secretary-energy-rick-perry-announces-36-million-projects-advance-carbon-capture.

12. Congressman Blumenauer educates Rick Perry on climate science, June 19, 2017. Accessed January 4, 2018 https://blumenauer.house.gov/media-center/press-releases/congressman-blumenauer-educates-rick-perry-climate-science.

13. EPA. This page is being updated. Accessed January 4, 2018 https://www.epa.gov/sites/production/files/signpost/cc.html.

14. Human fetal tissue research: Context and controversy. Majority staff report prepared for the use of the Committee on the Judiciary United States Senate One Hundred Fourteenth Congress second session, December 2016. Accessed January 5, 2018 https://www.judiciary.senate.gov/imo/media/doc/2016-12-13%20MAJORITY%20REPORT%20-%20Human%20Fetal%20Tissue%20Research%20-%20Context%20and%20Controversy.pdf.

15. Congresswoman Jan Schakowsky, U.S. House of Representatives. *The Facts About Fetal Tissue Research.* Accessed January 6, 2018 https://schakowsky.house.gov/uploads/The%20Facts%20about%20Fetal%20Tissue%20Research.pdf.

16. House investigation into planned parenthood. Accessed January 6, 2018 https://www.gop.gov/solution_content/plannedparenthood.

17. The facts versus fiction Planned Parenthood. *The House Committee on Oversight and Government Reform.* Accessed January 6, 2018 https://democrats-oversight.house.gov/planned-parenthood-fact-v-fiction.

18. Enforcement of Ethical Standards in Congress. Accessed January 6, 2018 http://archives-democrats-rules.house.gov/Archives/jcoc2ac.htm.

19. Code of Official Conduct. *Rules of the House of Representatives—114th Congress.* Accessed January 6, 2018 https://ethics.house.gov/publication/code-official-conduct.

20. National Institutes of Health Ethics Program. *Principles of Ethical Conduct for Government Officers and Employees.* Accessed January 7, 2018 https://ethics.od.nih.gov/principl.htm.
21. The Office of Special Counsel. *The Hatch Act: Frequently Asked Questions on Federal Employees and the Use of Social Media and Email.* Accessed January 8, 2018 https://osc.gov/Pages/The-Hatch-Act-Frequently-Asked-Questions-on-Federal-Employees-and-the-Use-of-Social-Media-and-Email.aspx.
22. National Science Board. 2016. *Science and Engineering Indicators 2016.* Arlington, VA: National Science Foundation (NSB-2016-1). Accessed January 15, 2018 https://www.nsf.gov/statistics/2016/nsb20161/#/report/overview.

Chapter 10

Observations on the Distribution of Extremist Propaganda

10.1 The Whirlpool of Extremist Propaganda

Extremist propaganda in the U.S. has its origins with Russian trolls and election meddlers, home-grown white supremacists, opposing political parties and many other places where it should not be, including with high-level elected officials and appointees in the U.S. Congress and even in the White House. It is also grown and disseminated from State Houses, places of worship, businesses, schools, and the very homes and families where people live. Some of this propaganda is targeted with limited distribution, but most of it is thrown into a cosmic whirlpool of information that is becoming increasingly populated with propaganda. Specific pieces of extremist propaganda may have been created with targets in mind, but generally propaganda has to go through a presort process before it eventually reaches its potential malleable target. Table 10.1 shows the various types of extremist propaganda creators.

Extremist propaganda, even when distributed through specific channels, will usually end up in a massive whirlpool of information with other propaganda and mixed with validated and reliable information. The propaganda will flow into non-exclusive streams, some created by media organizations seeking specific types of material, some through individual or group news feeds, some into the systems of

Table 10.1   Creators of Extremist Propaganda

Governments	Coalitions of terrorist supporting countries
	Individual terrorist supporting states
	Intelligence/counterintelligence agencies
	Military Intelligence/counterintelligence units
Business and commerce	Industry groups and consortiums
	Individual corporations
Ideological groups	Religions, sects, and sacred orders
	Special focus and interest groups
Hybrids	Aligned entities of different organization types
Insurgents	Insurgent groups
	Alliances of insurgent groups
	Rogue lone wolves

extremist propaganda redistributors, and some into the hands of legitimate analysts working to neutralize or counter extremists' propaganda. Thus, many organizations and individuals may be utilizing the same propaganda for different purposes. Table 10.2 shows an extremist propaganda sorting process and the goals that can be accomplished with different target audiences with the propaganda.

Even though extremist propaganda is consumed for different purposes by the various target audiences shown in Table 10.2, the propaganda is more effective when individuals are exposed to a blend of channels or feeds that are repeating the same propaganda. This repeated messaging through different channels can be effective in convincing individuals or groups exposed to the message that it is valid and legitimate. The channels blend the propaganda by cross-publishing each other's content through social media sharing and then back through reporting on who said what through their social media posts. A thread that may start as a single propaganda item can grow into a chain of items that increase the impact and value of one original piece of propaganda.

This process was readily apparent during the 2016 U.S. elections. Propaganda was disseminated by a political party or candidate by way of a speech or interview. That propaganda followed a consistent path through conservative TV news, publications, or websites. As it passed through redistributors, it was often enhanced with additional extremist propaganda or paired with already circulating propaganda. As new related propaganda became available, often from commentaries by political

Table 10.2   The Extremist Propaganda Sorting Process

Target audience	Propaganda goals		
Media outlets	Misinformation	Recruiting and indoctrination	Nullifying opposing perspectives and alternative messaging
Commentators			
Bloggers			
Aligned organizations	Influencing	Persuasion of fringe members	
Tribal leaders	Reinforcing		
Tribal members	Relationship building		
Fringe members			

candidates or high-profile supporters, the pieces of propaganda were combined into a story or a segment. Thus, starting with one piece of propaganda without any semblance of truth or fact, the bliss of U.S. voters was reinforced and perpetuated with little cost to the propagandist.

10.2   Extremist Propaganda Gets Funneled

Once a propaganda topic gets populated with items in various channels or outlets, the content items will get funneled into more specialized streams. Social media feeds set up by organizations, groups or individuals facilitate the funneling process. In addition, news feed items that social media applications populate feeds with based on the preferences and consumption patterns of specific social media accounts can create a rather narrowly scoped news feed. This helps maintain the blissfulness that an individual seeks by creating the custom news feed and blocking out opposing viewpoints.

A social media user's connections and contacts grow over time and personal networks of friends or followers most often attract like-minded individuals or observers that monitor various trends or activities. This of course facilitates the further spread and funneling of propaganda items. On Twitter, for example, a topic search or hashtag search will bring up a list, often a long list, of tweets and retweets containing the search words. It is easy then to follow the path of the retweets and determine the network relationships of the accounts spreading and funneling the propaganda. Realize, of course, that the spreaders of the extremist propaganda may not recognize that the content they are proliferating is propaganda; it is also unlikely they will ever question the validity of the content. That is how a blisstopian society works and why it works so well.

The distribution and funneling of extremist propaganda that occurs through this process helps build tribalism and group cohesion among the fans and followers. It also helps set the stage for group think where there is little if any room for insurgency. As this grows, tribal members do not even consider dissent because of the social cohesion of the tribe or group and the desire of the individual to hold membership. To gain status and recognition, the individual member will blissfully join in the distribution and funneling process. They may also discover new relevant items to redistribute to tribal or group members. Think of this as a merit badge-earning process.

The First Amendment in the U.S. protects free expression, but it also allows various groups that are a threat or a potential threat to homeland security to freely disseminate their extremist propaganda. There are many institutions and groups in the U.S. that contribute to unity, strength, stability, sustainability, and security. There are also many institutions and groups that oppose unity, weaken the nation, jeopardize stability and sustainability, and ultimately can and will compromise security. The following sections elaborate on circumstances that contribute to the later.

10.3 The Power of Rallies and Mass Events

Extremist propaganda is most effective in a context where recipients are malleable and easily manipulated. Political and ideological rallies are the ideal setting to leverage the power of existing extremist propaganda and to generate yet more propaganda to feed the process of dissemination and consumption of propaganda. Rallies also stimulate tribal tendencies, sending participants away in an excited and agitated state of mind and, through their natural response to peer pressure, they continue to spread the extremist propaganda to which they were exposed.

In 2017, there were numerous times when right wing extremist groups attempted to hold rallies on university campuses to leverage election results and tribal tendencies to spread their philosophies and make a call for action. Several of these attempts created situations where security and law and order became major issues. There were many demonstrations accompanied by isolated violence. There were also several planned rallies that were not given permits and a few that just did not draw an incredible amount of interest.

In August 2017, the loudest white supremacist rally of the year, the Unite the Right Rally, was a gathering of white nationalists and neo-Nazis, in Charlottesville, Virginia—it resulted in violence, death, and national embarrassment. On Friday night in Charlottesville, white supremacists with Tiki torches, rifles, and Confederate and swastika flags marched through the University of Virginia campus ahead of a Unite the Right rally on Saturday. Peaceful demonstrators gathered to protest this hate, but violence erupted. On Saturday, white supremacists and counter-protesters again gathered and a similar scene unfolded when, in an act of terrorism, a driver sped up and plowed his car into the crowd, killing one counter-protester and injuring nineteen people. Two police officers monitoring the events in Charlottesville also died when their helicopter crashed.

U.S. Senator Chris Murphy (Democrat-Connecticut) released a statement that read in part "What has happened in Charlottesville over the last 24 hours should be a call to action for every American who has grown complacent under the assumption that our nation's moral arc naturally bends toward inclusion and tolerance, Racism, anti-Semitism and homophobia are tragically alive and well in America today. And make no mistake—these insidious psychologies have been given license to be brought out in the open air by a president that openly seized upon these hatreds during his campaign and continues to traffic in divisive rhetoric and hateful policies in the White House" [1].

In the aftermath of the white supremacist Unite the Right rally and the domestic terrorist attack in Charlottesville, Virginia, Congresswoman Pramila Jayapal joined other members of Congress in introducing a resolution urging President Trump to strongly condemn white nationalists, the Ku Klux Klan, neo-Nazis and other hate groups responsible for the violence, and to remove from the White House and the Trump administration individuals, including Steve Bannon, Stephen Miller, and Sebastian Gorka, who support white supremacists. The cosponsors of the resolution are shown in Table 10.3 [2].

The other results of the white supremacist Unite the Right rally was a massive number of extremist propaganda social media posts with the hashtags #Charlottesville or #UniteTheRight. The white nationalist movement said it was feeling oppressed and discriminated against. Tweets stating that the mainstream media narrative was totally false and President Trump was blamed for stating that there was a group on one side that was bad, and you had a group on the other side that was also very violent. The white nationalist mantra of YOU WILL NOT REPLACE US became a rallying call for the white nationalists. This is far from over; the extremist propaganda will continue but it would be nice if it did not come from the White House.

Table 10.3   U.S. House of Representative Resolution Sponsors Condemning Fear-Mongering, Racism, Anti-Semitism, Bigotry, and Violence Perpetrated by Hate Groups

Representative's Name	State/District
Frank Pallone	NJ-06
Alcee Hastings	FL-20
Jerrold Nadler	NY-10
Nydia Velazquez	NY-07
Sheila Jackson Lee	TX-18
Earl Blumenauer	OR-03
Adam Smith	WA-09
Barbara Lee	CA-13
Grace Napolitano	CA-32
Raul Grijalva	AZ-03
Steve Cohen	TN-09
Hank Johnson	GA-04
Andre Carson	IN-07
Chellie Pingree	ME-01
Judy Chu	CA-27
Bill Foster	IL-11
Donald Payne Jr.	NJ-10
Carol Shea-Porter	NH-11
John Delaney	MD-06
Jared Huffman	CA-02
Mark Pocan	WI-02
Juan Vargas	CA-51
Don Beyer	VA-08
Brendan Boyle	PA-13
Mark DeSaulnier	CA-11
Debbie Dingell	MI-12
Seth Moulton	MA-06
Dwight Evans	PA-02
Ro Khanna	CA-17
Raja Krishnamoorthi	IL-08
Al Lawson	FL-05

10.4 Homeschooling Can Funnel Extremist Propaganda

Approximately one million elementary and secondary students are home schooled in the U.S. every year, of which 80% are white. These numbers vary from year to year but have been relatively constant for over a decade. In a 2003 survey, 31% of homeschoolers had parents who said the most important reason for homeschooling was concern about the environment of other schools. Thirty percent said the most important reason was to provide religious or moral instruction. The next reason was given about half as often; 16% of homeschooled students had parents who said dissatisfaction with the academic instruction available at other schools was their most important reason for homeschooling [3].

There are potential consequences from the motivations for homeschooling, especially when so many parents are concerned about school environment and want their children to have a religious and moral education. A U.S. Census Bureau study of self-described religious identification of the U.S. adult population showed that, in 1990, 86% identified themselves as Christian. In 2001, 76.7% identified themselves as Christian and, in 2008, 76% identified themselves as Christian. What this all comes down to is that parents want their children to have Christian beliefs and morals [4]. On the surface this sounds fine.

Since the terrorist attacks of September 11, 2001, and subsequent incidents where radicalized individuals have perpetrated attacks on civilians, there has been a growing *Islamophobia* in the U.S., accompanied by a spreading *xenophobia* and anti-immigrant sentiment. There is also a considerable Christian backlash against marriage equality and LGBTQ rights.

A major theme during the 2016 elections was that the Christian conservatives expressed anger and frustration about their faith not dominating thoughts and morals in the U.S. Candidate Trump managed to play out a large volume of extremist propaganda against minorities, especially Muslims, to sway the vote of the conservative Christians toward his presidency. That propaganda was a motivating factor during the election and remains so as the Christian conservatives have introduced legislation at the state level and lobbied for Congress to enable them to discriminate against those that are not white Christian conservatives. Christian conservative leaders are still spewing extremist propaganda against marriage equality and LGBTQ rights and many are opposed to Muslim immigration.

Homeschooling families in a Christian conservative culture probably view pro-LGBTQ and pro-inclusion material as extremist propaganda aimed at destroying their belief system, culture, and way of life. That concept can be applied to people that have opposing beliefs and what they view as extremism. The challenge becomes trying to overcome the propaganda funneling process to assure that students are exposed to more than a single perspective about life in a mass society. Public schools are always on the line and under scrutiny to not perpetuate racism, bigotry, exclusion, and bullying. Home schools and for that matter private schools of any persuasion are largely free from such pressure. Unfortunately, this lack of scrutiny can allow for the flow of extremist propaganda into the educational process and can result in the perpetuation of hate, bigotry and discrimination. That is a threat to homeland security, which is designed to protect all citizens, not just those who feel that manifest destiny has made them privileged, superior, or dominant.

10.5 Charter and Private Schools and the Perpetuation of Propaganda

The *charter school movement* is still in the early stages and there is not enough longitudinal research on the schools to determine if students will have greater success or even be more susceptible to extremist propaganda influence than in a mainstream public school. Charter schools are public schools operating under a charter, essentially a contract entered into between the school and its authorizing agency. In addition to allowing the school to open, the charter allows the school significant operational autonomy to pursue specific educational objectives. The autonomy granted under the charter agreement allows the school considerable decision-making authority over key matters of curriculum, personnel, and budget. Charter schools are often not a part of states' current districts and, therefore, have few if any zoning limitations. Therefore, students attend charter schools by the choice of their parents or guardians rather than by assignment to a school district.

Due to their lack of zoning, charter schools are usually funded in a manner that is distinct from how traditional schools are funded. However, nearly all charter schools receive public dollars. As public schools, charter schools are prohibited from charging tuition. If applications to attend a charter school exceed spaces available, enrollment is decided by lottery. In exchange for this autonomy, the charter school is subject to periodic performance review and may be closed for failing to meet agreed-upon outcomes. Charter schools are not exempt from federal laws that cover equal rights, access and discrimination.

The charter school movement has roots in a number of other education reform ideas, from alternative schools to site-based management, magnet schools, public school choice, privatization, and community-parental empowerment. Some of them were schools of choice. The idea was further refined in Minnesota where charter schools were developed according to three basic values: opportunity, choice, and responsibility for results. This was occurring at a time when greater accountability in education, oversight of public funds, and high-quality training for educators were priorities. Charter schools were seen as a way to meet these many goals.

Since the first Charter School Program grants in 1994, the federal government via the U.S. Department of Education has spent nearly $4 billion in support of charter schools. These funds have mostly been dispersed to state education agencies that then pass along the funds to charter schools for various expenses.

Startup expenses in particular are offset by these funds. The fiscal year 2016 budget included $333 million earmarked for charter schools. Additionally, congressional attempts to rewrite No Child Left Behind have also increased the amount of funding to charter schools. Having had consistent presidential backing since the Clinton administration to the present day, charter schools seem likely to continue their rapid expansion.

There is a wide array of charter school types. Charter schools may be specialized, either as to their programmatic focus (such as a STEM academy) or students served (prior drop-outs), though many simply serve mainstream populations with a distinct academic approach. There are charter schools in all sorts of settings—rural, urban, and suburban—and even online charter schools providing distance-learning opportunities. Some charter schools operate as neighborhood schools, having turned-around or converted traditional district schools. Charter-district collaboration, which usually takes the form of a charter school within a traditional school in the same building, has become more prevalent. These collaborations create a relationship by which charter schools and traditional school districts can learn from each other.

Charter schools continue to face limited access to resources and opportunities. Charter schools must secure funds to cover startup and other costs not faced by traditional schools. Acquiring a facility is a particular challenge. Charter schools typically rely on philanthropic, state, and federal grant programs to assist with these costs. However, these funding streams may be inadequate and unreliable for school needs. The sector also experiences narrow pipelines of human capital and talent. This includes qualified teachers, school leadership, executive leadership, and board members.

As one of the widest reaching school reform initiatives, charter schools have been the source of much debate. The primary question is whether charter schools are working or not, focusing on charter school impact on student achievement. The other topics of debate stem from the central tenet of charter schools, namely autonomy and the decentralization of accountability [5]. The very same autonomy and decentralization of accountability that charters enjoy can also make them more attractive targets of propagandists. It may also make it easier for staff and students to disseminate extremist propaganda and encourage extremist thought.

The same can be said for private elementary and secondary schools of all types. Private schools have been in operation since well before there were any public schools in the U.S.

Since 1989, the U.S. Bureau of the Census has conducted the biennial Private School Universe Survey (PSS) for the National Center for Education Statistics (NCES). PSS is designed to generate biennial data on the total number of private schools, students, and teachers, and to build a universe of private schools to serve as a sampling frame of private schools for NCES sample surveys. The target population for the PSS is all schools in the 50 states and the District of Columbia that are not supported primarily by public funds, provide classroom instruction for one or more of grades kindergarten through 12 (or comparable ungraded levels), and have one or more teachers. Organizations or institutions that provide support for homeschooling, but do not provide classroom instruction, are not included. Recent data shows that:

- In the fall of 2015, there were 34,576 private elementary and secondary schools with 4,903,596 students and 481,558 full-time equivalent (FTE) teachers in the United States.
- Sixty-seven percent of private schools, enrolling 78% of private school students and employing 70% of private school FTE teachers in 2015–2016, had a religious orientation or purpose.
- Sixty-eight percent of private schools in 2015–2016 emphasized a regular elementary/secondary program, 10% emphasized a Montessori program, 3% emphasized a special program, 5% emphasized a special education program, 3% emphasized an alternative program, and 10% emphasized an early childhood program.
- In 2015–2016, there were more private schools in suburban locations (12,662), followed by those in cities (11,476), followed by those in rural areas (7,539), and then by those in towns (2,900).
- More private school students in 2015–2016 were enrolled in schools located in cities (2,140,625), followed by those enrolled in suburban schools (1,903,824), followed by those in rural areas (557,148), and then by those in towns (301,999).
- More private school students in 2015–2016 were enrolled in kindergarten (466,475) than in any other grade level.
- The average school size in 2015–2016 was 142 students across all private schools. Private school size differed by instructional level. On average, elementary schools had 100 students, secondary schools had 263 students, and combined schools had 199 students. Forty-six percent of all private schools in 2015–2016 enrolled fewer than 50 students.
- Sixty-nine percent of private school students in 2015–2016 were White non-Hispanic; 10% were Hispanic or Latino, regardless of race; 9% were Black or African-American non-Hispanic; 6% were Asian non-Hispanic; 4% were of Two or more races non-Hispanic, and less than 1% was American Indian or Alaska Native non-Hispanic, or Native Hawaiian or other Pacific Islander non-Hispanic.
- Ninety-six percent of all private schools in 2015–2016 were coeducational, while 2% enrolled all girls and 2% enrolled all boys.
- Seventy-eight percent of private school teachers in 2015–2016 were full-time teachers; 5% taught less than full time, but at least three-quarter time; 9% taught less than three-quarter time, but at least one-half time; 5% taught less than one-half time, but at least one-quarter time; and 3% taught less than one-quarter time.

- The average pupil/teacher ratio in 2015–2016 was 10.2 across all private schools. Private school pupil/teacher ratios differed by instructional level. On average, the pupil/teacher ratio was 11.1 in secondary schools, 10.8 in elementary schools, and 9.3 in combined schools.
- Ninety-seven percent of 12th-graders enrolled in private schools around October 1, 2014 graduated in 2014–2015.
- Of the 343,252 private high school graduates in 2014–2015, some 65% attended 4-year colleges by the fall of 2015.
- In 2015–2016, there were 11,341 private schools that did not report membership in any private school association.
- In 2015–2016, there were 200,000 or more students enrolled in private schools in each of California, Florida, Illinois, New York, Pennsylvania, and Texas [6].

With a large percentage of private schools having a religious orientation, there is certainly room for concern that the private school environment could originate and perpetuate extremist propaganda targeting science, abortion rights, LGBTQ rights, immigration and other areas where religious conservatives have opposing extremist views.

10.6 Extremist Propaganda in Closed Societies

There are thousands of private social clubs in the U.S. that are not representative of open societies. There have been and still are many secret societies and hate groups, many of which are not registered in any manner with any government and there are thousands of private organizations that may be exempt under Internal Revenue Code section 501(c)(7), if they meet the requirements for exemption, including:

- College social/academic fraternities and sororities
- Country clubs
- Amateur hunting, fishing, tennis, swimming and other sport clubs
- Dinner clubs that provide a meeting place, library, and dining room for members
- Variety clubs
- Hobby clubs
- Homeowners or community associations whose primary function is to own and maintain recreational areas and facilities [7]

To be exempt under Internal Revenue Code (IRC) section 501(c)(8), a fraternal beneficiary society, order, or association must meet the following requirements:

- It must have a fraternal purpose. An organization has a fraternal purpose if membership is based on a common tie or the pursuit of a common object. The organization must also have a substantial program of fraternal activities.

- It must operate under the lodge system or for the exclusive benefit of the members of a fraternal organization itself operating under the lodge system. Operating under the lodge system requires, at a minimum, two active entities: (1) a parent organization and (2) a subordinate (called a lodge, branch, or the like) chartered by the parent and largely self-governing.
- It must provide for the payment of life, sick, accident or other benefits to the members of such society, order, or association or their dependents.
- An organization that provides benefits to some, but not all, of its members may qualify for exemption so long as most of the members are eligible for benefits, and criteria for excluding certain members are reasonable.

To be exempt under IRC 501(c)(10), a domestic fraternal society, order, or association must meet the following requirements:

- It must have a fraternal purpose. An organization has a fraternal purpose if membership is based on a common tie or the pursuit of a common object. The organization must also have a substantial program of fraternal activities.
- It must operate under the lodge system. Operating under the lodge system requires, at a minimum, two active entities: (1) a parent organization and (2) a subordinate organization (called a lodge, branch, or the like) chartered by the parent and largely self-governing.
- It must not provide for the payment of life, sick, accident or other benefits to its members. The organization may arrange with insurance companies to provide optional insurance to its members without jeopardizing its exempt status.
- It must devote its net earnings exclusively to religious, charitable, scientific, literary, educational, and fraternal purposes.
- It must be a domestic organization, that is, it must be organized in the U.S. [7].

The universal dynamic within these organizations is the opportunity for member contact and networking as well as having a substantial program of fraternal activities. Requirements for membership vary as does the ability of an individual to maintain membership. This creates opportunities for the creation or redistribution of extremist propaganda. Fraternal societies must devote their net earnings exclusively to religious, charitable, scientific, literary, educational, and fraternal purposes, but there are not many restrictions on the content of any material created to meet those goals. In addition, the closed nature of these organizations contributes to the perpetuation of monoculturalism, which sets the stage for xenophobia and reduces the possibility of cross-cultural relationship building.

10.7 Mental Health Conditions and Extremist Propaganda

The term *mental illness* refers collectively to all diagnosable mental disorders. Effects of the illness include sustained abnormal alterations in thinking, mood, or behavior associated with distress and impaired functioning. The effects of mental illnesses include disruptions of daily function; incapacitating personal, social, and occupational impairment; and premature death. The most common mental illnesses in adults are anxiety and mood disorders.

Mental health is a global issue that impacts the quality of life and the behavior of people as well as their ability to deal with daily life. It is also a threat to homeland security on a national level as well as to law enforcement personnel who must deal with often violent and radicalized people that are suffering from mental health conditions. A 2007 CDCP study showed that approximately 40% of persons in 35 states in the U.S. had serious psychological distress (SPD) during the last 30 days prior to their being interviewed or surveyed. Of those respondents indicating they had SPD, 37.7% received mental health services in the preceding year while 53.4% were currently not receiving treatment. Medically, respondents with SPD were more likely to be obese, to smoke, and to report being diagnosed with heart disease.

Historically, the economic burden of mental illness in the U.S. has been very substantial, costing about $300 billion per year, and about 25% of U.S. adults have had a mental illness. Data for 2004–2008 Health-Related Quality of Life (HRQOL), based on a period of in the past 30 days, showed that U.S. adults experienced an average of 3.4 mentally unhealthy days. An estimated 10.2% of U.S. adults experienced 14 or more mentally unhealthy days indicating Frequent Mental Distress (FMD). The Appalachian and the Mississippi Valley regions have high and increasing FMD prevalence, and the upper Midwest had low and decreasing FMD prevalence [8].

Many mental illnesses affect both men and women, but men may be less likely to talk about their feelings and seek help. Recognizing the signs that someone may have a mood or mental disorder is the first step toward getting treatment and living a better life. Warning signs of mental illness include:

- Anger, irritability or aggressiveness
- Noticeable changes in mood, energy level, or appetite
- Difficulty sleeping or sleeping too much
- Difficulty concentrating, feeling restless, or on edge
- Increased worry or feeling stressed
- A need for alcohol or drugs
- Sadness or hopelessness
- Suicidal thoughts
- Feeling flat or having trouble feeling positive emotions

- Engaging in high-risk activities
- Ongoing headaches, digestive issues, or pain
- Obsessive thinking or compulsive behavior
- Thoughts or behaviors that interfere with work, family, or social life
- Unusual thinking or behaviors that concern other people [9]

Anxiety disorders involve more than temporary worry or fear. For a person with an anxiety disorder, the anxiety does not go away and can get worse over time. The feelings can interfere with daily activities such as job performance, school work, and relationships. People with generalized anxiety disorder display excessive anxiety or worry for months and face several anxiety-related symptoms. There are several different types of anxiety disorders. Examples include generalized anxiety disorder, panic disorder, and social anxiety disorder.

People with panic disorder have recurrent unexpected panic attacks, which are sudden periods of intense fear that may include palpitations, pounding heart, or accelerated heart rate; sweating; trembling or shaking; sensations of shortness of breath, smothering, or choking; and feeling of impending doom. People with social anxiety disorder, sometimes called social phobia, have a marked fear of social or performance situations in which they expect to feel embarrassed, judged, rejected, or fearful of offending others [10].

Borderline personality disorder is a mental illness marked by an ongoing pattern of varying moods, self-image, and behavior. These symptoms often result in impulsive actions and problems in relationships. People with borderline personality disorder may experience intense episodes of anger, depression, and anxiety that can last from a few hours to days. People with borderline personality disorder may experience mood swings and display uncertainty about how they see themselves and their role in the world. As a result, their interests and values can change quickly.

People with borderline personality disorder also tend to view things in extremes, such as all good or all bad. Their opinions of other people can also change quickly. An individual who is seen as a friend one day may be considered an enemy or traitor the next. These shifting feelings can lead to intense and unstable relationships [11].

Schizophrenia is a chronic and severe mental disorder that affects how a person thinks, feels, and behaves. People with schizophrenia may seem like they have lost touch with reality. Although schizophrenia is not as common as other mental disorders, the symptoms can be very disabling. Symptoms of schizophrenia usually start between ages 16 and 30. In rare cases, children have schizophrenia too. The symptoms of schizophrenia fall into three categories: positive, negative, and cognitive.

Positive symptoms are psychotic behaviors not generally seen in healthy people. People with positive symptoms may lose touch with some aspects of reality. Symptoms include:

- Hallucinations
- Delusions

- Thought disorders (unusual or dysfunctional ways of thinking)
- Movement disorders (agitated body movements)

Negative symptoms are associated with disruptions to normal emotions and behaviors. Symptoms include:

- Flat affect (reduced expression of emotions via facial expression or voice tone)
- Reduced feelings of pleasure in everyday life
- Difficulty beginning and sustaining activities
- Reduced speaking

The cognitive symptoms of schizophrenia are subtle, but for others, they are more severe and patients may notice changes in their memory or other aspects of thinking. Symptoms include:

- Poor executive functioning (the ability to understand information and use it to make decisions)
- Trouble focusing or paying attention
- Problems with working memory (the ability to use information immediately after learning it)

There are several factors that contribute to the risk of developing schizophrenia. Scientists have long known that schizophrenia sometimes runs in families. However, there are many people who have schizophrenia who do not have a family member with the disorder and conversely, many people with one or more family members with the disorder who do not develop it themselves.

Scientists believe that many different genes may increase the risk of schizophrenia, but that no single gene causes the disorder by itself. It is not yet possible to use genetic information to predict who will develop schizophrenia. Scientists also think that an imbalance in the complex, interrelated chemical reactions of the brain involving the neurotransmitters (substances that brain cells use to communicate with each other) dopamine and glutamate, and possibly others, plays a role in schizophrenia. Some experts also think problems during brain development before birth may lead to faulty connections. The brain also undergoes major changes during puberty, and these changes could trigger psychotic symptoms in people who are vulnerable due to genetics or brain differences [12].

Other disorders include Attention Deficit Hyperactivity Disorder (ADHD, ADD), Autism Spectrum Disorders (ASD), Bipolar Disorder (Manic-Depressive Illness), Borderline Personality Disorder, Depression, Disruptive Mood Dysregulation Disorder, Eating Disorders, Obsessive-Compulsive Disorder (OCD), Post-Traumatic Stress Disorder (PTSD), and Seasonal Affective Disorder.

People with mental health disorders are more likely than people without mental health disorders to experience an alcohol or substance use disorder. Approximately

7.9 million adults in the U.S. had co-occurring disorders in 2014. Co-occurring disorders can be difficult to diagnose due to the complexity of symptoms, as both may vary in severity. In many cases, people receive treatment for one disorder while the other disorder remains untreated. This may occur because both mental and substance use disorders can have biological, psychological, and social components. Other reasons may be inadequate provider training or screening, an overlap of symptoms, or that other health issues need to be addressed first. In any case, the consequences of undiagnosed, untreated, or undertreated co-occurring disorders can lead to a higher likelihood of experiencing homelessness, incarceration, medical illnesses, suicide, or even early death.

People with co-occurring disorders are best served through integrated treatment. With integrated treatment, practitioners can address mental and substance use disorders at the same time, often lowering costs and creating better outcomes. Increasing awareness and building capacity in service systems are important in helping identify and treat co-occurring disorders. Early detection and treatment can improve treatment outcomes and the quality of life for those who need these services [13].

10.8 Summary

The world is a whirlpool of propaganda emanating from numerous media sources and is spread and validated by interactions between individuals and groups. It should also be recognized that people with diminished mental capacity and those that are in closed social environments may be more readily influenced by extremist propaganda. This chapter examines the circumstances that can make the distribution and reception of extremist propaganda effective. Key points covered include:

- Extremist propaganda in the U.S. has its origins with many sources, ranging from Russian trolls to members of the U.S. Congress.
- Many organizations and individuals may be utilizing the same propaganda for different purposes.
- The distribution and funneling of extremist propaganda help build tribalism and group cohesion among the fans and followers and can set the stage for group think, where there is little if any room for insurgency.
- One potential consequence of homeschooling when parents want religious and moral education is the children are a captive audience for the parents' choice of extremist propaganda.
- Charter and Private Schools are closed environments where the schools can determine the extremist propaganda to which students are exposed.
- Mental illness diminishes the mental capacity of individuals, which can make them more impressionable to the work of propagandists.

10.9 Course Activities

Course project number one: Identify a piece or related pieces of propaganda and the source of the propaganda and trace the distribution of that propaganda through social media and create a record of how it flowed and who redistributed it. Compare the results of the search with other members of the class.

Course project number two: Identify five private schools and analyze the propaganda content of their social media. Compare the results of the search with other members of the class.

Course project number three: Read and discuss Brave New World by Aldous Huxley and Fahrenheit 451 by Ray Bradbury.

References

1. Murphy statement on neo-Nazi rally in Charlottesville, August 12, 2017. Accessed January 10, 2018 https://www.murphy.senate.gov/newsroom/press-releases/murphy-statement-on-neo-nazi-rally-in-charlottesville/.
2. Congresswoman Pramila Jayapal. In response to racist terrorism in Charlottesville, Jayapal introduces resolution demanding President Trump fire white supremacists from the White House, August 15, 2017. Accessed January 10, 2018 https://jayapal.house.gov/media/press-releases/response-racist-terrorism-charlottesville-jayapal-introduces-resolution.
3. National Center for Education Statistics. 1.1 million homeschooled students in the United States in 2003. Accessed January 11, 2018 https://nces.ed.gov/nhes/homeschool/.
4. U.S. Census Bureau. *Self-described Religious Identification of Adult Population: 1990, 2001 and 2008.* Accessed January 11, 2018 http://www2.census.gov/library/publications/2011/compendia/statab/131ed/tables/12s0075.xls.
5. U.S. Department of Education. *What is a Charter School?* Accessed January 12, 2018 https://charterschoolcenter.ed.gov/.
6. U.S. Department of Education. *Characteristics of Private Schools in the United States: Results from the 2015–2016 Private School Universe Survey,* August 2017. Accessed January 12, 2018 https://nces.ed.gov/pubs2017/2017073.pdf.
7. U.S. IRS. *Examples of Tax-Exempt Social & Recreational Clubs.* Accessed January 12, 2018 https://www.irs.gov/charities-non-profits/other-non-profits/examples-of-tax-exempt-social-and-recreational-clubs.
8. CDCP. *Non-Specific Psychological Distress.* Accessed January 13, 2018 https://www.cdc.gov/mentalhealth/data_stats/nspd.htm.
9. CDCP. *Men and Mental Health Overview.* Accessed January 13, 2018 https://www.nimh.nih.gov/health/topics/men-and-mental-health/index.shtml.
10. CDCP. *Anxiety Disorders Overview.* Accessed January 13, 2018 https://www.nimh.nih.gov/health/topics/anxiety-disorders/index.shtml.
11. CDCP. *Borderline Personality Disorder Overview.* Accessed January 13, 2018 https://www.nimh.nih.gov/health/topics/borderline-personality-disorder/index.shtml.

12. CDCP. *Schizophrenia Overview*. Accessed January 13, 2018 https://www.nimh.nih.gov/health/topics/schizophrenia/index.shtml.
13. Substance Abuse and Mental Health Services Administration (SAMHSA). Co-occurring Disorders. Accessed January 13, 2018 https://www.samhsa.gov/disorders/co-occurring.

Chapter 11

Ten Reasons Why Propaganda Works

11.1 The Ten Reasons Propaganda Works So Well

The success of extremist propaganda in the twenty-first century is a subject that is coming under more detailed study and, as a result of the 2016 U.S. elections being extremist propaganda intensive, it will likely gain more attention over the next few decades. There is room for numerous disciplines to conduct research. Psychology, Social Psychology, Political Science, Sociology, Communications Studies, Advertising and Marketing, Law Enforcement, and Homeland Security all have a lot to explore.

The ten reasons propaganda works so well covered in this chapter were selected because a pattern emerged out of the interviews and observations. This in no way is meant to dismiss or disparage the existing research of the academic disciplines or the theories those disciplines will be testing in the future. The commentary on the ten reasons propaganda works so well is meant to provide those concerned about homeland security with alternative perspectives that will allow them to gain more insight into propaganda and why people so readily believe propaganda. Table 11.1 shows the 10 reasons covered in this chapter.

It is worthy of note that the U.S. government has engaged in numerous propaganda campaigns to win support for its activities at home and to counter threats abroad. These campaigns range from *white propaganda* or more overt factually based messages of clear authorship to *black propaganda* or covert unattributed messages of varying degrees of truthfulness. The U.S. National Archives has the most substantial collection of propaganda materials in the U.S. including films, audio recordings, leaflets, stickers, toys, posters, and magazines. This exhibit explores a

Table 11.1 Ten Reasons Why Propaganda Works

Blissfulness: Propaganda provides people a feeling of blissfulness and contentment

Easy to understand: Well-crafted propaganda is easy for people to understand and does not challenge their beliefs

Laziness: People are lazy and do not spend time analyzing or researching the validity of what they hear

Repetition: Propaganda is now spread through multiple channels over and over

Familiarity: People become familiar with and are comfortable with the message

Consistency: Well targeted propaganda is consistent with other beliefs people have

Lack of Knowledge: People do not have knowledge of a subject and accept easy explanations

Confusion: People confuse their beliefs for knowledge

Group expectations: People conform with the expectations as to what they believe

Peer pressure: People submit to pressure from others they are close to as to what they believe

fascinating array of materials that illuminate the image the U.S. has sought to impress upon itself and the world, as well as the tactics it has used in that pursuit.

The exhibition *Propaganda in Black & White: An Exploration of Overt and Covert U.S. Government Propaganda* provides the opportunity to gain essential knowledge about the history of the U.S. government's use of propaganda from the Revolutionary War to Operation Iraqi Freedom. The exhibit covers the evolving strategies, techniques, and technologies used by the U.S. government to win the hearts and minds of friends and destabilize enemies.

The term *propaganda* is most often associated with fascist and communist regimes. But the U.S. is no different from other world powers in its use of propaganda. U.S. propaganda campaigns have ranged from harmless such as encouraging people to visit National Parks to very deviously persuading enemy soldiers that their wives are being unfaithful in their absence. The exhibit relates the at-times shocking stories of secret OSS, CIA, and military operations [1]. For more information see https://www.archives.gov/files/exhibits/nates/files/propaganda.pdf.

11.2 Blissfulness and Consistency

The goal of any propaganda is to sway opinions or actions to a direction that is favorable to the creators of the propaganda. Successful propagandists must court their target and keep them locked into not just one message, but an ongoing campaign and stream of related messages designed to sway the target over a long period of time. Politicians are getting really good at this.

Well-crafted propaganda provides people a feeling of blissfulness and contentment with the messaging and they want to feel comfortable and related to through the messaging. Well-targeted propaganda is also consistent with other beliefs people have about the same or related issues. An analogy would be comfort food, that kind of food that makes people feel warm and cozy, take naps, and be lazy.

The interviews bore this out on several subjects, but the one that stands out most was the response to anti-Obama extremist propaganda. Those who were locked into, almost addicted to, anti-Obama messaging were blissful and content as long as there was a lack of counter messaging that suggested that Barack Obama was not evil or corrupt. Anti-Obama messaging was further bolstered by anti-Obamacare messaging.

The Red State lab rats for this research were predominantly Republican and not well educated. They also tended to be anti-science and anti-intellectual. Their knowledge of the presidency over time was nominal and the understanding of Obama care was generally limited to and focused on a few hot buttons. They opposed people being required to have insurance and several were opposed to the contraception mandate.

The Republican propagandists played on this as far and fast as they could. As the 2016 U.S. election seasoned opened, Barack Obama was blamed for everything that people felt was wrong with the world. He was blamed for things that happened well before he was president as well as for many things that never happened. The accusation that Obama was not a U.S. citizen and his birth certificate was a forgery rang in as true with the Republican constituents and was played on by presidential candidates and the conservative media.

The perspective that many of the interviewees often expressed is they did not like Barack Obama because he is an African-American and the U.S. should have a white president. About ten of those people observed during the field research used the N-word to describe the Obama family.

The anti-Obama propaganda never seemed to slow down while he was president; it remained consistent and it helped to fuel the Obama haters' response to further incidents. The night that Barack Obama was declared the winner of the election for his first term as president, a group of four men attacked and assaulted African-Americans on Staten Island, New York because they were dissatisfied with the election outcome. The four were convicted of hate crimes [2].

In August 2014, when 18-year-old Michael Brown was fatally shot by a police officer in Ferguson, Missouri, which was not far from the epicenter of the interviews, the white supremacists in Missouri—in a classic act of tribalism—began spewing anti-Obama propaganda along with an intense round of racist hate speech.

That, and the ensuing news coverage, fed the appetite for consistent messaging that African-Americans were bad people among the interviewees. They then participated in the hate fest and spreading more extremist propaganda. They were blissful, satisfied that they were proven superior and justified in their feelings and beliefs. It was rather ugly, as were the things they were saying about African-Americans and the Obama family. The majority of the interviewees responded to the racist propaganda in classic tribal fashion.

Darren Wilson, the police officer that killed Michael Brown, was considered a folk hero by the interviewees as well as most of the white people in Missouri. Everything about the story was skewed in a long stream of extremist propaganda. When Darren Wilson was not indicted by a grand jury, the white propaganda machine said he was found innocent. Two distinctively different conclusions, with the first being a fact and the second being propaganda that made white people comfortable and satisfied.

11.3 Lack of Knowledge, Confusion, and Laziness

During the course of the interviews, it became very apparent that there was generally a lack of knowledge on a wide range of current events and topics. This includes the electoral process and how government works. The more complex the events of the day were, the more likely it was for the interviewees to become confused and when they did they would substitute their beliefs for knowledge. This process made them more vulnerable to the propaganda because they wanted an easy-to-understand explanation and certainly were not going to let their beliefs be challenged.

Thus, well-crafted propaganda made it easy for people to claim an understanding. It was also apparent that they were lazy and did not want to spend time analyzing or researching the validity of what they hear or what they believe. Not surprisingly, the vast majority of the population did not read very much at all. As it turned out, many of them could not read very well and would gain what they considered to be knowledge from television or though social media news feeds.

Literacy was clearly an issue with the group of interviewees, but it is a growing concern nationwide in the U.S. In 2015, the percentage of 4th-grade students performing at or above the Basic achievement level (69%) was not measurably different from the percentage in 2013, but it was higher than the percentage in 1992 (62%). In addition, the percentage of 4th-grade students performing at or above the Proficient achievement level in 2015 (36%) was not measurably different from the percentage in 2013, but it was higher than the percentage in 1992 (29%). Among 8th-grade students, the percentage performing at or above Basic in 2015 (76%) was lower than in 2013 (78%). However, the percentage was higher in 2015 than in 1992 (69%). Similarly, a lower percentage of 8th-grade students performed at or above Proficient in 2015 (34%) than in 2013 (36%), but the percentage in 2015 was higher than in 1992 (29%). Among 12th-grade students, the percentage performing at or above Basic in 2015 (72%) was lower than the percentages in 2013 (75%) and 1992 (80%). The percentage of 12th-graders performing at or above Proficient in 2015 (37%) was not measurably different from the percentage in 2013, but it was lower than the percentage in 1992 (40%) [3].

The Program for the International Assessment of Adult Competencies (PIAAC) is a cyclical, large-scale study that was developed under the auspices of the Organization for Economic Cooperation and Development (OECD). Adults were surveyed in 24 participating countries in 2012 and 9 additional countries in 2014. PIAAC broadly defines literacy as understanding, evaluating, using, and engaging with written text to participate in society, to achieve one's goals, and to develop one's knowledge and potential. PIAAC results are reported as scale scores on a 0–500 scale. PIAAC reports five proficiency levels for literacy: Below Level 1, Level 1, Level 2, Level 3, and Level 4/5.

Compared with the PIAAC international average distribution of literacy skills, the U.S. had a larger percentage of adults performing at both the top and bottom of the distribution. Thirteen percent of U.S. adults age 16–65 performed at the highest proficiency level (4/5) on the PIAAC literacy scale, which was higher than the international average of 12%. Eighteen percent of U.S. adults performed at the lowest level of the PIAAC literacy scale (at or below Level 1), which was higher than the international average of 16%.

Average scores on the PIAAC literacy scale for adults age 16–65 ranged from 250 in Italy to 296 in Japan. The U.S. average score was 272, which was not significantly different from the PIAAC international average score. Compared with the U.S. average score, average scores in 7 countries were higher, in 6 countries they were lower, and in 8 countries they were not significantly different [4].

The problem with low reading scores is compounded because of the casual often unstructured language used in social media posts. If literacy continues to decline in large segments of the population, the ability to counter the impact of extremist propaganda will also decline as will the desire of individuals to more closely examine the validity of social media content.

11.4 Repetition, Familiarity, and Acceptance

Propagandists play their game well. The method of repetition by sending the same message again and again and spreading it through multiple channels over and over creates familiarity and people become comfortable with the message. The population interviewed during the project validated this approach. In addition to Barack Obama being bad, Hillary Clinton was added to the list of evil doers and those succumbing to the message joined the tribe in the mantra of Lock Her Up! Guilt was assumed without a trial based on endless streams of propaganda.

It was somewhat amusing to listen to explanations of what Hillary Clinton was allegedly guilty of doing. Some people said she stole money from the government and many said she was guilty because of the e-mail server. Statements

Table 11.2 Votes Cast in Missouri for Party Candidates in 2016 Presidential Election

Political Party Candidate	Votes Cast in Favor
Republican	1,594,511
Democratic	1,071,068
Libertarian	97,359
Green	25,419
Constitution	13,092
Write-in	7,156

Source: U.S. House of Representatives, Election statistics, 1920 to present, http://history.house.gov/Institution/Election-Statistics/Election-Statistics/, Accessed January 17, 2018.

assuming her guilt continued to assert, even after the FBI reported that they did not find clear evidence that Secretary Clinton or her colleagues intended to violate laws governing the handling of classified information, that there is evidence they were extremely careless in their handling of very sensitive, highly classified information [5].

Beyond knowing the consumption and repetition of extremist propaganda and results from the 2016 U.S. elections, it has still not been supported through structured and validated research that the propaganda was a primary driving force in the elections. In Missouri, the state where the interviews were conducted, the voting trends were still leaning toward the Republican ticket. How votes were cast in Missouri for the president in the 2016 election is shown in Table 11.2.

The propaganda on voter fraud during the 2016 election worked well and many of the interviewees repeated the propaganda and the accusations of fraud. This left a lasting impression that people of color were casting multiple votes for Hillary Clinton. In true tribal tradition the Trump supporters in the interviewee pool repeated many times that Trump had won the popular vote. Fortunately, they were less obsessed about this than Donald Trump.

Voting rates and patterns do change over time. Voting rates among young adults fell to 38.0% in 2012 from 44.3% in 2008, following increases in two consecutive presidential elections (2008 and 2004), according to a U.S. Census Bureau report on age and voting patterns. In every U.S. presidential election from 1964 on, 18- to 24-year-olds voted at lower rates than all other age groups. In contrast, Americans 65 and older have voted at higher rates than all other age groups since the 1996 election. Although 18- to 29-year-olds voted at lower levels than other age groups nationally in 2012, this result was not geographically uniform.

Voting rates have also varied according to age and gender. Women tend to vote at higher rates than men across most age groups. In every election since 1996, women age 18 through 29 voted at higher rates than men of the same age, with a difference of about 8.0 percentage points in 2008. For older Americans, a gender voting gap has operated in reverse, with men 65 and older voting at higher rates than women of that age in every election since 1996. At about 6.5 percentage points, this differential was larger in 1996 than in the two most recent elections, with older men voting at a higher rate than older women by about 3.7 percentage points, an indication that the gender divide among older voters may soon be a thing of the past [7].

11.5 Groups, Peers, and Belonging

During the interviews it also became apparent that people conform to the expectations of others as to what they should believe. The interviews showed that men were far more boasting in their opinions and declared how they would vote. Women were more subdued in their interpretation of extremist propaganda. Men tended to brag about their viewpoints, especially when there were two or more men involved in the conversation. The interviewees all lived in Jefferson County Missouri, which has very little diversity; this means that their peer groups and social groups probably did not have very much diversity. Table 11.3 shows recent census data for Jefferson County Missouri.

Interviewees were rather consistent in attributing creditability to propaganda based on input from their peers or a social group. This was especially true when it came to anti-LGBTQ extremist propaganda. Interviewees repeated statements ranging from all gay people are pedophiles to all gay people are infected by the human immunodeficiency virus (HIV) and have Acquired Immunodeficiency Syndrome (AIDS). Many of the interviewees were extremely paranoid and fearful of gay people and feared that they could get AIDS from just being near them.

However, it is well known that HIV is NOT transmitted:

- By hugging, shaking hands, sharing toilets, sharing dishes, or closed-mouth or *social* kissing with someone who is HIV-positive
- Through saliva, tears, or sweat that is not mixed with the blood of an HIV-positive person
- By mosquitoes, ticks, or other blood-sucking insects
- Through the air [8]

As the census data in Table 11.3 shows, there is virtually no diversity in the communities where the interviews took place, with the exception of there being Lutheran, Catholic, and Baptist churches. In other words, most of these people had never seen a Muslim let alone met a Muslim. Islamophobia and a simplistic hatred and fear of Muslims were a cultural norm. Several interviewees declared

Table 11.3 Jefferson County, Missouri Census Data

Population estimates, July 1, 2016	224,226
Population, Census, April 1, 2010	218,733
Population per square mile, 2010	333.1
Persons under 18 years, percent, July 1, 2016	23.6%
Persons 65 years and over, percent, July 1, 2016	14.3%
Female persons, percent, July 1, 2016	50.3%
White alone, percent, July 1, 2016	96.3%
Black or African-American alone, percent, July 1, 2016	1.1%
Veterans, 2012–2016	16,932
Housing units, July 1, 2016	89,434
Owner-occupied housing unit rate, 2012–2016	80.4%
Median value of owner-occupied housing units, 2012–2016	$152,300
Median gross rent, 2012–2016	$794
Persons per household, 2012–2016	2.68
High school graduate or higher, percent of persons age 25 years+, 2012–2016	87.5%
Bachelor's degree or higher, percent of persons age 25 years+, 2012–2016	18.4%
In civilian labor force, total, percent of population age 16 years+, 2012–2016	66.7%
Total health care and social assistance receipts/revenue, 2012 ($1,000)	478,710
Total manufacturers' shipments, 2012 ($1,000)	1,420,483
Total retail sales, 2012 ($1,000)	1,952,583
Total retail sales per capita, 2012	$8,867
Mean travel time to work (minutes), workers age 16 years+, 2012–2016	30.8
Median household income (in 2016 dollars), 2012–2016	$58,232
Persons in poverty, percent	10.1%

Source: U.S. Census Bureau, QuickFacts Jefferson County, Missouri, https://www.census.gov/quickfacts/fact/table/jeffersoncountymissouri/PST045216, Accessed January 18, 2018.

their hatred for Muslims but could not explain that hatred. They did confess to having never met a Muslim but were certain they were evil. Women were able to articulate their feelings and focused on the male dominance in Muslim religion and culture.

11.6 The Reason This Is Important

People are readily taken in by propaganda they are exposed to in any media, and the ability to customize a social media feed enables them to filter out anything that does not interest them. People are also strongly influenced by their peers and social groups in their acceptance of propaganda. Once propaganda is accepted, it is retransmitted to friends and family and can be passed on through generations. Children can end up believing the same propaganda that influenced their parents, and family life is where children first learn bigotry, prejudice, and other unpleasant beliefs that may be adhered to in their home.

It is widely accepted that children learn moral values and social conventions through a process of socialization, much of which involves parenting. Research has consistently shown that children do better in their educational settings when parents are more educated, when families' incomes are higher, when mothers had fewer or no symptoms of depression, and when families have well-organized routines, books, and play materials, and take part in learning activities [10].

The interviews, and daily news in the U.S., clearly reveal that there is incredible hypocrisy behind the behavior of many Americans. People that have extremist views towards people of color or different religions or from different countries and teach their children to have the same views ignore some of the fundamental ideas of the society in which they live. From the people interviewed in this chapter to the Halls of Congress to the White House, they pledge allegiance to their flag.

The Pledge of Allegiance was written for the 400th anniversary, in 1892, of the discovery of America. A national committee of educators and civic leaders planned a public-school celebration of Columbus Day to center around the flag. Included with the script for ceremonies that would culminate in the raising of the flag was the pledge [11]. So it was in October 1892, in Columbus Day programs, that school children across the country first recited the Pledge of Allegiance this way:

> *I pledge allegiance to my Flag and to the Republic for which it stands:*
> *one Nation indivisible, with Liberty and Justice for all.*

The Preamble to the Declaration of Independence reads: "We hold these truths to be self-evident, that all men are created equal, that they are endowed by their Creator with certain unalienable Rights, that among these are Life, Liberty and the pursuit of Happiness" [12].

It would be amiss to not mention that the opening of the immigrant processing station at Ellis Island in 1892, in the shadow of the Statue of Liberty, was facilitated by an immigrant association, as was the later popularity of Emma Lazarus's poem, *The New Colossus*. In 1883, Lazarus donated her poem to an auction raising funds for the construction of the Statue's pedestal. This poem vividly depicted the Statue of Liberty as offering refuge to new immigrants from the miseries of Europe. The poem received little attention at the time, but in 1903 was engraved on a bronze plaque and affixed to the base of the Statue; it reads in part: "Give me your tired, your poor, Your huddled masses yearning to breathe free, The wretched refuse of your teeming shore. Send these, the homeless, tempest-tost to me, I lift my lamp beside the golden door!" [13].

Many parents and educators still try to instill these types of values in the children or students. They are the good people. Then there are those that say things like we don't want people from shithole countries to come to the U.S. They are not the good guys.

11.7 Summary

Extremist propaganda is a twenty-first century success story around the world and certainly in the U.S. There are numerous reasons why extremist propaganda has been so successful, ranging from people having a lack of knowledge to people succumbing to peer pressure. This chapter presented ten reasons why propaganda works so well. Key points covered include:

■ There is room for numerous disciplines to conduct research. Psychology, Social Psychology, Political Science, Sociology, Communications Studies, Advertising and Marketing, Law Enforcement, and Homeland Security all have a lot to explore.
■ The ten reasons propaganda works so well covered in this chapter were selected because a pattern emerged out of the interviews and observations.
■ Successful propagandists must court their target and keep them locked into not just one message but an ongoing campaign and stream of related messages, designed to sway the target over a long period of time.
■ The method of repetition by sending the same message again and again and spreading it through multiple channels over and over creates familiarity and people become comfortable with the message.
■ The interviews showed that men were far more boasting in their opinions and declared how they would vote. Women were more subdued in their interpretation of extremist propaganda. Men tended to brag about their viewpoints, especially when there were two or more men involved in the conversation.
■ People are readily taken in by propaganda they are exposed to in any media and the ability to customize a social media feed enables them to filter out anything that does not interest them.

11.8 Course Activities

Course project number one: Each student should become familiar with at least one stream of extremist propaganda (i.e., anti-immigration, anti-science, anti-Muslim). Conduct three to five opened interviews with people you think may have a bias in the area you have studied. Do not lead the interviewee, just let them express their views.

Course project number two: Write up the results of the interviews and identify when the interviewee referred to fact-based information and when they just repeated propaganda.

Course project number three: Discuss the results of the research in a panel setting with all students presenting their results. Draw joint conclusions about the research findings.

References

1. National Archives Museum. Propaganda in Black & White: An Exploration of Overt and Covert U.S. Government Propaganda. Accessed January 16, 2018 https://www.archives.gov/files/exhibits/nates/files/propaganda.pdf.
2. U.S. Department of Justice Office of Public Affairs. *Final Defendant Pleads Guilty to Anti-Obama Assaults*. February 2, 2009. Accessed January 16, 2018 https://www.justice.gov/opa/pr/final-defendant-pleads-guilty-anti-obama-assaults.
3. U.S. Department of Education, National Center for Education Statistics. *The Condition of Education 2017 Reading Performance, 2017*. Accessed January 16, 2018 https://nces.ed.gov/fastfacts/display.asp?id=147.
4. U.S. Department of Education, National Center for Education Statistics. *Program for the International Assessment of Adult Competencies (PIAAC) 2012/2014 Results*, 2016. Accessed January 17, 2018 https://nces.ed.gov/fastfacts/display.asp?id=69.
5. FBI. Statement by FBI director James B. Comey on the investigation of Secretary Hillary Clinton's use of a personal e-mail system, July 5, 2016. Accessed January 19, 2018 https://www.fbi.gov/news/pressrel/press-releases/statement-by-fbi-director-james-b-comey-on-the-investigation-of-secretary-hillary-clinton2019s-use-of-a-personal-e-mail-system.
6. U.S. House of Representatives. *Election Statistics, 1920 to Present*. Accessed January 17, 2018 http://history.house.gov/Institution/Election-Statistics/Election-Statistics/.
7. U.S. Census Bureau. *Statistics Explore Voting Patterns of Young Adults*, April 24, 2014. Accessed January 17, 2018 https://www.census.gov/newsroom/press-releases/2014/cb14-74.html.
8. U.S. Department of Health & Human Services Secretary's Minority AIDS Initiative Fund (SMAIF). How is HIV Transmitted? Accessed January 18, 2018 https://www.hiv.gov/hiv-basics/overview/about-hiv-and-aids/how-is-hiv-transmitted.
9. U.S. Census Bureau. *QuickFacts Jefferson County, Missouri*. Accessed January 18, 2018 https://www.census.gov/quickfacts/fact/table/jeffersoncountymissouri/PST045216.
10. National Institutes of Health (NIH). *Family Characteristics have More Influence on Child Development than Does Experience in Child Care*, October 3, 2006. Accessed January 20, 2018 https://www.nih.gov/news-events/news-releases/family-characteristics-have-more-influence-child-development-does-experience-child-care.

11. U.S. Department of Veterans Affairs. *The Pledge of Allegiance.* Accessed January 20, 2018 https://www.va.gov/opa/publications/celebrate/pledge.pdf.
12. U.S. National Archives. *The Declaration of Independence.* Accessed January 20, 2018 https://www.archives.gov/founding-docs/declaration.
13. U.S. National Park Service. The Statue of Liberty. *The New Colossus*—full text. Accessed January 20, 2018 https://www.nps.gov/stli/learn/historyculture/colossus.htm.

Glossary of Key Terms

active deception: are measures designed to mislead by causing an object or situation to seem threatening when a threat does not exist and normally involves a calculated policy of disclosing half-truths supported by appropriate proof signals or other material evidence.

alternative master narratives: are designed to replace violent extremist narrative by offering an entire cultural, political, or social philosophy that eliminates the appeal of the extremist narrative.

alternative narratives: are those narratives that are designed to replace radical or extremist narratives that are intended to provide viable alternatives to radicalization.

automated accounts: are Twitter accounts that automatically respond to tweets from a specific user or with a specific topic.

automated engagement: occurs when bots are used to increase the visibility of a specific or group of tweets on the Twitter platform.

best practices: are techniques or methodologies that, through experience and research, have reliably led to a desired or optimum result.

black propaganda: is misinformation that identifies itself with one side of a conflict but is truly produced by the opposing side—like Franklin sending the letter from a German prince.

charter school movement: a national trend supported by parents and educators to open and support public schools operating under a charter, essentially a contract entered into between the school and its authorizing agency with the charter school having a great deal of autonomy in curriculum, teaching, and administration.

child exposed to violence: any individual who is not yet an adult (threshold age varies across jurisdictions, typically birth to either 18 or 21 years old) who is directly or indirectly exposed to violence that poses a real threat or a perceived threat to the individual's or an affiliated person's life or bodily integrity.

citizen journalist: is an individual that uses technology such as smart phones to record police or government representative actions and disseminate that evidence to the community at large as well as interested activists.

civil society leaders: are individuals who hold government, business, or religious positions that enable them to influence their societies, communities, and individuals.

community resilience: is the social beliefs and norms of a local population that enables the community to resist radicalization and neutralizes the impact of the radical narrative.

community-targeted approach: is a set of methods and techniques designed to engage individuals or groups in the communities where they live to diminish the possibility of radicalization and identify radicalized individuals or groups.

consumer-generated content: is digital content that is produced by self-publishers and sometimes picked up or referenced in traditional media.

content visibility: the exposure that a tweet or ad gets on the Twitter platform.

counter extremist content: media content that is designed to provide an alternative perspective to that of extremist content.

counter-messaging: is the process of matching radical extremist messages on a head-to-head basis in order mitigate the recruitment and radicalization to violent extremism.

counter-narrative to radicalization: is a narrative that neutralizes or invalidates the narrative designed to radicalize individuals or groups.

credible voices: are those voices of trusted community leaders, religious leaders, and intellectuals that can provide a positive influence on a society or community.

deceptive marketing: advertising or propaganda that misleads people about the true facts about a product, service, or corporate activity.

disinformation: is false and irrelevant information made available to deceive.

domestic antisocial groups: are groups of people or mini-societies that oppose the larger society in which they live and/or work.

domestic fanatics: are radical groups that are residents or citizens of the countries in which they kill, sabotage, or spread hate and fear.

eco-terrorists: are individuals or groups that oppose environmental policies or actions of governments and private companies who use a variety of methods to hinder or halt projects or operations.

election-related content: is any Twitter post related to any election in any country.

electronic aggression: is the use of any electronic device to commit such acts as cyberbullying, Internet harassment, and Internet bullying.

fetal tissue research: any research or development effort that uses fetal tissue in any manner.

following: a term that describes the process of one user deciding to follow the tweets of another Twitter user.

going dark: the process of concealing electronic communications and covertly interacting.

hashtags: are indicators that the content of a tweet is related to a specific topic.

hate messages: are social media posts that use obnoxious language to ridicule or discriminate against minority or ethnic groups.

ideological conflict: is the conflict perpetuated by radicalized groups against mainstream society and minority groups.

ideologically-motivated violence: is that violence that individuals or groups perpetrate towards targets because of their belief that those individuals or groups are inferior in some way and should be harmed or exterminated.

indigenous group: is a group or class of people that live in their area of origin.

information operations: is the integrated employment, during military operations, of information-related capabilities in concert with other lines of operation to influence, disrupt, corrupt, or usurp the decision making of adversaries and potential adversaries while protecting our own.

insider misconduct: conduct by an employee that is against organization policies or procedures or that otherwise can harm the employing organization.

intelligence operations: is the variety of intelligence and counterintelligence tasks that are carried out by various intelligence organizations and activities within the intelligence process.

international fanatics: are individuals, groups of people, or mini-societies that are greatly differentiated from the world around them by a belief system that is totally disconnected from larger realities in which they live and who have a tendency to act out those differences in violent ways or politically or economically disruptive manners. They are members of radical groups that cross borders or influence individuals or groups in other countries to kill, sabotage, or spread hate and fear.

islamophobia: is the dislike of or prejudice against or fear of Islam or Muslims, socially, politically, or based on religion.

lessons learned process: is a structured method of evaluating incidents or events and determining what individuals or organizations could have done better to deal with the situation and transforming that lesson into positive actions through employee training, improving procedures, or improving mitigation methods or technology.

media convergence: is the melding of different media types into multi-faceted streams of information and entertainment including video, text, photos, sound, and graphics, which were at one time all delivered from separate platforms and applications.

news feed: is a constantly updating, highly personalized list of stories, including status updates, photos, videos, links, and activity from the people and things you're connected to on Facebook. The goal of News Feed is to show people the stories that are most relevant to them.

online alias: is an online identity encompassing identifiers, such as name and date of birth, differing from the employee's actual identifiers that use a nongovernmental Internet Protocol address. Online aliases may be used to monitor activity on social media websites or to engage in authorized online undercover activity.

pages: Facebook Pages represent a wide range of people, places, and things, including causes, that people are interested in. Any user may create a Page to express support for or interest in a topic, but only official representatives can create a Page on behalf of an organization, business, brand, or public figure.

personal propaganda feed: the news, information, or content feed that individuals establish in their social media usage.

political correctness: the use of non-biased non-discriminatory words, phrases or images to communicate ideas or messages.

positive message promotional activities: are those that promote positive social behavior and counter negative messaging.

positive narratives: are designed to negate the violent extremist messages and provide powerful incentives for positive action.

price discounts paid to cigarette retailers: discounts paid in order to reduce the price of cigarettes to consumers, including off-invoice discounts, buy-downs, voluntary price reductions, and trade programs; but excluding retail-value-added expenditures for promotions involving free cigarettes and expenditures involving coupons.

promoted tweets: are those Twitter post that are paid for by the posting account to gain more exposure with Twitter users.

publicly available social media: is social media applications and content that can access and be viewed by a general public without restrictions.

radicalization: is the process of indoctrinating previously non-violent individuals or groups into antisocial violent ideologies and actions.

reasonable risk: is a risk that an event or incident could occur during the normal course of a day, week, or any other period without the presence of extraordinary circumstances.

recruiting and indoctrination: is the process of drawing people into a cause and teaching cause-related doctrine.

retweeted: a post on Twitter that has been resent to a Twitter account's followers.

Sabin: Albert Sabin developed live vaccines in the 1950s to fight polio. Neither Jonas Salk nor Albert Sabin patented their vaccines; they donated the rights as gifts to humanity.

Salem witch trials: a series of trials and prosecutions of people accused of witchcraft in Massachusetts in 1692 and 1693. The trials resulted in the execution of 20 people.

Salk: Jonas Salk developed killed vaccines in the 1950s to fight polio. Neither Jonas Salk nor Albert Sabin patented their vaccines; they donated the rights as gifts to humanity.

social media presence: is an organization's use of social media accounts and applications to communicate to individuals or groups as well as the mention, comments, discussions, and display of any material on any social media application that relates to or depicts an organization.

sociocultural analysis: is the analysis of adversaries and other relevant actors that integrates concepts, knowledge, and understanding of societies, populations, and other groups of people, including their activities, relationships, and perspectives across time and space at varying scales.

sovereign citizens: are anti-government extremists who believe that even though they physically reside in this country, they are separate or *sovereign* from the United States. As a result, they believe they don't have to answer to any government authority, including courts, taxing entities, motor vehicle departments, or law enforcement.

trends: are what topics are popular on Twitter at any given time.

unfollowing: a term that describes a Twitter user deciding to not further follow the tweets of a Twitter user that they previously decided to follow.

violence exposure: can be direct, where the victim or community of victims is the direct target of the intentional use of force or power, but it can also be indirect, where the victim or community of victims is witness to the intentional use of force or power or has lost a loved one to violence. Violence exposure results in significant short- and long-term debilitating and costly impacts on the victim's physical, emotional, cognitive, and social health and well-being.

visual content: is any photo, video, or illustration added to social media posts.

western-based extremists: are citizens or residents of western countries that engage or who want to engage in violence against the governments or residents in the countries in which they reside.

white propaganda: white propaganda openly identifies the source and uses gentle persuasion and public relations techniques to achieve a desired outcome. For example, during the Persian Gulf War, the CIA airdropped leaflets before some Allied bombing runs to allow civilians time to evacuate and encourage military units to surrender.

xenophobia: is the fear and hatred of strangers or foreigners or of anything that is strange or foreign.

Index

Note: Page numbers followed by t refer to table respectively.